AUSTRIA.

another recipient of a puppet theater
(Goethe, Renoir, Mann...)
renounces Judaism 1899, ca Nahum 1922
anti-feminist (sexual neurosis)

Heine blamed as father of feuilletonist, litterateur
Mutter facile, sentimental, corrupt press

A Nietzschean - hypocrisy → catastrophe

40-41 explanation of proliferating
ideologies in Vienna — forces of atomization
very powerful when class is added to
ethnic nationalism

Viennese Sensitlichkeit → makes KK's fierce-
ness

The Last Days of Mankind

KARL KRAUS AND HIS VIENNA

Frank Field

MACMILLAN · *London · Melbourne · Toronto*
ST MARTIN'S PRESS · *New York*
1 9 6 7

MACMILLAN AND COMPANY LIMITED
Little Essex Street London WC2
also Bombay Madras Calcutta Melbourne

THE MACMILLAN COMPANY OF CANADA
70 Bond Street Toronto 2

ST MARTIN'S PRESS
175 Fifth Avenue New York NY10010

Library of Congress catalog card no. 67–25439

Printed in Great Britain by
Western Printing Services Ltd, Bristol

To my parents

Acknowledgements

I SHOULD like to thank the many people who have helped me with their advice at various stages of the writing of this book, in particular, Dr. H. G. Schenk; Sir Isaiah Berlin; Mr. James Joll; Dr. Paul Schick; Dr. Rudolf Schlesinger; Mr. Francis Seton; Dr. Marie Jahoda; Dr. Ernst Jahoda; Professor Karl Deutsch; Professor Alexander Gerschenkron; Professor Paul Lazarsfeld; Mr. Donald Nicholl; Dr. John Eros. To Dr. J. P. Stern and Mr. Edward Timms I am greatly indebted for the loan of research material and for the benefit of their great knowledge of the literary significance of the work of Karl Kraus. To Mrs. L. Greaves I am extremely grateful for typing the manuscript. To my wife my indebtedness is beyond repayment.

Grateful acknowledgement is also made for permission to quote from the following works: to Curtis Brown Ltd. and the author for *Fallen Bastions* by G. E. R. Gedye; to Victor Gollancz Ltd. for *In Search of the Millennium* and *The Tragedy of Austria* by Julius Braunthal; to William Collins Ltd. for *Arrow in the Blue* by Arthur Koestler; to Faber and Faber Ltd. for *Collected Poems 1909–1962* by T. S. Eliot; to Putnam and Company for *The Disinherited Mind* by Erich Heller; to John Wiley and Sons Ltd. for *The Rise of Political Antisemitism in Germany and Austria* by P. G. J. Pulzer; to Cassell and Company for *The World of Yesterday* by Stefan Zweig. Particular acknowledgement must be made to Heinrich Fischer for permission to take quotations from *Die Fackel*, and to Kösel-Verlag, Munich, for quotations from their editions of *Die Letzten Tage der Menschheit*, *Die Dritte Walpurgisnacht* and *Worte in Versen*. Without their co-operation this book could not have been written.

Contents

List of Illustrations

Museen der Stadt, Vienna 1, 3 and 4; From the biography of *Karl Kraus* by kind permission of Dr. Paul Schick 2 and 6; By kind permission of Mrs. Walter Feilchenfeldt, Zurich 5; Karl Kraus archives of the Vienna City Library 7; Kosel Verlag 8; Nationalbibliothek, Vienna 9; Collection Viollet 10, 11 and 12; By kind permission of Mrs. Gertrud Jahn, Munich, and Dr. R. J. Jaray, from his film *Karl Kraus liest aus eigenen Schriften* 13; Foto Hilscher 14 and 16; Landesbildsteile, Vienna 15.

Introductory Note

THE cultural efflorescence which accompanied the decline of the Habsburg Empire has profoundly influenced the rest of the world. The fields of psychology, philosophy and music have been revolutionised by the contributions of Sigmund Freud and Alfred Adler, Ludwig Wittgenstein and the Vienna circle, Arnold Schoenberg and his pupils. Religious thought has been fertilised by the insights of Martin Buber. In literature, Rilke and Kafka, Hofmannsthal and Musil have now become part of the heritage of the English-speaking world. Liberated from their Central European context, the problems and anxieties of the intelligentsia of Prague and Vienna in the early years of the twentieth century have now attained a universal significance.

The object of this book is to investigate historically the society which provoked this extraordinary response and to do this through a study of the polemicist and satirist, Karl Kraus, editor from 1899 until his death in 1936 of the magazine *Die Fackel—The Torch*. Kraus, it is true, is not one of the great Viennese figures whose work is well-known in the English-speaking world. And yet the reasons for this neglect—the difficulties of translating his work and the fact that so much of his satire is concerned with a society that has now vanished—are precisely the reasons which make it fitting that the personality and achievement of Karl Kraus should be used as a focus for a study of Vienna in the first four decades of this century. There is also a further point: the singular quality which distinguishes his work from that of most other satirists is that his technique of satire both in *Die Fackel* and in his masterpiece on the First World War and the collapse of the Habsburg Empire, the play *The Last Days of Mankind*, was quotation, often without comment, from the press.

If it is true that almost by definition the satirist is more concerned with the nature of his social environment than is the poet or even perhaps the novelist, of no satirist is this more true than Kraus. His work was conditioned by the coffee-house life of Vienna, famous for its wit, its gossip and its intrigue. His satire was stimulated by the eagerness with which the patrons of the cafés devoured their daily newspapers, dissecting and relishing them as if they were the sugar pastries that accompanied their coffee and glasses of spring water.[1] In Kraus's hands, however, the wit and sophistication of the coffee-houses is brought face to face with the grim reality of the social and political problems of his time. The fact that Kraus was Jewish is of vital importance in understanding the particular extremism, the *Angst*, the sense of the apocalyptic, which pervades his work and gives it an inner consistency which transcends the satirist's outward changes of political allegiance. His satire was both intensely parochial and, at the same time, universal in its implications: Austria was to him the 'research laboratory for world destruction'.[2] Kraus did not live to see the Anschluss of Austria with Germany which took place under Nazi auspices in 1938, although in the document now known as *Die Dritte Walpurgisnacht* he had foreseen something of the unspeakable evil which was about to break loose.

'The understanding of my work', the satirist once proclaimed, 'is made more difficult by a knowledge of my material.'[3] It is not the intention of this study to use Kraus's work simply as a social or political document. Although he himself sometimes admitted that his writings could legitimately be used in this manner, he was also anxious to preserve their integrity as literature. His concern was primarily that of a poet, mourning over the decay of language in the midst of a decaying civilisation. It would be a complete misrepresentation of Kraus's achievement not to examine the nature of the satirist's involvement with language and the affinities between Kraus, Wittgenstein and Schoenberg in their attitude towards the problems of language. Still, the richness and variety of *Die Fackel* are not exhausted by any analysis which confines itself simply to the literary value of Kraus's contribution to the intellectual life of Vienna in this century. The satirist has much to say that is of interest to the historian, especially if the historian is prepared to accept the element of truth in Shelley's remark that poets are the unacknowledged legislators of the world.

Words strain,
Crack and sometimes break, under the burden,
Under the tension, slip, slide, perish,
Decay with imprecision, will not stay in place,
Will not stay still. Shrieking voices
Scolding, mocking, or merely chattering,
Always assail them. The Word in the desert
Is most attacked by voices of temptation,
The crying shadow in the funeral dance,
The loud lament of the disconsolate chimera.

T. S. Eliot, *Burnt Norton*

1 Karl Kraus, Portrait of the Artist

KARL KRAUS was born in Jičin in Bohemia in 1874. His father, Jakob Kraus, was a strict but affectionate parent, a devout Jew, and a prosperous paper manufacturer who moved his family to Vienna while his son Karl was still a small child. Even in infancy the son displayed a passion for the theatre and, while studying at the University of Vienna where he attended few lectures and spent most of his time in the theatre and in the literary cafés, he decided to become an actor. After an appearance in a disastrous production of Schiller's *Die Räuber* he abandoned this idea and became a journalist instead. Between 1895 and the founding of the satirical magazine *Die Fackel* in 1899, Kraus wrote for the magazine *Liebelei* under the pseudonym of 'Crêpe de Chine'. He also worked for a time for the leading newspaper of Vienna, the *Neue Freie Presse* and was its correspondent in Bad Ischl. Moritz Benedikt, the proprietor of the *Neue Freie Presse*, was so impressed by the talent of the young man that in 1898 he offered Kraus the position of chief satirical writer for the paper, a position which had been vacant since the death of the great Daniel Spitzer in 1893. Kraus refused this offer and instead founded the *Fackel* in 1899 to attack the activities of the Viennese press, activities which he had seen at very close quarters. After 1911 he dispensed with other contributors and henceforth, until his death in 1936, brought out the magazine by himself. Long before 1914 Kraus had established himself as the leading satirist of Vienna, worshipped by his admirers and detested by his equally numerous contingent of enemies.

During the First World War his position was one of

uncompromising hostility to the policies of the Central Powers, a position in which, for the first two years of the war, he was virtually alone among the public figures of Vienna. It was during and immediately after the First World War that he wrote the play *Die Letzten Tage der Menschheit* (*The Last Days of Mankind*) which appeared in its final form in 1922. In the course of the 1920s various attempts were made by French admirers of Kraus, together with Thomas Masaryk, the president of the Czechoslovakian republic, to secure a Nobel prize for the satirist, either for his contribution to literature or for his work for peace. This project fell through, partly because of the many enemies which Kraus had made in the literary and political circles of Central Europe, partly because the agitation for the union of Austria with Germany (in which the satirist took no part) alienated many prominent French intellectuals. The closing years of Kraus's life were rendered bitter by the rise of Hitler in Germany and the growing influence of the Nazis in Austria. The satirist was fortunate in dying two years before the Anschluss in 1938 when the wealthy Jewish intellectual world from which he sprang was utterly destroyed in Central Europe.

Such are the salient facts of Kraus's career. As both he and his admirers were concerned to emphasise, his work was his life. The satirist's public image was one of extreme arrogance and intransigence. To demonstrate his opposition to the customary effusiveness of the literary cliques of Vienna, Kraus refused to acknowledge greetings in the street but walked determinedly on. To assert his complete independence from the financial interests which stood behind much of the Viennese press, the satirist ostentatiously refused to accept advertisements for insertion in the *Fackel*. The considerable income which Kraus derived from his public recitals of poetry, drama, and satire, was, after the First World War, devoted entirely to charitable purposes. Each donation to charity was scrupulously detailed in the pages of his magazine, as was every reference to the *Fackel* and its editor in the press not merely of Central Europe, but also of France, Britain and the United States. The personal sacrifices which the satirist made to continue with his manifold activities were considerable: over many years Kraus slept for only five hours a day; apart from the time which he spent with his select circle of acquaintances in the cafés at night, it seemed to many of his friends that he lived at his desk.[1]

Like Freud and Schoenberg, Kraus could be extremely authoritarian in his relationship with his friends and disciples: and yet, again like Freud and Schoenberg, Kraus was idolised by these disciples. Successive generations of the intellectual youth of Vienna were attracted to his recitals by his wit, his gift for mimicry, his histrionic flair, and by a charisma that he generated of fanatical hatred towards all that was empty and corrupt in a civilisation that was moving, slowly but inexorably, towards its end. As they grew older many of Kraus's youthful admirers deserted him, either because they felt that his position was ultimately sterile, or because they were ruthlessly excommunicated by the master himself. Towards an enemy or an erring friend Kraus was implacable in his hatred. It would be impossible to enumerate the number of bitter personal vendettas and lawsuits which the satirist pursued in his lifetime. Dr. Oscar Samek, who was for a long time Kraus's legal adviser, died in New York in 1958 while he was in the process of writing a book on the years of litigation in which he had been engaged on Kraus's behalf.

The rôle which Kraus played in Vienna was in part the result of conscious choice and in part dictated for him by the actions of others. His onslaught on the Viennese press resulted in the newspapers bringing pressure to bear to prevent his using concert halls and lecture rooms for his public recitals; and although Kraus immediately had recourse to the law courts to stop this practice, this was both a slow and expensive process. Even more wounding was the deliberate and almost unbroken conspiracy of silence with which the Viennese press treated the activities and even the existence of Kraus and the *Fackel*: the satirist was, for example, particularly outraged because the *Neue Freie Presse* refused to mention the death of the poet and essayist Peter Altenberg in

1919 because Kraus had delivered a funeral oration at his grave-side. The one notable exception to the ostracism which the satirist experienced at the hands of the press was the sympathy extended to him by the Social Democrat *Arbeiter Zeitung*, although even in this newspaper they were enemies at hand. In reply to the charge of arrogance Kraus—again like Freud and Schoenberg—could only reply that it was forced upon him by the persecution which he had to endure.

It was equally true, however, that Kraus deliberately provoked persecution and relished the condition of martyrdom that was thrust upon him. Many attempts have been made to investigate the psychology of the satirist—not least by enemies who had once been admirers of his. Kraus's hatred of psychoanalysis for example was partly due to a ruthless dissection of his personality by the writer Fritz Wittels, a somewhat erratic disciple and subsequent biographer of Freud, and a former follower of Kraus.[2] The editor of the *Fackel* has been described by yet another of his ex-admirers as a neurotic and a retarded adolescent, a gifted sadist who broke with many of his youthful admirers because of a latent and unfulfilled inclination towards homo-sexuality.[3]

Although much of this sort of comment must be disregarded as part of the personal abuse apparently inevitable in any disagree-ment in the intellectual and political world of Central Europe, there *was* a dark obsessional aspect of Kraus's character at which some of his lifelong friends have hinted. Germaine Goblot, the French scholar who for many years worked on a study of Kraus which was unfortunately incomplete at the time of her death, once commented on the way in which, whenever the satirist ventured out of Austria or Germany, his whole being would gradually relax and the tensions within him would disappear: 'It is another world,' he smilingly remarked to her about Paris. The drawing of Kraus by Kokoschka clearly brings out the strange mingling of ruthlessness and naïvety within the satirist's personality. The reader of Kraus is constantly reminded of an anecdote that concerns the satirist's childhood. When his family

moved to Vienna in 1877, Kraus at the age of three was terrified
by the noise and bustle of the great city. Whenever he and his
elder brother, Richard, were taken for a walk in the park by their
governess, he was frightened that they would never return
home. Consequently he always carried under his arm the one
thing he loved most in the world—his marionette theatre.[4]

Perhaps it was the child in Kraus that was responsible both for
the satirist's cruelty and the vividness of his imagination. The
theatrical producer, Heinrich Fischer, who knew the satirist
intimately for the last thirteen years of his life, has written of
Kraus's response to his daily reading of the newspapers:

> It was a unique experience to see his thoughts now in full
> flood; Kraus was scarcely able to control and fix them. With
> the stump of a pencil he would hastily scribble notes in the
> margin of the newspaper and then thrust it back into his
> pocket; that fellow was dealt with and could not escape any
> more. At such times it was clear that polemic was for Kraus
> both a moral and aesthetic necessity. Whatever malice or
> stupidity the day brought within his purview left him no
> peace until it had been dealt with. Nothing weighed more
> heavily upon him than the thought of the thousands of news-
> papers in his room which still awaited their transmutation
> into satirical art. The same obsession impelled him incessantly
> to remould and file his written words.[5]

Dr. Fischer provides a further vignette from the period after the
accession of Hitler to power in Germany:

> With Kraus it was always the unusually vivid imaginative
> powers of his mind and heart that gave birth to satire: satire
> arose from his faculty of experiencing the sufferings of others
> as an injustice done to himself. I remember how he would turn
> pale, how the veins in his forehead would swell, how he gazed
> with a look of incomprehending astonishment at the news-
> paper in which he now read day after day of things more
> frightening than the worst carnage of the last war.[6]

If, however, the satirist was capable of pursuing an enemy
with a hatred that was demonic in its intensity, there was a

redeeming facet of his personality: he was possessed of an extraordinary quality of empathy towards the world of animals and children, a world with which much of his poetry is concerned. Kraus was deeply attached to his mother, and the depth and intensity of his grief at her death in 1891 was a cause of anxiety to his friends. Towards women in general his attitude—as befitted a product of the neo-romantic movement of the 1890s—was a mixture of extreme intellectualism, inhibition and spontaneity. Kraus was the heir of the misogyny of Schopenhauer and Nietzsche, who feared the irrationalism and elemental sensuality which they claimed to see in woman; and the satirist often employed his sardonic wit to attack any movement for feminine emancipation, a movement which he and a number of his Viennese contemporaries claimed was a hysterical response to sexual neurosis. On the other hand, it is equally clear that Kraus came more and more not merely to accept but even to exalt the feminine qualities as a necessary corrective to the arid rationalism of man, a rationalism which, he felt, was responsible for the worship of the values of science and technology in modern civilisation. Indeed in the course of his career the satirist's hatred of the dehumanising implications of man's greed for material power led him further and further beyond Schopenhauer and Nietzsche back to Goethe's conception of the eternal feminine principle as the secret source of the renewal of life and the artistic imagination.

In any case Kraus was obviously fascinated by the erotic licence of the theatrical and literary world of Vienna and by the spectacle of an aristocratic civilisation in Austria in which, by the end of the nineteenth century, social barriers, hitherto rigid, were now in the process of decay. His own relationships with women were facilitated by this process. Many women found the satirist attractive, despite the physical peculiarities—in particular, the deformity of his shoulders—which gave him a pronounced stoop. Although Kraus never married, his first major love affair was with the gifted young actress Annie Kalmar, who died of tuberculosis in Hamburg in 1901 at the early age of

twenty-three: her memory was a constant source of inspiration
for the poems which the satirist printed in the pages of the *Fackel*.
The most important relationship of his life, however, was the
long liaison which existed between Kraus and the Baroness
Sidonie Nadherny to whom most of his most intimate love poetry
is dedicated. Although it is doubtful whether the satirist's
devotion to his mission would ever have allowed anything like a
normal marriage between the two, it seems that Kraus did
indeed propose marriage to the baroness on several occasions
between 1913 and 1915 and that on the advice of the poet Rilke
(who had many friends amongst the aristocracy) she turned these
proposals down.[7] There followed an interval of several years
during which the baroness was married and then divorced.
Although the relationship between Kraus and Sidonie Nadherny
was then resumed and lasted without further interruption until
the satirist's death in 1936, for most of the time they led separate
lives—he in Vienna, she at her country seat of Janovice, south of
Prague. Their voluminous correspondence was lost when the
baroness was compelled to flee from Czechoslovakia after the
Communist coup in 1948. She died in a nursing home near
Denham in Buckinghamshire in 1950, a prosaic setting far
removed from the Central European scene and the passions
which informed it.

It is of course difficult for the English reader fully to compre-
hend so alien an environment as that of Karl Kraus. But it is not
difficult for that reader to appreciate the fact that the personality
of the satirist was infinitely more devious and complex than that
which was suggested by his public image. There were areas of
the satirist's private life which were to astonish the readers of
Die Fackel when he felt prepared to reveal them. In 1922, for
example, Kraus, who had renounced Judaism as early as 1899,
announced that he had left the Catholic Church in protest against
the association of the Church with the inauguration of the
Salzburg Festival.[8] This was the first intimation that the satirist
gave his readers that he had been a Catholic for the last eleven
years. And even behind this surprising and unexpected apostasy

there was a further motive at work—Kraus's personal animosity towards the theatrical producer Max Reinhardt.

The incident would be dismissed as being totally absurd unless it is taken as a not entirely uncharacteristic symptom of the over-strained and neurotic atmosphere in which the Viennese artist and intellectual was accustomed to work. 'I am thrice homeless,' Gustav Mahler once said. 'As a Bohemian among Austrians, as an Austrian among Germans, as a Jew throughout the world. Everywhere an intruder, never welcomed.'[9] In his remorseless perfectionism, his intolerance of the traditional Austrian qualities of *Schlamperei* and *Gemütlichkeit*, Kraus resembled Mahler in many respects. The creative tension which inspired both these men sprang in part from the encounter between an emancipated Jewish intellectual and a baroque civilisation now far gone in decline. Like Mahler, Kraus was full of contradictions: an artist who lived on his nerves and on the nerves of others, a creature of the city and yet a hater of city life; a dictator in personal relationships but a dictator peculiarly vulnerable to criticism; a Jew who had renounced Judaism and yet, for that very reason, felt even more acutely Jewish than before. Mahler was by temperament a mystic and a solitary whose innermost feelings were released only in his music. With Kraus also artistic creation was a spiritual necessity. For the satirist *Die Fackel* was at the same time an autobiographical fragment, an analysis of society, and the vehicle for a remarkable aesthetic achievement. It is to the aesthetic achievement that attention must now be directed.

The alienation of the creative artist from his society has been a common theme in European literature since the time of the French Revolution. The decline of religious belief, the impact of industrialisation and mass democracy in the twentieth century, have only accelerated a process that was already apparent to many of the key figures in the great renaissance of German culture that took place between 1770 and 1830. The theme of alienation was a commonplace among German intellectuals for obvious reasons; the enormous gulf that existed between the world of *Macht* and the world of *Geist* in a Germany that was still disunited; the isolation of the intellectual in the stagnant and parochial atmosphere of the petty states; the catastrophic consequences of the loss of religious faith in a society in which so many of its poets and philosophers—Herder, Hegel and Hölderlin, for example—had been profoundly influenced by the Lutheran tradition. In the neo-romantic movement of the 1890s which followed the impact of Nietzsche on the German mind, a movement which directly affected the work of Karl Kraus, there was a rediscovery and a reinterpretation of the dilemmas and achievements of those earlier generations of Germans who had experienced an acute sense of isolation within their society.

Austria, it is true, had escaped many of the evils which had plagued the rest of the Holy Roman Empire in the sixteenth and seventeenth centuries. The disintegrating tendencies of the Reformation had been checked, even though the price for this was the forcible conversion of thousands of heretic Czechs. In addition to the unifying principle provided by Catholicism, Austria also possessed a marked political advantage over the Germans: in the Habsburg dynasty she enjoyed a succession of conscientious if unimaginative rulers who, by their power and by their imperial pretensions, were capable of inspiring a loyalty which far surpassed that accorded to the kings and princes of the rest of the Empire.

This situation changed however in the course of the nineteenth century. The rise of nationalism and democracy, in particular the national awakening of the Magyar and Slav peoples, was fatal for the survival of the Habsburgs, deprived as they were of their dominating position within Germany first by Napoleon and then subsequently by the unification of Germany under Prussia in 1866 and 1871. By the end of the nineteenth century significant elements of the German population in Bohemia and Austria were looking to Berlin for protection against the rising tide of Slav national feeling. It is an ironical commentary on any materialist explanation of history that it was in the period in which the political decline of Austria became increasingly apparent that her literature achieved its final maturity. Like so many other civilisations in the past, that of Austria achieved self-awareness and definition only on the eve of collapse.

Until this time, Austrian literature enjoyed only a provincial status within the German-speaking world. The product of a culture which had close links with Italy as well as Southern Germany, the Viennese imagination was pictorial and musical rather than literary. It was no accident, therefore, that, within the realm of literature, it was the art of the theatre which was most highly developed in Austria. Partly as a result of the cultural cohesion provided by Catholicism, Austria, in contrast to Northern Germany, preserved in the seventeenth and eighteenth centuries a tradition of popular drama which flourished, with undiminished vigour, far into the nineteenth century, and reached its apotheosis in Mozart's *The Magic Flute* and in the plays of Raimund, Anzengruber, and Nestroy. A characteristic feature of the Viennese theatre was the magic comedy (*Zauberposse*), a typical baroque art-form combining the fairy story with elements of social criticism. Through Nestroy, the last and most accomplished exponent of the magic comedy, Kraus was heir to a long dramatic tradition.

The folk drama was never really accorded the dignity of imperial approval. The Emperor Joseph II—that most enlightened if least successful of the Enlightened Despots—certainly wished to foster the arts in Vienna: and it was largely due to his inspiration that in 1776 there was established the most famous of Viennese theatres, the Burgtheater. Its repertoire, however, was heavily slanted away from the local drama of Vienna in favour of the Classical theatre of Lessing, Goethe and Schiller. As a result of this situation, Austrian dramatists such as Raimund and Grillparzer were faced with an agonising choice: should they remain faithful to the immediate source of their inspiration or should they emulate the achievements of the Classical drama of Germany? Nestroy, it will be seen, avoided this difficulty. Others were not so fortunate: all too often Grillparzer, the

greatest Austrian dramatist of the nineteenth century, sounds
like a pale Viennese imitation of Goethe's Weimar.

Austrian literature, in fact, only came into its own towards the
end of the nineteenth century when, in the poetry and plays of
the Impressionist movement, it produced a major challenge to
German domination. No incident more clearly demonstrated the
emancipation of Austrian literature than the polite but firm
refusal of Hugo von Hofmannsthal, the most brilliant and most
precocious talent of the Impressionist school, to accept the
patronage of the great poet Stefan George, a disciple of Nietzsche
and an artist whose work was the expression of a much more
narrowly German genius. Impressionism, by contrast, was a true
manifestation of the Austrian spirit, both playful and serious,
aristocratic and at the same time sentimental, sensual and
melancholic, intensely mannered and self-consciously aesthetic
and yet containing within itself the seeds of a larger concern for
humanity. This last quality is particularly marked in the work of
Hofmannsthal, who moved from the Impressionist period of his
youth to a remarkable dramatic output in his later years—the
opera libretti for Richard Strauss and the plays written for the
Salzburg Festival—which won for the Austrian drama a European reputation.

Before Hofmannsthal reached the second great creative phase
of his artistic life, however, he was condemned to encounter deep
despair. The historian, Jakob Burckhardt, once pointed out that,
in periods of great crisis, everything that was formerly accepted
now loses its meaning, and that this process is mirrored in the
disintegration of language.[10] Hofmannsthal, too, was to make
this discovery: after the astonishing outburst of inspiration which
had, in his adolescence, produced his finest lyrical poetry, he
underwent a serious psychological crisis in which he found that
his loss of confidence was mirrored before his eyes in the disintegration of the meaning of language. The words which he had
used so prodigally and unthinkingly in the past had now become
devoid of sense:

For me, everything disintegrated into parts, those parts again into parts; no longer would anything let itself be encompassed by a single idea. Single words floated around me; they congealed into eyes which stared at me and into which I was forced to stare back—whirlpools which gave me vertigo and, reeling incessantly, led into the void.[11]

Realising that the aesthetic Impressionism of his youth led only to sterility, Hofmannsthal abandoned lyrical poetry for the medium of drama in an attempt to reintegrate himself into a civilisation which he was passionately concerned to save.

There were responses even more extreme than that of Hofmannsthal to the spiritual crisis, the crisis of communication, which accompanied the decay of Austrian civilisation. The limitations of language did not escape the critical inquiry of Sigmund Freud.[12] Kafka has a parable concerning royal messengers rushing through the world with messages that no longer have meaning because the monarchy came to an end long before.[13] There was the Vienna of Wittgenstein, of Buber, of Schoenberg and the revolt against tonality in music. In philosophy, music and literature there occurred both a ruthless analysis of language and a single-minded determination to rid that language of all its hypocrisies and evasions, its irrelevant ornamentation, its imprecision. This was also the Vienna of Karl Kraus.

For, like Wittgenstein and Schoenberg, both of whom admired his work greatly, the satirist was obsessed with problems of language. To Kraus language is not merely the medium of thought: thought and language are related in a complex and semi-mystical dialectic which he, as a poet, was never concerned to analyse in any philosophical way. Thought, he asserts, does not possess an independent existence in this world, but through the prism of the material circumstances of life is dispersed and scattered among the elements of language. Or, to vary the metaphor, the world is sifted through the sieve of language.[14] Above all, the function of words is not decorative: this is the burden of the satirist's attack on the Impressionists in Austria, an attack exemplified by Kraus's description of Hofmannsthal in his attempt to revivify the baroque drama as 'living among golden goblets in which there is no wine'.[15]

Kraus practised what he preached. With a style of extraordinary concentration, allusiveness and wit, with a moral fanaticism that bordered on the pathological, the satirist elevated language to apocalyptic significance and intensity. Since he was convinced that words are possessed of an innate magical potency by which they can revenge themselves on societies and individuals who pervert them or use them idly, Kraus would agonise for hours over the revision of his work and claimed in one of his epigrams that he worked longer on a single word than other men on a novel.[16] Certainly his obsessive concern with every detail of proof-reading and punctuation (every comma in *Die Fackel* had to be placed exactly half-way between the words it separated) was to drive his printers to distraction.[17] For years the pages of Kraus's magazine were enlivened by the masterly replies which the satirist sent to his readers who wrote to him on questions of grammar and syntax: his book *Die Sprache* had its origins in the prolonged seminar which Kraus conducted with his readers on these problems. But while a perfectionist in matters of form and style, the satirist was an opponent of any kind of grammatical or philological pedantry. His critics might complain that the cult of language by Kraus and his disciples was a substitute for the declining convictions of conventional religious belief, but the satirist replied that, on the contrary, a sensitivity to the mysteries of language was a necessary condition of religious awareness. For indeed, in his own encounter with language, Kraus experienced something of the miseries and ecstasies of the religious mystic: as he once said to his friend Sigismund von Radecki, 'I have never wept so much in all my life as during my work yesterday.'[18] 'I am only the master of the language of others,' the satirist explained on yet another occasion. 'My own does with me what it likes.'[19]

As has already been seen, Kraus's characteristic method of satire, which emerged about 1908 from his replies to readers' letters, was that of quotation, followed usually by his own comment. Often, however, any further remark of his own would have been superfluous; this was to prove particularly effective in combatting the censor during the First World War. 'My business', he once said, 'is to pin down the Age between quotation marks.'[20] In its definitive form, Kraus's work is apocalyptic: not, however, in the sense of Nietzsche or Stefan George who looked to the future for the realisation of their intuitions of catastrophe and rebirth. On the contrary, the satire of Kraus is directed from a cosmic standpoint from which is captured the timeless significance of each passing moment, each detail which catches the eye of the poet. Through this process incidents, often tiny in themselves, become magnified into terrible portents of impending doom: and by their relationship to specific events and personalities in Viennese life, these incidents can be built up from the pages of *Die Fackel* into a cumulative picture of the disintegration of Viennese society and the alienation of the satirist from that society. The world of Kraus is a quotation from reality and is yet a nightmarish abstraction from reality, a world in which the Jewish-owned *Neues Wiener Journal* (which had joined with anti-semites to hound Mahler from the directorship of the State Opera) sheds crocodile tears over the return of the dying composer to Vienna in 1911.[21] It is a world in which the *Neue Freie Presse* claims that 'The *Titanic* is as good as unsinkable' and praises the building of the ship as a triumph of modern science and technology. To Kraus the sinking of the *Titanic* was the death-knell of the false optimism that pervaded the world before 1914, a world in which the real foundations of society and culture were being undermined by the forces of 'Progress'.[22] Nowhere could this be more clearly seen than in an Austria where the casual words of commendation, with which the Emperor Franz Josef commented on the exhibits at a fashion display, were taken down by newspaper reporters and sold to the exhibiting firms to be used as advertising material.[23]

Polemic and satire were by no means unknown in the Viennese press before the advent of Kraus. It was a tribute to the journalistic sophistication of the *Neue Freie Presse* that, every week for twenty years in that newspaper, Daniel Spitzer in his column 'Viennese walks' had attacked the corruption of parliament and the greed of the capitalist class in Austria. Some of Spitzer's epigrams became deservedly famous, such as his comment that the Austrian Foreign Minister, Count Andrássy, by occupying Bosnia-Herzegovina in 1878, had increased the population of the Empire by a million insurgents. But the wit and irony of Spitzer, however cutting—and he could be particularly savage towards the music and philosophy of Richard Wagner—could never go too far without putting into question the fundamental assumptions upon which the *Neue Freie Presse* was built. Kraus's refusal to accept Spitzer's position on that newspaper can thus be seen as the most important decision of his life: he was determined to launch his campaign against the insincerities of the world of journalism from a vantage point outside it.

The satirist's hatred of the press was due not merely to the corrupt nature of many of the newspapers of Central Europe: he found the *Neue Freie Presse* to be pernicious precisely because its financial corruption was allied with a journalistic excellence for which it strove unceasingly. Not only did this newspaper provide excellent coverage of the world of Art and Music by attracting a number of famous contributors (including the great music critic, Edward Hanslick, who for many years championed Brahms against Wagner and was to be satirised by the latter in the character of Beckmesser in *Die Meistersinger*), the *Neue Freie Presse* also printed regular contributions from such leading Viennese literary personalities as Hofmannsthal, Schnitzler, Richard Beer-Hofmann and Hermann Bahr. The Viennese press, indeed, brought to perfection that fusion of the worlds of literature and journalism which must always present a threat to the integrity of the creative artist. A characteristic feature of the literary pages was the feuilleton, a form of journalism of which Arthur Koestler has written that 'it was a perverse blend of travelogue, essay and short story, bringing out the worst side of each'.[24] Skilled as he himself was in all the arts and tricks of the feuilletoniste, Kraus, in countless quotations in the

Fackel, mercilessly exposed the whimsy, the sentimentality, the play on words, the essential *aestheticism* of this journalistic medium.

The responsibility for the cult of the feuilleton in Central Europe Kraus largely attributed to the influence of the poet, Heinrich Heine, of whose reputation he was constantly critical.[25] Heine was indeed the prototype of a whole species of nineteenth-century German and Austrian littérateur, no longer able or willing to be the pensioner of a wealthy patron but seeking the financial independence which would enable him to continue his writing by entering the world of journalism. There was however a special reason why Kraus was so hostile towards Heine: during his long exile in France the latter had acquired a great admiration for French literature and civilisation, an admiration which profoundly affected his own work and through that work exerted a peculiar fascination on those German writers who came after him. Whereas the French language, in Kraus's view, permitted anyone with sufficient intelligence and sensitivity to become a stylist, the very intractability of German meant that only the chosen few could hope to excel in it. But Heine through his imitation of the order and clarity of French literature had shown the way in which German—and in particular German prose—could be written with an amazing and dangerous facility. The German language might be the most profound but German speech was the most superficial: the lack of formalisation which enabled German, in contrast to French, to preserve a considerable flexibility, was itself, according to Kraus, a further reason for the corruption of the German language at the hands of those imitators of Heine who worked in the fashionable press of Berlin and Vienna.

The function of art, Kraus maintained, is to upset the simple platitudes by which men live, to reveal the elemental chaos in which human life must be spent. How can the artist do this and at the same time make weekly contributions to the press? The feuilletonistes of the *Neue Freie Presse* might enjoy the same popularity as actors at the Burgtheater and singers at the Opera, and yet the satirist saw a deep contradiction at the heart of their work: for all their aesthetic disdain for modern capitalistic civilisation and the emergence of the great city, many members of the Impressionist circle in Vienna were, by the fact of publishing their work in the newspapers, in grave danger of succumbing to the very values which they so ostentatiously despised. In fact, it is only with a knowledge of the pretentious and narcissistic character of the literary and journalistic fashion prevailing in Vienna in 1899 that the initial impact of *Die Fackel* can be fully appreciated. Erich Heller has likened it to the 'arrival of an elemental spiritual force into a beauty parlour of the soul'.[26] Already in 1896, three years before the first edition of *Die Fackel*, Kraus had published the pamphlet *Die demolirte Litteratur* in which he had shown his growing alienation from the Impressionist 'Jung Wien' circle around Hofmannsthal and Bahr and his sympathy for the Naturalist movement stemming from Berlin and Northern Europe, a movement which insisted, with at times tedious honesty, on facing the realities of life. The occasion for the publication of this pamphlet was particularly apt—the pulling down of the Café Griensteidl (which was the headquarters of the Impressionist circle) to make way for street improvements. 'Vienna has been demolished into a big city,' was the famous opening line of this pamphlet in which, for the first time, Kraus revealed his hostility towards Hermann Bahr. It was to become a famous feud.

The antipathy between the satirist and Hermann Bahr was soon exacerbated in the very early years of the *Fackel* when Kraus accused Bahr of using his contacts as a freemason to undermine the independence of dramatic critics from the theatre managers; the satirist lost the libel case which ensued, one of the few defeats that he was to suffer in years of constant litigation, and had to pay 1,800 crowns in damages.[27] Bahr was, however, an individual whom it was difficult to hate. It was true that his influence within Vienna was enormous, extending as it did from the literary cliques to the Burgtheater (of which for several years he was director) and the Opera (of which his wife, the famous soprano Anna Bahr-Mildenburg was a prominent member). But even Kraus's dislike of Bahr was tinged with a certain affection for a personality whose foibles were so evident that he could so easily be inflated into the rôle of one of the great comic figures of *Die Fackel*. The unfortunate Bahr certainly left himself open to Kraus's attack by his perpetual concern to climb on every possible aesthetic or political bandwagon: he started off his career as a moderate Socialist but became successively an atheist, a Pan-German, a Realist, an Impressionist, a Liberal, dying as a Monarchist and a Catholic. This talented and volatile impresario of ideas seemed perfectly to epitomise the essential rootlessness of the Viennese littérateur. No wonder that Kraus's readers delighted in his gibe that Hermann Bahr changed his views like other men changed their shirts![28]

Adolf Loos, one of the satirist's most intimate friends, fought all his life for simplicity and purity of line and brought upon himself years of persecution and neglect for his constant opposition to the pompous and over-ornate building style which was characteristic of Vienna before 1914. What Loos attacked in architecture, Kraus attacked in literature and society. In the very first issue of *Die Fackel* the satirist announced his uncompromising hostility to all that was empty or corrupt in Austrian life, explaining that his political programme was not a portentous 'What we bring' (*Was wir bringen*), but the more honourable 'What we destroy' (*Was wir umbringen*). The criterion which *Die Fackel* would apply to literature, politics and the press would be that of language:

What has been laid down here is nothing else than a drainage system for the broad marshes of phraseology.[29]

Kraus conceived it his duty to fight against everything that was falsely regarded by foreigners to be picturesquely 'Viennese'. And yet, of course, there were many genuinely Viennese elements in the satirist's own work. He was the heir of the tradition of coffee-house wit with its outrageous epigrams and paradoxes, a tradition which reached its apotheosis in the work of his friend, the writer Alfred Polgar: Kraus was also the friend of the bohemian and disreputable coffee-house poet, Peter Altenberg, whose special gift was for short sketches, photographic in their accuracy, of Viennese life and morals. Even more important was the debt owed by Kraus to the tradition of the Austrian folk drama and in particular to the plays of Johann Nestroy for the dramatic element which underlay the whole of his satirical art.

Nestroy had avoided the temptation to which Raimund and Grillparzer had succumbed of trying to imitate the Classical theatre of Germany. Instead, he had sharpened and perfected the magic comedy into an instrument of highly sophisticated and devastating social satire, employing as his main technique his extraordinarily acute ear for dialogue and the play of language. The penalty which Nestroy had to pay for popular success was the misunderstanding to which this work was subjected by literary critics during his lifetime; he was blamed for the decline of the folk drama which took place in the middle of the nineteenth century, a decline for which indeed not he but the impact of social change within Austria was largely responsible; he was dismissed as a dialect writer but, on the contrary, he was, as Kraus pointed out, the first German satirist to use the ambiguities and diversity of language as the starting point for his satire; he was attacked for his indifference towards politics, whereas in fact, claimed Kraus, he was more passionately concerned with the society of his time than either politicians or those historians who have tried to dismiss the contradictions within his work by naïvely complaining that he was frightened of the police. Nestroy, affirmed Kraus, was conscious of standing at the end of an epoch which rejected Art and which forced the literary artist into the last medium in which he could find refuge—that of satire. The duty of the satirist was to organise the flight of culture from the world of humanity; after the satirist comes the deluge.[30]

It was Kraus who was largely responsible for the rediscovery of Nestroy that took place in Austria in the early years of this century; and it would be foolish to deny that there were considerable affinities between the two satirists. There were, however, important differences. Whereas Nestroy was primarily a craftsman of the theatre and was accustomed to a great deal of improvisation in the writing and performance of his plays, Kraus was far more of a selfconscious artist. Although the latter was passionately interested in the theatre and for many years hoped that a rebirth of the folk drama might be found in the plays of the Expressionist movement, he became more and more convinced that the theatre of his own day was no longer suitable for the kind of work in which he was interested. In the years before 1914 Kraus constantly lamented the decline that had taken place in the quality of the Viennese theatre and in particular of the Burgtheater which had in the nineteenth century, under the directorship of Heinrich Laube, paid special attention to the excellence of the spoken word. By the beginning of the twentieth century the reputation of the Burgtheater was being undermined by the loss of many of the best Viennese actors to the lively and experimental German stage. It was also being destroyed—at least as far as Kraus was concerned—by the importation of theatrical innovations which had originated in the Theater in der Josefstadt, the original home of the gifted Viennese producer Max Reinhardt who, in the satirist's eyes, was perpetually concerned to sacrifice the spiritual and poetic content of drama for all sorts of visual tricks and devices designed to titillate his audiences. Kraus's campaign against Max Reinhardt was lifelong in its duration: it was pursued even after the latter, following Hitler's accession to power in 1933, left Germany to divide his time between Salzburg and Hollywood.

Convinced as he was that the spoken word was now at a discount in the theatre, Kraus was determined to practise his dramatic art outside the theatre. It was in this way that there originated those famous public recitals—over seven hundred of them in all—which the satirist gave during his lifetime in most of the major cities of Central Europe. Numerous accounts of Kraus's recitals are in existence, largely of course because he

Karl Kraus

Die demolirte LITTERATUR

von

KARL KRAUS

WIEN, 1897.

VERLAG VON A. BAUER.

Preis 40 Kreuzer.

Cover of Die Demolirte Litteratur.
The figure in the middle is Hermann Bahr

printed them in full in *Die Fackel*. The gramophone records which after the First World War the satirist made of readings from his own works can give the listener only a faint impression of what the atmosphere was like at one of his public gatherings. They served, above all, as a meeting-place of the avant-garde intellectual youth of the cities which he visited, a youth that exulted in the master's witty and ironic attacks on conventional sexual morals and bourgeois society, the hypocrisies of politicians and the lies of the press. Kraus was not content merely to advertise his own work: the repertoire of his recitals was constantly extended. After the First World War there appeared the satirist's enormously ambitious programme of a 'Theatre of Poetry', in which Kraus was to show his disdain for all the techniques of the contemporary theatrical impresarios by giving one-man performances of the poetry of Goethe, the operettas of Offenbach, the plays of Shakespeare, Nestroy and Brecht—all without any scenery, costumes or special lighting, relying merely on his own voice and the power of the spoken word. There were, it was true, many critics of his recitals of Offenbach: there were complaints that Kraus had no singing voice and that he relied instead on a form of *Sprechgesang*. These criticisms did not, however, affect the enormous success of these evenings. In the Offenbach operettas Kraus discovered a world in which satire yields to fantasy, and in which there occurs that release of art from its material environment which he had always claimed was a necessary prerequisite for an understanding of his own work. As for the charge that he did not understand Offenbach's music, it was the composer Alban Berg, an old friend and devoted admirer of Kraus, who pointed out the enormous intuitive feeling for musical rhythm which the satirist displayed on these occasions.[31]

But the main attraction at these recitals was the revelation of a personality of an intense and, at times, frightening moral fanaticism. At his recitals Kraus appeared as a creature possessed and transformed by his mission:

All lights were extinguished. Only above on the table with the green cover were two solitary candles burning. Their flames glittered strangely. Then Kraus came in. Young, with long awkward limbs, nervous as a bat, he moved towards the table, entrenched himself behind it, crossed his legs, smoothed his forehead, blew his nose, collected himself together like a beast of prey about to pounce, listened, waited, opened his mouth as if to bite, closed it again, waited. . . . If he had spoken in Chinese or Persian, his words would have been followed with the same excitement. His inner ardour had the same impact as the movement of a locomotive across the dry summer prairie: everything caught fire as he spoke.[32]

Nestroy had exerted a similar fascination over the audiences who saw him acting in his plays. But Nestroy was a changed man off the stage, a mild and inoffensive individual, completely under the domination of his wife. It is clear that behind Kraus's personality there stood a much greater and more tragic figure than that earlier satirist of Viennese society.

On the death of Friedrich Nietzsche in 1900, Kraus had attacked the *Neue Freie Presse* for belittling his reputation in its obituary and had himself described the German philosopher as 'the most penetrating mind of the century'.[33] From Nietzsche's personality, Kraus took a pattern for his own psychological extremism: from Nietzsche's work, a *Weltanschauung* which, however aesthetic in its emphasis, was based fundamentally on a moral repudiation of the inhuman tendencies at work within modern civilisation. The cultural pessimism expressed in Kraus's work, the antithesis which he constantly made between *Kultur* and *Zivilisation* to the detriment of the latter, was derived from a tradition of German thought which ran back through Nietzsche and Schopenhauer ultimately to Kant. Nor was that all that Kraus owed to Nietzsche. The influence of Schopenhauer and Nietzsche in Germany towards the end of the nineteenth century led to a rediscovery of the world of the German Romantics, of the work of Novalis, Tieck and the brothers Schlegel, who had found in the spirit of the German language one of the few great unifying principles which existed amidst the bewildering variety and complexity of the German cultural and political experience.

From the neo-romantic movement at the end of the nineteenth century, therefore, Kraus derived inspiration not merely for his concern with the driving force of sexuality in human existence, but also for his corrosive examination of the nature and limitations of language. Nietzsche's acute sensibility towards literary form and style, his trenchant aphorisms, his hatred of the prostitution of the German language by philosophical abstractions (a hatred expressed in essays such as 'Schopenhauer as Educator' and 'On the Future of our Educational Institutions'), adumbrated themes which Kraus was to carry much further. The quite unforced and spontaneous mingling in Kraus's work of the influence of Nestroy on the one hand and Nietzsche and Schopenhauer on the other demonstrates once again the fact that by the end of the nineteenth century Austrian literature had shed its inferiority complex *vis-à-vis* that of Germany.

The influence of Nietzsche on Kraus was, then, profound. But despite his repudiation of Judaism, despite the eagerness with which Kraus, like so many Jewish intellectuals, rushed to assimilate themselves into the world of German culture, there were elements in his Jewish inheritance which he could never completely deny. However much the satirist might be possessed of a bitter and neurotic hatred of the influence of the Jews in Vienna and their association in Central Europe with those forces of materialism and capitalism which he, as a Nietzschean, must regard as inimical to aesthetic and spiritual values, Kraus was and remained intensely Jewish. His vision of language was, in the final analysis, rooted in the specifically Judaic concept of the revelation of the will of God through the Word, the Word of power which brings what it says to pass. Although in their lives and their work Kraus and his Viennese contemporary Martin Buber were to follow very different paths, both were greatly influenced by Nietzsche and yet both were possessed by a passionate search for moral truth which could never be satisfactorily appeased by Nietzsche's repudiation of religious belief.

It was this factor which was responsible for the impact that was made on both Kraus and Buber by the rediscovery of Kierkegaard which took place in the years before 1914 largely as a result of Theodor Haecker's writings on the significance of the Danish philosopher. In Kierkegaard Kraus discovered not only an ally in his fight against the press as a manifestation of the heresy of modern 'Progress', not only a pathological individualism and a hatred of all the abstractions and ideologies which afflicted the world, but also the necessary religious alternative to the siren calls of Nietzschean atheism. It was partly because of his indebtedness to Kierkegaard that Kraus and his work were frequently defended against hostile attack by the Innsbruck literary and intellectual magazine *Der Brenner* which in the years before 1914 occupied a seminal position in the diffusion of existentialist attitudes within Austrian culture by encouraging all those talents—Adolf Loos in architecture, Kokoschka in painting, Schoenberg and Berg in music, Kraus and Trakl in literature—which were directed against the dominant movement of Impressionism. Just how far-reaching was the influence exercised by *Der Brenner* before the First World War can be seen from the fact that, in July 1914, Ludwig Wittgenstein secretly gave 100,000 Austrian crowns—a substantial part of his inheritance—to Ludwig von Ficker, the editor of this magazine, to distribute as he thought fit to promising young talent. Wittgenstein did this out of admiration for the work of Kraus and Ficker's discernment in encouraging that work.[34]

Mention has, of course, already been made of the respect in which Wittgenstein and Schoenberg held Kraus's work and personality. The relationship between Kraus's approach to language and that of Wittgenstein, especially the later Wittgenstein of the *Philosophical Investigations*, has been pointed out by Erich Heller.[35] Wittgenstein's famous description of the aim of philosophy as being like the release of a fly from a flybottle has rightly been seen by the historian, Friedrich Heer, as an expression of the dilemma of the twentieth-century Austrian intellectual, trapped in a society which long ago had lost all cohesion and meaning.[36] What was true of literature and philosophy was also true of the world of music. Before the outbreak of the First World War Vienna produced not only the early philosophy of Wittgenstein but also the first compositions of Arnold Schoenberg who in the course of his career was to push the chromaticism prevalent in music after the death of Wagner up to, and then finally beyond, the frontiers of tonality, creating in the process a new kind of musical language. In the dedication which he sent to Kraus with a copy of his *Harmonielehre*, Schoenberg wrote, 'I have learnt more perhaps from you than one can learn if one is to remain independent.'[37]

That there was a deep affinity in temperament between Wittgenstein, Schoenberg and Kraus is quite clear: in their hatred of all that was slovenly or imprecise in the means of expression at their disposal, in their intransigence towards opposition or contradiction, in their at times hidden but very real humility, all three were inspired by an Angst which was fundamentally ethical and even, one might say, religious in nature. But there are certain qualifications that must be made if one is tempted to see too close a relationship between their work.[38] Kraus was a poet and not a philosopher: it is not legitimate to see in his scattered essays and aphorisms any systematic theory on the nature of language. Nor was he a musician. Despite the intuitive musicality which Alban Berg praised in his work, Kraus himself testified to the fact that he did not possess any formal understanding of music; and certainly as far as Schoenberg's music was concerned the satirist's attitude seems to have been one of benevolent incomprehension. Although Schoenberg, faced with the extremism and intolerance of some of his disciples, was in his later years to complain that he was not an atonal composer, it is undeniable that, as has been previously pointed out, certain elements in his work can be viewed as the beginnings of a breakthrough to an entirely new kind of musical language. The same cannot be said of the relationship between Kraus and German literature: the satirist's obsession with language, although possessed of radical—and even anarchic—implications, was always the expression of a deeper conservatism.

This respect for tradition can be seen in many ways. Throughout his career Kraus was concerned to demonstrate his indebtedness to such past masters of the German language as Jean Paul, Lichtenberg, and Schopenhauer. Towards Nietzsche and towards Nietzsche's posthumous influence on German literature, the satirist's sympathies were divided: although he was, for example, to support and encourage many members of the Expressionist movement before 1914, seeing in the work of such writers as Wedekind, Trakl, and Else Lasker-Schüler, a necessary reaction against the cloistered aestheticism of the Impressionists, Kraus's enthusiasm soon evaporated when, in the course of the First World War, in the work of a number of writers the violent and destructive element always near the surface in Expressionism erupted into a wild and uncontrolled disregard for considerations of form and meaning. Although most writers whose work may loosely be regarded as Expressionist in manner were to be supporters of the extreme left in German politics in the 1920s, only a small number of individuals, including Brecht, were to be exempt from the satirist's attack during that decade. Indeed Kraus was bitterly to compare the spiritual nihilism which characterised the work of a number of Expressionists with that of writers who stood near to the Nazis. When in 1933 the satirist was to be confronted with a régime in Germany which claimed a vulgarised and distorted Nietzsche as one of its principal intellectual antecedents, he reacted by condemning those elements in Nietzsche's work which made such misrepresentation possible, complaining of 'the flight of Zarathustra from civilisation into a chaos of metaphors'.[39]

'I am only one of the epigones living in the old house of language,' Kraus wrote in one of his poems.[40] It is in his lyrical poetry and his translations of Shakespeare and Offenbach that the conservative orientation of the satirist can be most clearly seen. Freed from the necessity of attacking the outside world through the medium of polemic and satire, Kraus found in his poetry an outlet for those impulses of love, fear and wonder which found only a frustrated expression in his other work. The satirist often took the same incident—some episode during the First World War for example—which provoked one of his most savage polemics, and then transmuted it into a work of satirical art, a commentary on some human folly which will long outlive the circumstances which brought it to pass. Kraus moves a stage further in his poetry: now language is permitted its fullest freedom from material necessity. In that masterly essay 'Der Reim' which he included in his book *Die Sprache*, the satirist attacked those poets to whom the function of rhyme is not central to whole meaning and significance of a poem. In his own poetry rhyme and meaning are fused inseparably together; Kraus retreats into a still and ordered world in which he clearly demonstrates his allegiance to periods of German culture earlier than his own, the era of Goethe and Hölderlin, and the era of the German Romantics. It would not be an exaggeration to say that, even when it seems to have achieved its most spontaneous level of expression, Kraus's poetry has the concentrated but sterile beauty of a tradition that has come to an end. As Erich Heller has written:

> He is not a 'modern' poet. His subjects, images, rhymes and rhythms are traditional. . . . But they are made of brittler stuff than their traditional appearance would suggest. Their material seems purified in the purgatory of the satirist's experience and hardened by the determination of one who was called to defend what is left of the innocence of the world.[41]

Already in the middle of the nineteenth century, Grillparzer had sounded the note of cosmic pessimism which, in varying degrees, was characteristic of the Viennese intellectual scene before 1914: 'I am', he had written, 'the poet of the last things.' It was Grillparzer, too, who had related his pessimism to the political and social situation which surrounded him when he lamented the coming journey of mankind from humanism through nationalism to bestiality. For all the sparkle of his wit Nestroy, too, Kraus maintained, was possessed of the tragic vision. The novelist Hermann Broch writing on Hofmannsthal and his epoch rightly characterised the last quarter of the nineteenth century in Vienna as 'the façade era' in which the superlative but insubstantial music of Johann Strauss epitomised the evaporation of the spiritual content of Viennese culture just as surely as did the cult of the feuilleton in the press.[42]

In reaction the Viennese writer indulged in melancholic introspection and nostalgia for the happier period of Vormärz, the period before the revolutions of 1848. The only solution that seemed to offer itself to the growing sense of isolation which the writer experienced in his society was an aesthetic withdrawal into a cult of the self. The Impressionist movement was in part a response to this situation. Hermann Bahr attempted to provide intellectual justification for this position by using the theories of the philosopher, Ernst Mach, who had taught at the University of Vienna in the closing years of the nineteenth century, to point to the intensely subjective nature of man's perception of the world outside that relatively small area of knowledge where truth was scientifically verifiable. Hofmannsthal, it is true, after recovering from the crisis which had provoked the 'Chandos Letter' attempted to reintegrate himself into his society by means of the drama and an attachment to the Catholic Church. The position of political and cultural conservatism to which he moved, however, bore little relation to the realities of the Austrian situation, as Kraus was constantly to point out: in *The Austrian Idea* published in 1917, Hofmannsthal's apologia for Austrian civilisation as the bridge which united all the great cultures of Europe—German, Latin and Slav—contrasted sharply with the increasing subjugation of Austria to Germany in the third year of the First World War.

The influence of Ernst Mach and of the contemporary revolution in psychology penetrated into all aspects of the Viennese literary scene, whether the writer accepted or rejected Freud's particular contribution to the latter field.[43] Both influences can be very clearly seen at work in Robert Musil's novel *The Man*

Without Qualities. Set in the year 1913–14 against a richly
detailed background of the preparations for the celebrations to
be held in 1918 of the seventieth anniversary of the accession of
the Emperor Franz Josef, the novel examines the progressive
withdrawal of the principal character, Ulrich, from all social
contacts and human relationships within a Vienna that, in its
shapelessness and futility, has become to him increasingly unreal.
In order that Ulrich shall survive a society that is about to perish,
he must divest himself of all those 'qualities' which that society
has imprinted on him. Thus Musil's 'solution' to the dilemma of
the sensitive individual is one in which salvation is to be achieved
by a process of radical alienation: in the soft and yielding
atmosphere of Musil's Vienna, the influence of Nietzsche is once
more discernible.

The theatrical quality of so much Viennese life, the sense of
the individual as a marionette acting out a destiny over which he
has little control, is characteristic also of the work of Arthur
Schnitzler. His play *Doctor Bernhardi* (1912) vividly illustrates
the difficulties of the Jews in a society where their every action
is open to misrepresentation. Bernhardi provokes a political
outcry because of his decision to deny a priest access to a dying
girl on the grounds that she is ignorant of her condition and
would die more peacefully if she were left in this state of
ignorance; as a result of his action the doctor is condemned to
two months' imprisonment. Schnitzler's novel *Der Weg ins
Freie* (The Path to Freedom, 1908) deals with a number of
Viennese individuals aware that they are drifting through life
towards some end which is as yet unknown. For each of these
individuals the moment arrives for some decision to be taken in
respect of creeds and ideologies as well as in personal relationships:
the principal Jewish character, for example, decides after a long
period of soul-searching to become a Zionist, and the aristocrat,
Georg, abandons his mistress in the belief that he can best find
himself in his artistic pursuits. And yet it is clear that the novelist
himself did not believe that any of his characters had really
solved their problems. His message is fatalist: 'The paths to

freedom do not run through the lands out yonder, but rather through our inner selves.'[44] Schnitzler did not indicate any great conviction that freedom could be found even there, except the ability to live with reality.

Amongst writers such as Schnitzler and Musil whose relationship towards Vienna was a more subtle blend of attraction and repulsion than his own, the demonic element in Kraus's personality could inspire a lasting hostility. Musil, on one occasion, compared the fanaticism of Kraus's disciples with that of Hitler's.[45] Kraus reciprocated this hostility: he once, for example, maliciously accused Schnitzler of writing for Jewish intellectuals suffering from fatty degeneration of the mind.[46] The satirist's own relationship with his society was at the same time more negative and more positive than that of most of his contemporaries: it is this ambivalence at the heart of his life and work which imparts to that work its peculiar fascination. His attitude to politics is a very good illustration of the kind of problem to be faced. Any purely aesthetic approach to Kraus's work must continually take into account the fact that so much of it was inspired by the passions of his day and could not have been written without an intense interest in the politics of his society. On the other hand, of course, the satirist never ceased to heap contempt upon all political parties and politicians. How little Kraus was interested in politics defined in any narrow way is shown by the following anecdote which dates from the period just before his death. In answer to the charge that he was occupied with problems concerning commas while the Japanese were bombarding Shanghai, Kraus replied:

> I know it is all pointless when the house is on fire. But I must do this as long as it is possible for, if the people responsible had always taken care that all the commas were in the right place, Shanghai would not be burning.[47]

It is hardly surprising, therefore, that the satirist's ventures into the political arena—his vociferous campaign to secure the dismissal of the Viennese police chief, Johannes Schober, in 1927, for example, or his sudden, almost overnight, switch from an extreme left wing position to one of support for the Dollfuss régime in 1932—could not but seem quixotic if not malevolently perverse, if viewed from any orthodox political standpoint. Constantly the charge was made against him that his political positions were the *reductio ad absurdum* of his excessively aesthetic approach to human experience.

Many of the criticisms that have been made against Kraus in this respect have some justification. But they are also in part irrelevant. The very nature of the satirist's 'ridiculous' interventions in the political arena, his absurd belief that an individual could—almost single-handed—bring down governments and influence policies, is itself a most illuminating comment on the society in which he lived. That a writer whose chosen realm was that of *Geist* should have decided that the only way in which he could fulfil himself was through a savage denunciation of an environment which made any other literary activity futile, and that this writer should, in the pursuit of his mission, be drawn into an active involvement in the political process which he so vehemently despised—all this reveals in the most striking way the neurotic character both of the satirist and the society which nurtured him. It was the same society, albeit in a very different cultural milieu, in which the young Hitler spent most of the years from 1907 to 1913, acknowledging it to be 'a hard school for me; but it taught me the most profound lessons of my life'.[48] Hitler emerged from a society in which, despite the brittle and deceptive charm of the pleasure-loving Viennese, hysteria was never very far from the surface. Kraus illustrated very well the difference between the atmosphere of Berlin and that of Vienna before 1914 when he described Prussia as a place where one was free to move but one's mouth was gagged, Austria as an isolation cell in which one was allowed to scream.[49]

2 'Research Laboratory for World Destruction': Austria, 1899–1914

ALTHOUGH the Habsburg Empire was to collapse catastrophically at the end of the First World War, only a small minority of its fifty million inhabitants wished, before that fateful year of 1918, to see the break-up of this remarkable political entity that united the many different nationalities living between the Alps, the Carpathians, and the Adriatic Sea. The problem which faced the rulers of Austria-Hungary in the second half of the nineteenth century was how their dominions should be transformed from a purely dynastic agglomeration of kingdoms and principalities into a modern political organisation viable in an age of industrialisation and mass democracy. All attempts to achieve this transformation ended in failure.

There were many reasons for this. The mission of Austria in the seventeenth and eighteenth centuries had been the defence of Catholicism and resistance to the Turk. In the nineteenth century Metternich had tried, not altogether unsuccessfully, to use Vienna as the centre for European opposition to the principles of nationalism and democracy. But what mission would the Empire fulfil if it attempted to come to terms with the demands of its peoples? Although practically everyone wished to see the Empire continue, no one could agree on the form in which this renewal should take place. Each group within the Empire hoped to capture the Habsburgs as the instruments of their ambitions; the Catholic Church wished the dynasty to uphold and maintain its dominant position among the religions of the Empire; the Social Democrats wanted the Emperor to ally with them to bring socialism to the peoples of Central and Eastern Europe; those

Slavs who disliked the brutal and reactionary nature of the Tsarist régime in Russia hoped to transform the Habsburg Empire into a liberal Slav-dominated confederation which would serve as a beacon to the oppressed masses of the East.

The one national group which came nearest to obtaining its political demands was the Hungarians. Having attempted to secure their complete independence from the Habsburgs in 1848, the Hungarians had been crushed by the dynasty (with the aid of Russian troops) in the next year. For some time after this the Emperor attempted to rule his Empire in a centralised form directly from Vienna. Not only did this attempt prove increasingly difficult in the face of continuing Hungarian opposition, the necessity for a broader base of popular support for the dynasty was underlined by the Austrian defeat at the hands of the Prussians in the war of 1866. By the *Ausgleich* or Compromise of 1867, which divided the Empire into two parts, one part ruled from Vienna and the other from Budapest, the Habsburgs were therefore compelled to grant widespread autonomy to the most highly organised and politically effective nationality within the Empire. One result of the *Ausgleich* was the subordination of the non-Hungarian peoples of one half of the Empire to the rule of the Magyars. Although the numbers of these other nationalities amounted to over half the total population of the Hungarian part of the Empire, the minorities were deeply divided amongst themselves, and many potential leaders of a movement against domination from Budapest were attracted away from championing the cause of their own people by the willingness of the Hungarians to accept into their nation anyone who was prepared to learn their language and assimilate themselves into Hungarian culture. This was the one liberal aspect of an otherwise extremely illiberal policy of Magyarisation which was implemented against the Serbs, the Slovaks, and the Rumanians

The minorities were not the only group to suffer from the high-handedness of the Hungarian ruling class. As the imperial government in Vienna became progressively weaker towards the end of the nineteenth century, the radical nationalists within

Hungary continually chafed at the restrictions placed upon their freedom by the *Ausgleich* of 1867: persistently they demanded that Hungary should be allowed to control its own separate army and conduct its own foreign policy without reference to Vienna. The relations between the Emperor and the Hungarians were perpetually under varying degrees of strain over these points despite the fact that the latter always exercised considerable influence over the foreign policy pursued by the imperial government; indeed, after 1867 a number of the foreign ministers of the Empire were drawn from the ranks of the Hungarian ruling class.

Within the Austrian part of the Empire the German-speaking population never enjoyed the same degree of authority which the Hungarians exercised from Budapest. One factor responsible for this was the active presence in Vienna of the Emperor, who wielded far more power in Austria than in a Hungary of which he was the distant and largely ineffectual king. Furthermore, the minorities within the Austrian half of the Empire—the Poles, the Czechs, the Italians, for example—were never so easily dominated as the Slovaks or the Rumanians. The Poles, indeed, enjoyed many privileges denied to other minorities and in many practical affairs were largely independent of the imperial government. The Czechs were the most educated and industrialised Slav nation within the Empire, a people whose growing wealth in the nineteenth century resulted in the gradual displacement from power of the hitherto dominant German minority within Bohemia and Moravia. As far as the Italians were concerned, after the creation of the kingdom of Italy in 1859 and the cession of Venetia by Austria in 1866, the nationalist movement amongst the Italians of Trieste and the South Tyrol was amongst the most recalcitrant with which the Habsburgs had to deal. How were all these peoples to be reconciled to the imperial throne?

The Emperor Franz Josef, whose long reign was to last from 1848 to 1916, was a dynast whose only interest was to preserve his inheritance from those forces of social and political change by which it was threatened. Although he could be regarded as a German member of an essentially German line of rulers, Franz Josef belonged spiritually to an era of European history that existed long before the rise of nationalism and racialism. Having been compelled in 1867 to abandon millions of his subjects to the domination of the Hungarians, the Emperor henceforth was determined never to identify himself too closely with the claims and aspirations of that other traditional 'master race', the German population within the Austrian part of the Empire. In 1879 he withdrew his support from the German Liberals, who had dominated Austrian politics since 1867 and chose as his prime minister Count Taaffe, who was to remain at the helm until 1893. Taaffe's avowed policy of keeping all the nationalities in a 'balanced state of dissatisfaction' by alternately making threats and concessions to the various conflicting groups, was based on the support of the Poles, the Czechs and those Austrian Germans to whom Catholicism and allegiance to the Emperor were more important than the claims of German nationalism. The fall of Taaffe in 1893, however, and—even more—the inability of Franz Josef in 1897 to implement the schemes of his minister Badeni to grant equal rights to the Czech and German languages in Bohemia, indicated that the room for imperial manoeuvre was being drastically reduced.

The failure of Badeni's language ordinances was largely due to the violent street demonstrations which his policies provoked in Vienna, demonstrations in which a prominent rôle was played by the racialist Pan-German movement under Georg von Schoenerer. The rise of this movement was an extreme example of the difficulties with which Franz Josef had to contend by the end of the nineteenth century. Schoenerer had publicly repudiated his loyalty to the Emperor and his allegiance to the Catholic Church, since he felt that both were betraying the interests of the German element within the Empire in order to appease the demands of Slav nationalism; in reaction to this situation, he looked increasingly towards the eventual break-up of the Empire and the union of the Austrian Germans with the powerful German Reich of Wilhelm II. This was a striking change from the situation at the beginning of the nineteenth century when, faced with the choice between Berlin and Vienna as a focus for resistance to the expansionist ambitions of Napoleonic France, many German intellectuals had opted for the latter. Nevertheless, although Pan-Germanism was a far more important factor in Austrian life than might be suggested by the small numbers of the lunatic fringe around Schoenerer himself, it is important to note that down to the final collapse of 1918 the dynasty retained the loyalty of the great majority of the Austrian Germans.

The parties of this majority were the Christian Socialists and the Social Democrats. The former emerged in the last quarter of the nineteenth century as the vehicle for the political aspirations of the lower middle class of Vienna and the peasantry of Lower Austria. The ideology of the party was Catholic, pro-Habsburg and anti-semitic: it was hostile to the power of both the big financial concerns inside Austria (which were largely Jewish) and the Austrian Social Democrats (many of whose leaders were also Jewish). But ideological considerations never played a major part in Christian Socialist policies. The party's most prominent leader, Karl Lueger, Mayor of Vienna from 1897 (after years in which his appointment had been blocked by Franz Josef) until his death in 1910, was a demagogue of genius, an opportunist and a practical politician who did much to improve the municipal amenities of Vienna during his period of office. His antisemitism was partly serious, partly theatrical: Lueger counted a number of wealthy Viennese Jews amongst his sympathisers and even his circle of friends. His flexibility in tactics and his abilities as an orator made a profound impression on the young Hitler. If the latter disapproved of Lueger's fidelity to the Habsburgs and the ambivalent nature of his stance on the Jewish question, Hitler did realise that Lueger was a more effective political figure than an ideologue like Schoenerer and that his policies enabled the Christian Socialist party to adapt itself to changing circumstances far more easily than was the case with the Pan-Germans or, for that matter, the Social Democrats. On the other hand for this advantage there was a heavy price to pay: the weakness of the Christian Socialist position lay in the hostility that existed between the various social strata in what was essentially a confessional party, a hostility that was reflected in the continual tensions between the party leadership in Vienna and that of the provinces. More than most other political parties in Austria the fortunes of the Christian Socialists were greatly dependent on the personality and flair of their leadership: between the death of Lueger and the emergence of Seipel in the 1920s, for example, the morale and effectiveness of the party declined markedly.

In 1911, one year after Lueger's death, the Christian Socialists lost their overall majority on the city council of Vienna. Seven years later, at the end of the First World War, the Social Democrats gained control of the Austrian capital, remaining in power ever since—except for the period between 1934 and 1945 when the party was proscribed first by the Dollfuss dictatorship and then by the Nazis. The Viennese Social Democrats included within their ranks many personalities of wide cultural sympathies and considerable intellectual sophistication, and produced in the theoretical works of Friedrich Adler, Max Adler, Karl Renner, Otto Bauer and Rudolf Hilferding a remarkable amalgam of both orthodox and revisionist Marxist literature that has been given the collective and misleading description of 'Austro-Marxism'. Misleading because there were important differences of principles and temperament between these thinkers, differences which were to be shown most clearly in the long rivalry which existed between Karl Renner and Otto Bauer.

Both these men adopted a broadly similar position in the work which they did before the First World War on the nationality problem in the Habsburg Empire: both hoped that Austria-Hungary could be transformed into a modern supra-national political organisation by co-operation between the dynasty and the peoples. But whereas Renner's socialism derived ultimately from Lassalle's acceptance of the power of the state as the prerequisite for social advance, the socialism of Otto Bauer was of a more radical and libertarian nature. Once the First World War had broken out the divergence between Renner and Bauer became apparent. The former stubbornly maintained his belief in a Greater Austria which could be achieved if socialists collaborated with the Emperor against the divisive forces of nationalism. Bauer, on the other hand, became progressively more sceptical of the wisdom of preserving an Empire which was increasingly incapable of protecting its minority peoples and moved towards a position favouring the independence of all the nationalities, including the right of the Austrian Germans to opt for union with a democratic and socialist Germany. As will be seen later, the differences between these two men continued to affect the policies of the Social Democratic party in the course of the 1920s and down to the temporary eclipse of the party after the inauguration of the Dollfuss dictatorship and the riots of February 1934. In some ways the conflict that went on within the Social Democratic organisation may be seen as a microcosm of the much larger conflict of loyalties to which the Austrian racial mixture was condemned. Bauer was a Jewish intellectual who saw in socialism the only effective solution to the inhumanity of man to man, to the hatred between Gentile and Jew. He came to dominate the party through the energy and brilliance of his personality and through his passionate concern for humanitarian values. The function of Renner, the son of a poor Moravian peasant, became to inject into the party debates a sense of realism, a realism which, however sordid on occasion, was particularly necessary after the fascination which Bauer exerted by his feats of dialectical skill.

It was a constant source of amazement to foreign observers of the Viennese scene that two opponents so different from each other as Bauer and Renner could remain together within the same party. There was an explanation for this: under Viktor Adler, who until his death in 1918 was its first leader, the Social Democratic party had been instilled with the idea that its overriding concern should be with internal unity. Such a consideration had been particularly important in the 1880s and

1890s when the Socialist cause was plagued with intense
conflicts between followers of Marx, Lassalle and Bakunin and
was faced with the external threat of repression and persecution
by the imperial government. The need for unity was further
demonstrated even after the era of persecution had come to an
end: after 1900, the party, although rapidly increasing in
strength, was subjected to those centrifugal forces of nationalism
which were afflicting the Empire at large, forces which were
eventually responsible for the split into distinctive Austrian,
German, Czech and Polish parties which took place within the
Social Democratic movement in the years before the outbreak
of the First World War. That the morale of the party was not
fatally impaired during this period of disintegration and that the
Austrian Social Democrats during the First World War did not
experience that tragic division between Majority Socialist, Independent Socialists and Spartacists, which marked the beginning
of the decline of Social Democracy in Germany, was due very
largely to the policies pursued by Viktor Adler.

Adler's work was indeed impressive. The Austrian party prided
itself on the size and wealth of its organisation and on the high
morale of its members to whom it offered facilities of every kind;
opportunities for further education, singing and dramatic
societies, youth associations, special magazines for women. Not
for nothing did the Austrian Social Democrats, like their
counterparts in Germany, pride themselves on being a 'state
within a state'. But there were dangers in this situation. The
deeply conservative character of Viennese society expressed itself
not merely in the caste system of the Habsburg court but also in
the deep respect for hierarchy which characterised the Social
Democratic party and was reflected both in the sophistication of
the leadership and in the gulf which existed between the leadership and the rank and file. There was even further point to
the comparisons that were sometimes jokingly made between the
position of Viktor Adler and that of Franz Josef: just as the
Habsburg Emperor tried to reconcile the irreconcilable tensions
within his Empire, so the Social Democratic leadership attempted

39

to transcend not only the nationalist and separatist forces within its ranks but also the very real ideological divisions which afflicted the socialist movement in every European country in the years before the outbreak of the First World War.

As so often happens in this sort of situation, the party as a whole was influenced as much by the vices as by the virtues of the different factions within its ranks. If the policies of the moderates were rendered ineffectual by the doctrinaire attitude of the radicals, the latter in their turn were forced in the name of party unity to accept responsibility for manoeuvres which made them appear both inconsistent and hypocritical. This problem was exacerbated by the growth in power and organisation of the party after 1918, a process that was accompanied by a marked decline in that generosity of spirit and receptivity to new ideas which had been characteristic of the era of Viktor Adler. In the 1920s there emerged a type of Social Democratic functionary whose whole life had been spent within the political organisation and ideological framework of the party, a type whose main loyalty was focused on the party machine almost as an end in itself.

The rise of the Social Democratic party was yet another example of the proliferation of ideologies which occurred in Austrian life towards the end of the nineteenth century. Ideologies were of course to spread in all countries during this period: and yet the conditions for such a development were particularly favourable in Austria. For Vienna was not a great capital city in the same sense as Paris or Berlin: it was, rather, an enormously overgrown Versailles, whose civilisation had depended on constant fertilisation from every part of Europe over which the Habsburgs had ruled. As Erich Heller has pointed out, the very virtues of Viennese society laid it open to corruption:

> Its very generosity and blissful lack of formulated moral convictions, its baroque taste for untidiness, its sense of drama and dramatic upheavals, and its childlike trust in its own everlastingness made it the more susceptible to the poison of industrialisation and commercialisation. A people in whom

faith had always had preponderance over the intellect enthusiastically embraced political ideologies which offered a substitute for the evaporating convictions of religion.[1]

It is only against the background of a society in the process of fragmentation, and indeed, of atomisation, that it is possible to understand the inflated claims of the political ideologies—Pan-Germanism, Pan-Slavism, Marxism, Christian Socialism, Zionism, to name only a few—which met at the heart of the Habsburg Empire in its decline. The paradox was that the growing crisis within Viennese society was concealed by that indefinable quality of *Gemütlichkeit*, the reluctance of the majority of Viennese ever to push matters to their logical conclusion. The situation was always 'desperate, but not serious'. Even the most bitter satirist of this society was constantly in danger of being accepted—and dismissed—as a literary entertainer. It was this which provoked the extremism of Kraus's attack.

The first issue of *Die Fackel* appeared in Vienna early in April 1899. The title of this new venture was derived from that of *La Lanterne*, the satirical magazine in which Henri Rochefort had castigated the follies of the Second Empire in France. A more immediate model for Kraus was *Die Zukunft* (The Future), published by the journalist, Maximilian Harden, in Berlin.[2] A man with wide interests in politics and literature, Harden, who was Jewish by extraction, was the most feared by all the journalists of Wilhelmine Germany having formed early in his career an alliance with the dismissed Bismarck to attack the policies and pretensions of the young Kaiser, Wilhelm II. If the violence of Harden's attacks on the German Kaiser shook the hard-boiled political and literary world of Berlin, all the greater was the impact of Kraus's onslaught on the Viennese press. The first small red-covered issue of *Die Fackel* caused such an immediate sensation in the coffee-houses that a second printing of several thousand was immediately rushed out.

The *Neue Freie Presse* which was the main object of Kraus's attack was the leading organ of the Jewish Liberal bourgeoisie of the Austrian part of the Empire, its counterpart in Hungary being the *Pester Lloyd*. It had been founded in 1864 by August Zang with the aim of representing the economic and political interests of the middle clasess in the era of the constitutional experiments which the Emperor initiated in the period between the failure of the repressive policies of the 1850s and the conclusion of the Compromise of 1867. In the methods which he employed in operating the *Neue Freie Presse*, Zang evolved a newspaper which became a model for the rest of the Viennese press: he established the closest of relations with the great industrial and banking interests in Austria and his newspaper constantly defended the interests of this group. It was characteristic of Zang that he once half-seriously confided that he dreamt of the day when every column of his newspaper had been paid for by an outside body. During the forty years from 1880 to 1920 which marked the editorship of his successor, Moritz Benedikt, greater emphasis was laid on the purely journalistic aspect of the newspaper. Benedikt was an editor of superlative gifts and was once described by one of his former employees who subsequently supported the Nazis as 'an incarnation of the newspaper'.[3] Under such an editor the *Neue Freie Presse* became—as it was bound to become in a state like Austria where, with the exception of the brief period from 1867 to 1879, the Liberals had not achieved effective political power—the most important political instrument of big business and the Stock Exchange. The position of the Viennese press thus had no close parallel with that of England, France, or America where the existence of powerful representative institutions afforded an alternative means for the exercise of political pressure on the part of the middle class. This fact was commented upon by the experienced English journalist Wickham Steed in his book on the Habsburg Monarchy first published in 1913.[4]

Politically, the evolution of the *Neue Freie Presse* followed the rapid development of national consciousness amongst the German-speaking members of the Habsburg Empire in the last two decades of the nineteenth century, a development which was itself a reaction to the growth of Slav nationalism, especially among the Czechs. As would be expected, however, the *Neue Freie Presse* vigorously opposed the antisemitism of the Pan-German movement and the less extreme antisemitism of the Christian Socialists. Nevertheless, in response to this antisemitism the *Neue Freie Presse* was made even more stridently nationalist in tone. The Jewish press in Budapest was xenophobic for similar reasons—only in this case from a Magyar point of view. As far as foreign policy was concerned, Benedikt constantly advocated closer links with the German Empire and, as the dependence of the Habsburg Empire on the German Reich increased in the years before 1914, the relations between Benedikt and the anti-Serb war party at court—men like the Austrian Chief of staff, Conrad von Hötzendorf—grew closer.

The Austrian government had always maintained close links with the press, links that were both formal and informal, so that foreign opinion came to regard the views of the *Neue Freie Presse* as indicative of the policies of the government; it was this newspaper, instead of the official *Fremdenblatt*, which the government used when it did not wish to associate itself directly with a policy. The links between government and press in Austria were all the closer because of a factor that has already been pointed out—the lack of any effective centre of political power. If the groups in the Austrian parliament, the Reichsrat, did not control the government (which was especially true after the Emperor's dismissal of Beck, the prime minister, in 1908), neither could the collection of bureaucrats and courtiers entrusted with the destinies of the Empire rule without some measure of popular support. Within the Reichsrat this meant the manipulation of the parties by the use of the carrot and the stick: outside, it meant the mobilisation of support within the press by the same methods. Such a system bred irresponsibility. The Austrian press, unlike that of France, was largely independent of direct financial bribes from the government, but it feared the considerable powers of censorship which the government possesed.

Furthermore, the press could be won over by government concessions to the financial interests which stood behind the newspapers.[5] With the decline in political power of the Liberals and the rise of the two great mass parties of the Christian Socialists and the Social Democrats, the Liberal Jewish press was obviously drawn more and more into seeking indirect political influence behind the scenes. The paradoxical result was that the influence of Moritz Benedikt increased as the government, fearful of the rise of mass democracy, grew weaker. Thus Wickham Steed reported that it was jokingly but not untruthfully said that, next to Moritz Benedikt, the Emperor was the most important man in the country.[6] It was indeed with full approval that Kraus once quoted the statement of Bismarck (who certainly knew all the arts of newspaper manipulation) that the influence of the Viennese press was more pernicious than that of Prussian journalism.[7]

It was a view shared by many Austrians themselves. They certainly enjoyed the technical excellence and journalistic verve of the *Neue Freie Presse*, a newspaper which prided itself on its unique position within Viennese life and regarded itself as worthy to be mentioned in the same context as *The Times*. Yet another of those Viennese witticisms which reveal the reluctant admiration which Benedikt's newspaper commanded was that some people inscribed on their visiting cards after their name the description 'subscriber to the *Neue Freie Presse*'. That this ornament of the Viennese press was corrupt was widely known and accepted as a fact of life. Popular resentment against the press was focused not so much on the *Neue Freie Presse* as on the more popular boulevard sheets such as the *Neues Wiener Journal* and the *Neues Wiener Tagblatt*, whose links with major industrial and banking interests were handled much less discreetly.

If the Christian Socialists were never consistent opponents of the Jewish press since Lueger was concerned to cultivate a close relationship with a number of press proprietors including Jakob Lippowitz of the *Neues Wiener Journal*, the hostility of the Pan-

Germans was a far more serious and violent affair and led in 1888 to a notorious incident in which the *Neues Wiener Tagblatt* was involved. After prematurely reporting the death of Kaiser Wilhelm I of Germany in an extra edition on the evening of 8 March 1888, that newspaper came out with a further extra edition around midnight declaring that the first report was false and the Kaiser was still alive. Schoenerer and his followers who had been singing a memorial ode to the German Kaiser, burst into the editorial offices of the newspaper. A fracas ensued in which a number of people were injured and a considerable amount of property was damaged. The 'Jewish devils', whom Schoenerer had accused of making capital out of the death of His Germanic Majesty, appealed to the courts who rewarded Schoenerer with expulsion from the Reichsrat and four months' imprisonment. A feature of the case, however, was the widespread sympathy aroused on behalf of the Pan-German leader for his reaction to the activities of the Jewish press. [8]

It is against this sort of background that Kraus's hatred of sections of the Jewish press of Vienna and his position during the Dreyfus Affair must be seen. It is not often realised the anti-semitism generated by the Affair in France caused tremendous excitement among the Jews of Germany and Austria and was, as will be seen later, largely responsible in converting the distinguished Viennese journalist Theodor Herzl to the cause of Zionism. The *Neue Freie Presse* and the Liberal press in Germany took every opportunity to declare their belief in the innocence of Captain Dreyfus and in this stand they were supported by the bulk of Austrian and German Social Democrats. One exception, however, was Wilhelm Liebknecht, one of the leading figures of German Social Democracy. Liebknecht himself was inclined to believe that Dreyfus might be guilty and that the outcry against France conducted in the Central European press would fan the winds of militarism. He was also convinced of the hypocrisy of a press which concentrated on evils abroad and was blind to those at home. Faced by the overwhelmingly Dreyfusard sympathies of the German and Austrian parties and press,

Liebknecht chose to state his position in the *Fackel* of 1899.[9] A further point which he made in his articles was that, by ostentatiously backing Dreyfus, Liberals and Social Democrats were in grave danger of increasing antisemitism at home.

The storm which was provoked by these articles raged long after the death of Liebknecht in 1900. To write for a magazine that was in no sense an official organ of the Socialist movement was regarded as a particularly heinous transgression against the canons of party discipline. Naturally enough, after Liebknecht's death, Kraus came in for most of the blame. Friedrich Adler, the son of Viktor Adler, the leader of the Austrian Social Democrats, attacked *Die Fackel* in the *Arbeiter Zeitung*: and at the Dresden Congress of the German Social Democratic party in 1903 it was claimed by Karl Kautsky, the leading ideologist of the party, that Liebknecht had written for the *Fackel* in ignorance of the fact that it was not an official organ of the Austrian party. The fury of Socialists both in France as well as in Central Europe was undoubtedly exacerbated by the fact that the French novelist Maurice Barrès translated the Liebknecht articles and published his translations in the militantly anti-Dreyfusard and monarchist *Revue de l'Action Française*.[10] Nor were the Social Democrats appeased by Kraus's reply to the charges made at Dresden, in which he pointed out that Liebknecht, an admirer of the *Fackel*, wrote his articles in full knowledge that it lacked official connections with the Austrian party. On the contrary, the dispute became more acrimonious when Kraus printed various letters from Liebknecht showing that he had been extremely critical of the standards of the Social Democratic press in Germany and Austria, even though he would not offend the discipline of his party by attacking these newspapers openly by name.[11]

The Christian Socialists of course were able to make great use of the Dreyfus Affair in fanning popular resentment in Austria against the Jewish banking and financial groups which held such a strong grip on the commanding heights of the economy. Further fuel for antisemitism had been gathered during the long fight which had been fought in the 1860s and 1870s to prevent the sale of the Wienerwald—that remarkable green belt which Vienna has preserved to the present day—to a group of building speculators led by the Jewish financier Moritz Hirschl. From an early contributor to the *Fackel*, Joseph Schöffel, a former imperial official turned politician who could in no way be described as an anti-semite, came the revelation that the acclaim which he and others had recently received from the *Neue Freie Presse* and the *Neues Wiener Journal* for the part he and his supporters had played in preventing the sale of the Wienerwald was completely hypocritical; from the inception of the campaign August Zang, the then proprietor of the *Neue Freie Presse*, had been one of its most ardent opponents.[12]

Yet another of the innumerable concerns of the early *Fackel* was the necessity for nationalising the privately owned railways in Austria. These had largely been built with the aid of Jewish financiers amongst whom the Rothschilds were prominent. In the 1880s, when the railways were profitable, the question of nationalisation had been constantly raised in antisemitic political circles. The necessity for some action to be taken over this problem was underlined when, at the end of the century, the railways began to run at an ever-increasing loss: government subsidies were then forthcoming and there was the inevitable claim of corruption to be made—it was well known, for example, that large sections of the Viennese press were in the pay of the Südbahn. Despite political pressure by both the Social Democrats and the Christian Socialists, the Austrian railways were not to be fully nationalised until after the collapse of the Empire when the infant republic was faced with a large deficit accruing not merely from the inefficiency of the railways, but also from the enormous number of officials who had formerly been employed on the system throughout the Empire and now demanded alternative positions or pensions. It was indeed one of the major achievements of Dollfuss, in his ascent to the position of Chancellor, that he made a determined attempt to put the railways on an economic footing.[13]

What united Kraus with the Social Democrats in this early

period of the *Fackel* was their common opposition to the *laissez-faire* economic and social policies advocated by the *Neue Freie Presse*. Up to 1904 the *Fackel* gave general support to the Social Democratic party, although Kraus's attitude at the time of the Dreyfus Affair had shown the complete independence which the satirist demanded. Equally he refused to be influenced by the fact that the majority of those who bought the *Fackel* were supporters of or sympathisers with the Social Democrats: Kraus prided himself that his was the only magazine in Austria which was not written to please the readers. Having dispensed with advertisements in order to demonstrate his utter alienation from the world of capitalism, the satirist constantly attacked the *Arbeiter Zeitung* for the advertisements from which it drew much-needed revenue.[14] The Social Democrats also came in for perpetual criticism for their innate respect for authority, for their reliance for support on the stupidity and prejudices of the masses, for their addiction to empty phraseology and for their reactionary views on the relationship of Art and Literature to the world of politics.[15]

On the other hand, the Christian Socialist party with its parochialism, its demagogic antisemitism and its use of religion for political purposes held no attraction for Kraus; it was, he proclaimed, a compound of all the defects of the Habsburg Empire.[16] As far as the nationalities problem within Austria-Hungary was concerned, the satirist was in general agreement with the position taken by the Social Democrats. He was strongly opposed to the increasing nationalism of the Germans in Bohemia, a nationalism which was, of course, supported by both the *Neue Freie Presse* and the Christian Socialists: on the language problem in Bohemia the significant point which struck him was that, whatever language the Czech and German politicians quarrelled in, they were bound to debase it.[17] On the nationalities problem in Slovenia, Kraus was opposed to the strident espousal by the *Neue Freie Presse* of the German cause in that province and advocated economic development to help solve the social tensions in such a backward area. In matters of foreign

policy the main object of the satirist's attack in these early years
was the policy of Count Goluchowski, the Austrian Foreign
Minister, of backing the cruel and corrupt King Milan of Serbia
against those elements of his people which were hostile to an
Empire in which so many Serbs lived.[18]

The years from 1904 to 1906, however, show Kraus's increasing disillusionment with the world of politics.[19] Even in the
beginning, of course, his attacks on the press had not been
directed primarily at its political evils but at its perversion of
culture and its prostitution of language. From the earliest years,
too, the satirist was greatly concerned with a matter which could
only in a marginal sense be regarded as political—the reform of
the laws relating to sexual offences. Nevertheless, Kraus's
movement away from politics after 1904 was to come as a shock
to many of his friends on the Left. The issue came to a head in
the controversy in the *Fackel* between the satirist and his friend
the writer Robert Scheu, over the question of the campaign by the
Social Democrats to secure universal suffrage in Austria, a campaign which was crowned with success in 1907.

The Social Democrats regarded the outcome of this campaign
as being of crucial importance to the future of Austria. They
believed that it would both destroy the power of the imperial
bureaucrats over the Reichsrat and weaken the forces of
nationalism which were destroying the Empire, forces which,
they felt, were primarily expressions of bourgeois discontent. If
universal suffrage was granted, the Social Democrats believed,
the way would then be open for co-operation among the races of
the Empire to work for the establishment of democratic socialism.
'Austria must first die in order to live,' Viktor Adler had proclaimed:

> She must be divided into her national elements, which
> might then be integrated, if possible, into a new entity. The
> old feudalism must go; and absolutism must be broken, for
> the integration of the nationally autonomous elements of

Austria is only possible on the basis of an honest, thorough democracy.[20]

For a start, however, the Social Democrats had to be satisfied with universal suffrage within the Austrian part of the Empire only. The ruling group in Budapest had prevented the introduction of universal suffrage there in return for a promise to co-operate with the dynasty again after the political crisis which had arisen in the early years of the century over the demand of the Magyar extremists that there should be a separate Hungarian army independent of Vienna. It was, incidentally, a remarkable illustration of the lengths to which a Habsburg would go to maintain his position that Franz Josef, the incarnation of the spirit of the ancien régime throughout Europe, had not scrupled to threaten to destroy the power of the Hungarian aristocracy and gentry by extending universal suffrage to their part of the Empire if they did not come to heel over the question of the common army. The decision by the Hungarian ruling class to sacrifice sentiment for a prolongation of their political power over the minorities was received with mingled relief and dismay in Vienna, dismay predominating within progressive circles.

Before the question of universal suffrage was settled, however, the debate between Kraus and Robert Scheu had taken place.[21] The aim of the latter was to point out the inconsistency between the radicalism displayed by the satirist in his attacks on the bourgeois press and the power of capitalism and his refusal to ally himself with the progressive forces within Austria who were agitating for political democracy. Instead, Scheu complained, the satirist had by 1906 retreated into an ivory tower of aestheticism and was filled with nostalgia for an aristocratic ideal that in Austria was only represented by ennobled business men and barons who were addicted to sport; in reality there was no practical alternative open to Kraus except a choice between supporting the existing order or allying himself with the Left. In his reply, the satirist agreed that the aristocracy of which he dreamt did not exist but he believed that he had as much right as the Social Democrats to be Utopian in his ideals. He was, he explained, fanatically unpolitical because politics was basically a matter of empty slogans: the only practical result of the extension of the suffrage would be an increase in tension between the nationalities of the Empire. As for the choice which Scheu had presented to him: 'If I must choose the lesser of two evils, I will choose neither.'

In the event, the introduction of universal suffrage in Austria did not solve the fundamental social and national conflicts that were destroying the Empire: the political parties could not combine for periods long enough to force any coherent policy upon the government and, after the dismissal of the prime minister Beck in 1908, rule by imperial decree and administration by bureaucrats once again took the place of effective political activity. Deeper and more sinister forces were at work in the world, Kraus believed, forces of science and dehumanisation against which the panaceas of the Social Democrats were irrelevant.[22] Austrians were living in a world in which there were constant demonstrations at the University of Vienna, demonstrations, not of physical and physiological experiments, the satirist lamented, but political demonstrations and fights which reflected the tensions within a dying Empire.[23]

The apocalyptic note which came increasingly to the fore in Kraus's work after 1904 can be detected very clearly in the article which he wrote in 1909 attacking the political activities of the eminent Austrian historian, Professor Heinrich Friedjung. Between 1908 and 1909 there had arisen a major diplomatic crisis between Austria and Russia over the formal annexation by Austria of the Turkish provinces of Bosnia and Herzegovina, provinces which had been occupied by Austrian troops since 1878. Aehrenthal, the Austrian Foreign Minister, had secured an agreement with Russia whereby the latter would agree to the Austrian annexation provided that Austria in return supported the Russian desire to secure the opening up of the Straits at Constantinople for the regular use of the Russian fleet. Both governments wished to bolster up their declining prestige and effectiveness at home by a striking diplomatic success abroad. In the event Isvolski, the Russian Foreign Minister, frustrated in his own plans by the opposition of England and France, attempted to deny the two provinces to Austria by supporting the opposition of the Serbian government to an annexation which would include an even greater number of Slavs within the Habsburg Empire, an empire to which the Serbs were now openly hostile following the murder in 1903 of King Alexander (the son of the notorious Milan) and the accession of the pro-Russian Peter Karageorgević. The crisis of 1908 and 1909 nearly erupted into war but did not finally do so for two reasons; in the first place Germany announced her support of Austria, Wilhelm II seeing himself as a 'knight in shining armour' eager to come to the aid of his ally; secondly, Russia herself had no desire for war since Stolypin, her prime minister, was far more concerned to concentrate his energies on the more pressing problems of domestic policy.

However, on several occasions during the months of crisis it had seemed that the war party in the Austrian government, a party whose main moving spirit was Conrad von Hötzendorf, would succeed in plunging Austria-Hungary into a war that would crush Serbia for all time. One legacy of the crisis was that, as an excuse for the proposed war against Serbia, charges of treasonable relations with the Serbian government had been made against the leaders of the Serbo-Croat coalition in Croatia. Although there was an element of truth in the charges against some of the Slav leaders, the evidence on which they were subsequently tried and convicted was so blatantly spurious that they were immediately pardoned by the Emperor. But this was not the end of the affair: Aehrenthal had persuaded Friedjung, a Pan-German, to write articles in the *Neue Freie Presse* in 1908 backing up the charges of treason with documents supplied by the Austrian Foreign Office.[24] As these documents were, in fact, crude forgeries, the Serbo-Croat politicians had no difficulty in winning damages against Friedjung by an action for libel. The Czech nationalist leader Thomas Masaryk was able to use the

Interior of the Café Griensteidl

The first issue of Die Fackel

Friedjung Affair as a highly effective propaganda weapon against the anti-Slav policies of the Austrian government.

To Kraus, who secured the lifelong friendship of Masaryk for his attitude during the affair, the whole business was a further example of the disastrous nature of the alliance between government and press in Austria.[25] In a sustained and savage piece of polemic he accused Friedjung, who had not scrutinised the documents on which he based his articles, of ignoring the most elementary principles of his discipline. The case of Friedjung symbolised the corrupting influence of the press upon literature and scholarship: professors now prostituted their learning by indulging in journalism. The whole episode was a further example of the mixture of immorality and *Schlamperei* which was leading Austria to destruction. Nowhere was the emptiness of Austrian life more clearly shown than in the fact that nothing followed from this incident—nothing was done to punish Friedjung, Aehrenthal and the *Neue Freie Presse* for what they had done. No amount of *Heurigenmusik*—accordeon and violin music played in the picturesque wine-producing villages around Vienna—could conceal from the rest of the world that Austria was a land where no consequences were ever drawn from actions.[26]

The political decay of Austria was made even more apparent during the Balkan wars of 1912 and 1913 when first Serbia, Greece and Bulgaria defeated the Turks and then Greece and Serbia attacked Bulgaria which had taken the lion's share of the gains in the encounter with the Turks. The maintenance of the Turkish Empire had been for years a cardinal principle of Austrian foreign policy, a principle which was based on the need to keep the Balkan peoples weak and divided so that they could not provide strong focal points for nationalist sentiment within the Habsburg Empire. During the Balkan wars, however, Austria was condemned to stand by helplessly while the Turks were almost completely evicted from Europe. Instead of the military intervention which he wanted, Conrad von Hötzendorf had to be content with giving interviews to the press and to be photographed studying the map of the Balkans: had he never before studied a map of the Balkans, Kraus wondered?[27]

It was a symbol of Austrian impotence that the only way in which she could preserve the fiction of herself as a great power was, by repeated mobilisations and threats to Serbia, to insist upon the independence of the backward inhabitants of Albania. The *Neue Freie Presse* constantly reminded Serbia of the might of Germany and Italy behind Austria ('We are in favour of peace, but not peace at any price.'), while at the same time it maintained that Austria did not grudge Serbia her territorial gains at the expense of the Turks.[28] On the occasion of the expulsion of the Serbs from Scutari, an expulsion that was accompanied by much suffering and cruelty, the leading article of that newspaper condemned the atrocities which had taken place as an affront to civilised Europe: on the second page, however, there was a report of the festivities in Vienna on the news of the town's fall.[29] Denied a victory of their own—the troops marching through the streets of Vienna during the frequent mobilisations had been at last ridiculed by the crowds—the Austrians had to look elsewhere. Kraus was also concerned to point out the insensitivity of the Viennese reporters sent to report on the Balkan wars; their commenting on the war from the safety of military headquarters; their intrusion into hospitals in search of interview material from the wounded Turks; their detailed description of corpses. The *Neue Freie Presse* correspondent reported from the Bulgarian army headquarters at Stara Zagora that repeated bombardments had turned the sky to red, while at the same time it was clear from his report that the foreign military attachés and newspaper correspondents were toasting one another in the cafés of the town. 'The sky south of Zagora', wrote the satirist, 'is blood-red with shame. Austria is represented in the Balkans by impressionists.' In the same piece Kraus contrasted the conviviality of the Austrian, Hungarian and German journalists drinking bottles of Hungarian champagne in their coupé at the Turkish headquarters, while Moslem soldiers performed their religious devotions at dusk.[30]

The whole business had its ridiculous side of course. The Viennese press was beside itself with delight when its protégé, the Prince of Albania, visited Vienna soon afterwards: he was trailed around the streets by a crowd of reporters who followed him from the Burgtheater to the Opera where scores of opera glasses were trained upon him as he entered his box. Outrage was expressed in 1914, however, when the Prince failed to greet members of the staff of the Univeristy of Vienna when they put in at Durazzo after a cruise of the Adriatic. It was the least thing that could be expected, the newspapers commented, when Austria had spent so much money on defending the integrity of his country: a state that was so primitive and had only recently formulated a new alphabet might have been expected to be anxious to receive the good wishes of a delegation from 'the seat of the highest form of culture'.[31]

Despite the help and encouragement which Kraus had received from Maximilian Harden in the early years of the *Fackel*, the relations between two such individualists could never be easy and came under increasing strain as the years passed. Although Harden had exposed individual examples of financial corruption among the Berlin press, he was not a systematic opponent of press activities in the same sense as Kraus: he was indifferent to many of the evils to which Kraus pointed in the Viennese newspapers with whose editors, indeed, Harden was anxious to be on good terms. Neither was Harden interested in the nature of language and his own style had a pretentious facility which Kraus was to label in later years 'Desperanto'. After the final breach with Harden, Kraus was to press home his attacks by 'translating' Harden's style into German in the pages of the *Fackel*.[32]

The break with Harden occurred in 1904 when the latter, as part of his campaign against Wilhelm II, exposed the fact that homosexuality was rife among the Kaiser's entourage. The charge of homosexuality was often hurled about in the vicious polemics of Central European politics, especially during the

Weimar Republic. The result of Harden's accusation was that the prestige of the Kaiser was gravely impaired and the career of his close friend, Count Eulenburg, was smashed. Not only was the affair an example to Kraus of the worst kind of press intrusion into the details of the private lives of prominent personalities, it was also a symptom of the fact that the age of democracy had finally triumphed over that aristocratic ideal which by this time the satirist cherished in politics as well as in culture. 'What is happening now in Germany,' Kraus wrote, 'is a revolt of the footmen':[33] the Eulenburg affair was a 'victory of information over culture'.[34] Harden was not content to pontificate on questions of peace and war but had now to report on victories and defeat in bed; he now saw the world through a key-hole.[35]

The attack which Kraus levelled at the sexual hypocrisy of bourgeois society grew out of his campaign against all kinds of injustices in the legal system, a campaign in which the satirist had enlisted the support of Wilhelm Liebknecht until this was cut short by the latter's death in 1900. Since the God to whom Kraus subscribed was the God of Justice, it was natural that one of the main themes of the *Fackel* in the years before 1914 should be the urgent need for the reform of laws relating to sexual offences. 'A trial involving sexual morality,' the satirist wrote in one of his most famous aphorisms, 'is a deliberate step from individual to general immorality.'[36] He was particularly incensed by the persecution and blackmail of prostitutes by the police as a result of the fact that only a small minority of the prostitutes of Vienna complied with the law of 1873 which required them to register with the police for taxation purposes and for medical examination by a police doctor—an examination which was in itself an opportunity for bribery and corruption to occur.[37] The presence of a prostitute in the dock was, to the satirist, a confrontation of the realities of life with a hypocritical society: the prostitute and the diseases of the prostitute were the product of traditional Judaeo-Christian morality.[38]

The revolt against conventional sexual mores was characteristic of the *fin de siécle* in Europe and the views which Kraus held were common in intellectual and literary circles in Vienna. In his autobiography the Viennese writer Stefan Zweig vividly described the contrast between the rigidity of bourgeois morality and the blatant prostitution carried on in the main streets of the Austrian capital.[39] The eroticism which permeated the literary and artistic world of Vienna at the turn of the century particularly fascinated those young men who reacted with a special kind of extremism against the austerity of a Judaism which they had renounced. This mood is brilliantly captured in the work of Kraus's great friend, the poet and essayist, Peter Altenberg. Surrounded by his admirers and a crowd of prostitutes, the latter was the doyen of the bohemian cafés, cynically depicting in his stories the relationships between the sons of respectable families and the *Wiener Mädel*, that type of Viennese shop-girl or domestic servant who afforded sexual satisfaction without the complications of marriage. When Kraus wrote that it was high time for children to enlighten their parents about the secrets of sex, he was rebelling against the code of his father's generation. Themselves of middle-class origin, both Kraus and Altenberg were attacking a code of behaviour to which large sections of the aristocracy and the working class did not subscribe.[40]

And yet, understandably, the movement towards sexual freedom created as many problems as it solved. Kraus was particularly disturbed by the suicide in 1903 of his friend the philosopher Otto Weininger who took his life at the age of twenty-three because of his distress at the seemingly irreconcilable gulf between the facts of sexual desire and the moral codes of Judaism, Christianity and the philosophy of Immanuel Kant. Weininger reflected and magnified in himself all those tensions which afflicted the Jewish intellectuals of Vienna. Already in the year of his death he had caused a sensation by the publication of his important work *Geschlecht und Charakter* (Sex and Character). In this book Weininger postulated a fundamental and tragic conflict between the sexes, between the rationalist impulse dominant in man and the sensuality inherent in woman. It has already been seen that Kraus, too, was deeply influenced by the antithesis between male and female which had been made in that tradition of German thought which descended from Schopenhauer and Nietzsche, a tradition to which the dramatist Strindberg had given further expression in the corrosive misogyny of his plays. Weininger's position, however, was even more despairing than that of Strindberg: he could reconcile himself neither to the incompatibility between Man and Woman nor to that between the masculine and feminine elements within Man himself. Whereas, however, Weininger was driven by hatred of the feminine principle to the point of self-destruction, Kraus welcomed that principle as belonging to a world of unself-conscious innocence, a world of children, animals and Nature, to which he devoted much of his poetry. While Weininger carried Schopenhauer's misogyny and pessimism to their logical conclusion, Kraus believed that it was possible for the individual to transcend the nihilism that perpetually haunted existence and affirm, as Nietzsche had done, the beauty and terror of life.

The attack which the satirist levelled at the sexual hypocrisies of Viennese society earned him the admiration of Sigmund Freud, who confessed that he read the *Fackel* with great pleasure.[41] Kraus himself held Freud in great personal esteem, and after Moritz Benedikt had called in the *Neue Freie Presse* for homosexuals to consent to their own castration, he appealed to the work of Freud to protest against the stupidity and inhumanity of such a proposal.[42] The hypocrisy of the *Neue Freie Presse* was all the more blatant because, like so many other newspapers in Central Europe, it regularly carried whole pages of advertisements in which men sought women or other men as 'companions': other advertisements concerning the services offered by 'masseuses' were a constant source of scandal to Kraus in these years.

But although on issues which concerned society's interference with the private sexual life of the adult individual the satirist felt close to the position taken up by Freud, he had many reservations on the wider issue of psychoanalysis and the more extreme claims made for it by Freud's disciples. Kraus was irritated, for example, by the psychoanalytical approach to religion and culture, feeling that such an approach was basically irreverent towards the central mysteries of life. In such plays as *Traumstück* and *Traumtheater* the satirist was concerned not only to ridicule the inflated claims of the new psychology, but also to defend the autonomy of dreams and the unconscious against interference from the doctor and the scientist. As he once remarked, 'I would rather go back to childhood with Jean Paul than with Sigmund Freud.' As far as sexual repression was concerned Kraus believed that, under the pretence of healing sexual neuroses, psychoanalysts still carried over into their approach the Jewish and Christian idea that sex was fundamentally sinful: they aimed unconsciously at intensifying the atmosphere of guilt and shame in which the subject was shrouded. [43] In other words, 'Psychoanalysis is the disease of which it pretends to be the cure.' [44]

Of course this was unfair. It was indeed from the position of an artist, anxious to preseve the wholeness of human experience in an age of increasing specialisation, that much of the satire of Kraus was directed. But the distinction between satire and polemic was often obscured in his work by a marked element of personal and social animosity. It has already been seen that one of the reasons for Kraus's attack on psychoanalysis was the analysis of his own personality that was performed by a member of Freud's circle. When the satirist expressed his fear that, in the hands of men less devoted to the integrity of their profession as Freud himself, psychoanalysis might become merely a lucrative source of income derived from the unhappiness of mankind, he was certainly maliciously underlining the fact that the overwhelming majority of the practitioners of psychoanalysis were Jewish. The incident might seem trivial if it were not part of a pattern. Kraus's position over the Dreyfus Affair has already been noted. So have his attacks on the Jewish press of Vienna. Now he is seen making remarks about Freud's circle which, if they came from a non-Jew, would be regarded as anti-semitic.

What forces within Viennese society influenced the satirist to behave in this fashion?

The rise of antisemitism as a powerful political force within Austria was the result of the influence possessed by the Jewish community. Although the Jewish element within the Austrian part of the Empire amounted to only 4.33 per cent of the total population in 1880, most of it was concentrated in the towns, principally the cities of Bohemia, Moravia, Galicia and the capital city of the Empire, Vienna.[45] The Jewish population of Vienna rose from 40,277 in 1869 to 175,294 or 8.7 per cent of the total number of inhabitants by 1910.[46] Higher estimates of this population have often been given. The confusion has arisen as a result of two factors: the proportion of Jews fluctuated from one census to another, reaching a figure of 10.8 per cent in 1923[47] when the population of Vienna was swollen by the influx of Jews from Galicia and Hungary following the political upheavals which marked the end of the Empire; furthermore, the census defined a person as Jewish according to his religion and obviously could not take into account the number of Jews who had renounced the religion of their fathers and had married outside the Jewish community.

Statistics, then, can be somewhat unreliable; particularly so when a numerically small proportion of the population exercises an influence out of all proportion to its numbers. Some indication has already been given of the particular concentration of the Jewish element of Vienna in the ranks of the upper middle class which drew its wealth from the banks, the finance houses, the professions and the press: 33.6 per cent of the university students were Jewish in 1890, and Jewish students were especially to be found in the faculties of medicine and law. In 1913 Wickham Steed, who was sometimes less than charitable towards the Jews, in his study of the Habsburg Monarchy quoted an estimate that 75 per cent of the journalists of Vienna were Jewish.[48]

Given this sort of situation the growth of antisemitism of one kind or another was tragically inevitable. The antisemitism of the Christian Socialists usually manifested itself in efforts to reduce the influx of Jews into the educational system. In the period between the end of the nineteenth century and the rise of Nazism many attempts were made to ensure a smaller entry of Jewish students into the University of Vienna which already by the end of the nineteenth century had become a hot-bed of Pan-Germanism. In the years before the *Anschluss* the Dollfuss and Schuschnigg dictatorships enacted a certain amount of legislation—legislation that was mild compared with what was to happen later under the Nazis—to segregate Jewish and non-Jewish children in the state schools. But the policies of the Christian Socialists never satisfied those extremists whose antisemitism was reinforced by racial hatred: from the end of the nineteenth century there were periodic outbursts of anti-Jewish riots in Vienna, notably during the World Zionist Congress in 1925 and in the immediate aftermath of the *Anschluss* in 1938 when a hideous pogrom accompanied the Nazi victory.

The Jews were not, of course, the creators of the Jewish 'problem'. For centuries the Jewish people had been the victims of persecution and discriminatory legislation. Freed completely from legal disabilities within the Austrian Empire only in 1867, the Jews even after this date still found it virtually impossible to rise very high in the bureaucracy and army. It was natural therefore that, given their long and enforced experience of financial and economic affairs, the Jews of Central Europe should have played the important part which they did in the Industrial Revolution. That the period of Jewish emancipation in Austria and Germany should also have been the epoch of the great social and political changes which accompanied the process of urbanisation was to be the source alike of both the initial success and the eventual failure of the attempt made by the Jews to integrate themselves successfully into their adopted society. For although the backward and under-developed areas of Eastern Europe were to remain in the nineteenth century as the classic home of anti-Jewish persecution, it was in Germany and Austria in the same century that antisemitism was developed into a modern ideology compounded of economic resentment, racialist argument, and the romantic rejection of materialism.[49]

In some respects Vienna was an especially fertile ground for the dissemination of such doctrines: the Jewish population of Vienna was greater in numbers than that of any other German-speaking city, and the influence of this population was enhanced in the course of the nineteenth century by the reluctance of many Austrians to come to terms with the fact that the state in which they lived was no longer a semi-feudal creation of the Habsburgs and their attendant aristocracy and clergy but was rapidly being transformed into a modern and highly complex political and social organisation. The concentration of so many of the palaces and churches of Vienna in the Inner City bounded by the Ringstrasse, the accessibility of the Emperor to any of his subjects who wished to petition him, the easy informality between all classes of the population, an informality which was only really possible in a deeply hierarchical society—all these features of an older civilisation seemed threatened by a new scale of values based on individual energy and enterprise, on the Stock Exchange and Jewish financial expertise.

Only a minority of extremists, however, saw in the wealth and influence of the Jewish community of Vienna a justification for systematic racial hatred of a whole people. The indolence and tolerance that was characteristic of so much of the Viennese scene did much to mitigate the effects of a potentially dangerous situation. However much the anti-semite might deplore the changes that seemed to be making Vienna into a soulless *Grossstadt*, he could not deny that in material terms there was a lot to be said for the process. As Lueger once unblushingly said to the leaders of Viennese Jewry:

> I dislike the Hungarian Jews even more than I do the Hungarians, but I am no enemy of our Viennese Jews; they are not so bad and we cannot do without them. My Viennese always want to have a good rest, the Jews are the only ones who always want to be active.[50]

It was one of the ironies of the position of the Jews in Austrian society that during the long years of Liberal domination in Vienna no Jews were appointed to important positions within the municipality because the Liberals were widely regarded to be the party of the wealthy Jews. It was only during Lueger's period of power that Julius Porzer, who was partly Jewish, became deputy mayor of Vienna in 1904.

If there were many different kinds of antisemitism in nineteenth-century Vienna, the Jewish response to this situation was itself one of infinite diversity and complexity. Mention has been made of the German nationalist fervour of the Liberal Jewish press which attempted to counter the challenge of anti-semitism by demonstrating to the full the assimilationist ambitions of the Jewish population. After 1918, indeed, a small but powerful minority of the wealthy Jewish middle-class was to give its support to the Christian Socialists as defenders of the social and economic status quo within Austria. Assimilation, too, was the aim of the many Jewish members of the Social Democratic party. Not all these individuals were café intellectuals and the sons of wealthy families: again, the anti-semite conveniently forgot that there were large numbers of poor Jews in Vienna, living in the area called the Leopoldstadt, the old ghetto of Vienna between the Danube canal and the river. The Social Democrats constantly expressed their hostility to the Jewish financial interests which were so powerful in Austria but demanded that the party should struggle against *all* exploiters, regardless of their race, nationality or religion. While the element of truth in many of Kraus's attacks on the wealthy Jews of Vienna must be recorded, it must also be remembered that, with the virtual disappearance of the Liberals as a political force after 1918, the majority of Viennese Jews were supporters of Social Democracy as the only political movement which accepted them as equal members of society.[51]

Faced, however, with the challenge of the racialist anti-semitism of the Pan-Germans, there were elements within the Viennese Jewish community which came to the conclusion that assimilation was no longer possible. It was in Vienna that, under the inspiration of Theodor Herzl, Zionism was created as a modern political force. Herzl was convinced that the Jewish problem must be solved by drastic action. His first and somewhat melodramatic solution was that the Jews of Vienna should take part in a ceremony of mass conversion to Catholicism in St. Stephen's cathedral. After the disillusionment of this particular ideal, Herzl was finally driven to question the wisdom of assimilation after he had been sent to France by Moritz Benedikt to cover the Dreyfus Affair and had experienced the wave of anti-semitism which accompanied that Affair. Herzl's ambition to build up a Zionist movement in Europe which would work for a Jewish 'National Home'—Palestine was not yet mentioned—achieved its first success in 1897 when, as a result of his efforts, the first Zionist conference met at Basle in Switzerland. After a promising beginning, however, the progress of the Zionist idea was painfully slow: difficulties soon emerged in the movement between those who saw the Jewish future in essentially political and secular terms and those who wished even more for a revival of Judaism. Herzl himself, as his published diaries clearly show, was greatly distressed by the rancour of the sectarian disputes to which his movement was prone before his death in 1904.

The founder of modern Zionism was also to be sickened by the refusal of the assimilationist Jews to show any sympathy towards his policies by which, indeed, they were greatly embarrassed. Moritz Benedikt, for example, although anxious to retain Herzl on his staff, refused to allow him to make any mention of Zionism in his newspaper: 'For the *Neue Freie Presse*', Benedikt on one occasion magisterially proclaimed, 'the Jewish problem does not exist.' Equally hostile were the Jewish members of the Social Democratic party who agreed with much of the Zionist critique of the unhealthy concentration of Jews in urban life but accused Herzl of advocating a nationalist solution to what was essentially a social problem: it was nationalism which was threatening the survival of the Habsburg Empire, and all that Herzl could offer was yet another variety of this destructive force. Although the

Zionist cause attracted a number of distinguished converts among the Jewish intellectuals of Vienna in the years before 1914—notably, of course, the young philosopher Martin Buber— the overwhelming majority of Viennese Jews held themselves aloof. The main victories of Zionism were to be achieved not among the assimilationist community of Austria and Germany, but among the backward and oppressed Jewry of Eastern Europe, who clung to their religion with a devotion certainly not paralleled in Berlin, Frankfurt, Prague or Vienna.

If Zionism was widely regarded as an extremist response to the Jewish problem, there were assimilationist responses that could be regarded as equally extreme. In the 1880s, for example, a number of Jews had been attracted to the Austrian Pan-German movement before the racialist and anti-semitic implications of the Pan-German ideology had become fully apparent. After all, for many Jews it was easier to assimilate into a German civilisation which they deeply admired for its Protestant and idealistic emphasis, than into the Catholic and cosmopolitan traditions of the Austrian capital. Before embracing the Social Democratic faith Viktor Adler had collaborated with Schönerer and Professor Friedjung in producing the so-called Linz Programme of 1882 which put forward the demands of the Austrian Germans for a more positively German nationalist policy to be pursued in the Austrian part of the Empire. Some Jews, Friedjung being a prominent example, remained supporters of the Pan-German idea although they were soon forced to disassociate themselves from Schönerer. The most tragic victim of the fascination which the Germanic ideal exercised over a number of Jewish intellectuals was undoubtedly the philosopher Otto Weininger, whose suicide has already been discussed. Quite apart from his anguish over the seemingly irrelevant character of traditional codes of morality, there was yet another problem which drove him in despair to take his own life. This was his attraction to the mixture of Aryan racialism and romanticised Christianity which was to be found in the writings of the composer Richard Wagner and his son-in-law, the philosopher Houston Stewart Chamberlain.

In response to this situation, Weininger became possessed of a violent hatred of his Jewishness and renounced Judaism in favour of Protestantism only to find that the Aryan *Weltanschauung*, to which he was so attracted, denied the possibility of Jewish assimilation.[52] Needless to add, the suicide was to be hailed by anti-semites—not least by the Nazis—as the only logical step which could be taken by a Jew anxious to solve the Jewish problem.[53] His death was to be cited by Theodor Lessing, a German philosopher of Jewish extraction, as evidence corroborating his theory of the self-hatred which, he believed, afflicted a large number of Jews in Central Europe.[54]

There was some truth in Lessing's theory. Masochistic anti-semitism was a characteristic feature of many German and Austrian Jews. Examples of this can certainly be found in the life and work of such different personalities as Heinrich Heine, Karl Marx, Ferdinand Lassalle, Walther Rathenau, Maximilian Harden and Theodor Lessing himself. Kraus was also a product of this tradition. A close friend of Weininger, he too had abandoned Judaism at an early age and was famed for the merciless nature of his attacks on the failings of other Jews. But although, in his diary, the novelist Franz Kafka claimed that Kraus belonged to that type of Jew who had turned against things Jewish out of hatred of his parents, there is no evidence to suggest that the satirist had any personal antipathy towards his father: on the contrary, on several occasions he defended his father's memory against attack from enemies of his own who were attempting to show that Jakob Kraus had exploited his work people. His alienation from Judaism seems to have been far more the result of pressures at work within his society, pressures reflected in the bitter and neurotic attacks on the 'Judaisation' of German culture which are frequently to be found in *Die Fackel*. It is no wonder then that Lessing singled out Kraus as a particularly significant example of Jewish self-hatred.[56] Further evidence to substantiate Lessing's judgement might be found in the fact that Houston Stewart Chamberlain was an early contributor to *Die Fackel*;[57] and that, in a questionnaire which the magazine *Der Brenner* circulated in 1913, the Viennese racialist propagandist Lanz von Liebenfels, editor of the magazine *Ostara*, had saluted Kraus as 'the greatest living writer of German prose', and as a writer whose attacks on the Jewish domination in the press had rendered considerable services to the Aryan cause.[58] Perhaps the most cruel blow of fate which the satirist had to endure was that the last years of his life were to be made wretched by the knowledge that a number of his works had not been placed on the Nazi index of banned publications because of their attacks on the Jews. A rumour also reached his ears that a section of the Austrian Nazis intended to make use of him for propaganda purposes if he was still alive when the *Anschluss* came.[59]

It would of course be absurd to pass a judgement on Kraus's attitude to the Jewish question based on the misunderstanding of his work by such confused individuals as Lanz von Liebenfels and members of the Austrian Nazi movement. For racialism of any kind Kraus had nothing but contempt. Neither can anything necessarily sinister be read into the articles which Chamberlain contributed to *Die Fackel* attacking the journalistic writings of the historian Theodor Mommsen and pointing out the low intellectual calibre of Catholic universities. Kraus's magazine was in its early years extraordinarily wide in the range of its contributors: when the Social Democrat Wilhelm Liebknecht wrote his articles on the Dreyfus Affair for the *Fackel*, one of the reasons he chose this magazine was that, in his own words, he judged it to be 'neither political nor anti-semitic'.[60] If this was true in 1899, it was even more true twenty years later: after the First World War Kraus was to moderate his attacks on a number of individuals—Maximilian Harden, for example—so that his position on the Jewish question could not possibly be misinterpreted.[61] It seems hardly necessary to add that his whole life and work were directed against those values which were to triumph under Hitler. In 1933 the satirist was concerned to point out the absurdity of the charge that the anti-semitic policies of the German government were a fulfilment of his attacks on the

Jewish press of Central Europe. He revealed that he had received a request from the Westdeutsche Rundfunk at Cologne to send a copy of his recently published translation of Shakespeare sonnets for review on the radio programme 'Die Welt im Buch'. In his reply of 21 April 1933 Kraus pointed out that there seemed to be some discrepancy between the request for his translation and the cultural policies followed by the German government. Certainly the Kraus translation was in German, but perhaps it was not realised that it was a translation from the Hebrew: if a direct translation into German was required, it would be better to refer to that of Stefan George.[62]

The fact however remains that Kraus went to extreme lengths to distance himself from his Jewishness. This hatred of his origins was not simply a harmless matter of the satirist's social snobbery—although the pleasure which he derived from his friendship with members of the Austrian aristocracy was always the subject of pained comment from his friends on the Left. Nor was it merely the expression of Kraus's dislike of the corruption and dishonesty of the press: his repudiation of the Jews, as indeed his repudiation of modern Man, was of an infinitely more serious character than that. The truly terrifying element in Kraus's 'antisemitism' was only to be fully revealed during the First World War when he attacked the Jewish people *collectively* for their similarity with the Germans in their ruthless pursuit of material power combined with their belief that they were the Chosen People,[63] an attack which reached its culmination in the poem 'Prayer to the sun of Gibeon' in which Kraus called down the vengeance of Jehovah on the Jewish people for their worship of false gods.[64]

This, then, was the root of Kraus's hostility to the Jews. He attacked his own people in the same way that the prophets of the Old Testament had castigated the unworthiness of the Israelites for the trust which God had placed in them. However much the satirist might wish to dissociate himself from his Jewish inheritance, the bitterness of his alienation was itself a symptom of the importance which that inheritance played in the formation of his personality. Like Heine, Lassalle, Harden and many others, Kraus was both the victim and the critic of the situation of the Central European Jewish intellectual, alienated from a Judaism which they regarded as parochial, greatly attracted by the single-mindedness and relentless moral serious-ness of a German cultural tradition which had profound affinities with that of the Jews themselves—and yet aware that the society in which they lived was one in which they could never be fully accepted. Lassalle once said that he hated two things, Jews and littérateurs—and he had the misfortune to be both.[65] Kraus's ambivalent attitude towards Heine, the paradigm case of the German-Jewish symbiosis, must be seen against this background. The crime of which Kraus accused Heine was not primarily that of vulgarity and a superficial cosmopolitanism. Heine's real crime was that of facetiousness, a repudiation of the moral seriousness not merely of the German, but also of the Jewish tradition: Heine was a Moses who struck the rock of the German language with his rod, but all that flowed out was Eau de Cologne.[66]

Caught as they were between the claim of the Jewish tradi-tion and their love-hate relationship with the society in which they wished to assimilate themselves, Jewish intellectuals found that their dilemma became even more acute in the second half of the nineteenth century when emancipation was followed by the rise of political antisemitism. Despite the lack of success which the antisemites of Central Europe experienced in the years before the First World War, it became increasingly evident that the position of the Jews in Austria and Germany was still a precarious one. For whatever solution the Jews adopted to remedy this situation was to prove fruitless; if they supported the political forces of the Right, they were accused of all the vices of finance capitalism; if they found salvation in the parties of the Left, they were labelled as harbingers of the Red Peril. Despite themselves Central European Jews were brought face to face with the problem of their Jewishness and the relationship which they must try to establish with their past. The Zionist response to this situation had already been indicated. The poignancy of this response can however only be fully appreciated if it is remembered that Zionism itself derived much of its inspiration from the very civilisations—German and Russian principally—which it was being compelled to repudiate. Before moving to his rediscovery of the spiritual treasures of Hassidism, even Martin Buber, it must be remembered, had experienced all the temptations of the assimilationist position in the Vienna of his youth. In his revolt against modern materialism and the emergence of the Grossstadt, in his search for moral certitude in the values of a reinvigorated Judaism, Buber was greatly indebted to nineteenth-century German Romanticism and the thought of Friedrich Nietzsche. When attempts are made to trace too direct a relationship between nineteenth-century German thought and the ideology of Nazism, it is salutary to meditate on the contribution of that thought to the formation of modern Israel.

The return of the Jewish intellectual back towards his roots can, however, be seen in circles far removed from those of Zionism. In 1900 Sigmund Freud chose to affirm that, in a secular sense at least, he regarded himself as Jewish by joining the Vienna lodge of the B'nai B'rith society. Thirty years later he told one of his visitors,

> My language is German. My culture, my attainments are German. I considered myself a German intellectual, until I noticed the growth of anti-semite prejudice in German Austria. Since that time, I considered myself no longer a German. I prefer to call myself a Jew.[67]

Freud was not alone in this sentiment. Under the influence of his friend Max Brod, Franz Kafka came to an increasingly deeper understanding of his Jewish inheritance and reacted with increasing violence against the degree to which the Jews of Bohemia identified themselves with the opposition of the German population towards the Czechs.[68] The Viennese poet Richard Beer-Hofmann, after starting off his career as a devoted adherent of the Impressionist movement, ultimately discovered this position to be aesthetically and morally unsatisfactory and, slowly and painfully, worked back from his support of assimilation to a moving proclamation of his faith in his destiny as a Jewish artist. The same process can be seen in the career of Kraus's friend, the composer Arnold Schoenberg. The latter, although Jewish by origin, had been brought up as a Catholic and was converted to Protestantism at the age of eighteen. Under the impact of the challenge of antisemitism on the one hand and by his own growing interest in religious matters on the other, Schoenberg embarked on that long spiritual Odyssey which began with the unfinished oratorio *Jacob's Ladder* dating from the period 1913–15. By the time of writing his opera *Moses and Aaron* in the late 1920s, his religious evolution was almost complete. After the advent of Hitler to power in Germany and his own exile from Germany after 1933, Schoenberg took the final step: in a special ceremony in Paris in the same year he was received back into the fold of Judaism.[69]

Kraus never made any such dramatic return to the religion of his fathers. After 1918, however, there are many signs that the satirist's own involvement with the tradition of Jewish self-hatred was on the decline. His change of attitude towards Theodor Herzl was indicative of this process. It was during the period of his youth when he was strongly influenced by the policies of the Social Democrats that Kraus attacked Zionism in his pamphlet *Eine Krone für Zion* (A Crown for Zion), published in 1898. Only through a policy of socialism and assimilation, Kraus maintained, could the backward and oppressed Jews of Eastern Europe, to whom Zionism mainly appealed, become truly free. He mocked at the contrast between the poverty of these people and the wealth of the smart emancipated littérateurs of Vienna who, like Herzl, had formulated the Zionist ideology. In this pamphlet, as in the early *Fackel*, the satirist was persistently critical of the Napoleonic ambitions of which he believed Herzl to be possessed. After the First World War, however, Kraus was to admit that, in attacking Herzl, he had been concerned to attack him primarily as an employee of Moritz Benedikt on the *Neue Freie Presse*, as the man who, in his capacity as literary editor, was responsible for the feuilletons. After reading the published diaries of Herzl the satirist was increasingly impressed by the integrity and vision of the man, and was to admit in 1924 that many of his earlier attacks had been unfair.[70]

On the other hand Kraus never expressly repudiated his earlier position on the Jewish question: to the end of his life he remained faithful to the ideal of complete assimilation and like many other Viennese Jews he moved after 1932 to a position of support for the Dollfuss and Schuschnigg governments as the only effective barrier against the rising power of the Nazis. It might indeed be argued that in no period of his career was Kraus so obviously reconciled to the traditional values of Austrian civilisation as in the closing years of his life. And yet no one had so clearly demonstrated the emptiness of these traditional values. Despite his cult of Nestroy, despite all the obviously Viennese characteristics of his work, it is difficult to resist the impression that, faced with the political and intellectual vacuum that had been created in Austria during his lifetime, Kraus, perhaps unconsciously, sought refuge in the Jewish tradition into which he had been born and which he would never completely repudiate. In the epitaph which he once wrote to apply to himself, the satirist complained, 'How empty it is here in my position.'[71] His condition was indeed one of loneliness: unable to break through his isolation back to the living faith of his people, Kraus nevertheless brought the passions of a Jewish prophet to bear on a Viennese civilisation which was perishing before his eyes. As the Austrian critic Friedrich Torberg has commented, Kraus was the only writer of his time

> by whom Austrian self-judgement legitimately became judgement of the world and vice versa. . . . Kraus felt responsible for everything that happened inside and outside Austria—whether it was only to the extent that he could not prevent it from happening.[72]

* * *

A noted opponent of the power of the Jews in Austrian life was Franz Josef's heir, the Archduke Franz Ferdinand, whose death at Sarajevo in 1914 was to lead to the outbreak of the First World War. The murder was planned by anti-Austrian elements within Serbia, elements whose intentions were certainly known to, if not shared by, the Serbian government which had warned Vienna that an attempt was likely to be made on the Archduke's life. The Austrian government ignored these warnings and even derived a malicious pleasure in seeing the heir to the throne put into a dangerous situation. For the Archduke, a violent and unbalanced personality who was widely regarded as a creature of the reactionary forces within the Austrian army and the Catholic Church, was extremely unpopular. That he was also a close personal friend of Conrad von Hötzendorf, with whom he shared a burning desire for some resolute action—in both domestic and foreign policy—which would revitalise the Empire, made him even more of an object of suspicion to the Left.

This suspicion was not altogether justified. Although a bitter opponent of the forces of political liberalism, Franz Ferdinand was an even more determined opponent of the Compromise of 1867: when he succeeded to the throne he hoped to bring the Slav elements within the Empire into play against the hegemony not only of the Austrian Germans but also of the Magyars, whom he particularly disliked because of their defiance of the House of Habsburg in the past. The policies of the Archduke were thus a mixture of self-interest and perhaps a genuine concern for those peoples within the Empire who were oppressed by the traditional master races. In any case, his bark was very much worse than his bite: his reactionary outbursts were largely due to his impatience to succeed to the throne and break the political deadlock apparent since 1908. His dislike of Jews was also far more verbal than real, an expression of his sense of caste and of his irritation with the wealthy newspaper proprietors of Budapest and Vienna who championed the claims of the Hungarians and the Austrian Germans. Indeed, a number of Jewish intellectuals sympathetic to Catholicism, amongst whom the novelist Franz Werfel was a prominent example, moved in circles close to the heir of the Austrian throne. A final mitigating feature of the Archduke's personality was the fact that although he was sometimes described as a member of the war party in Austria and certainly had on occasion wished for a preventive war against Italy, Franz Ferdinand became after the Bosnian crisis of 1908–9 a supporter of conciliatory tactics towards Serbia and an opponent of the anti-Serb policy of Field-Marshal Conrad. Perhaps this last factor contributed to the feelings of profound relief with which the news of the Archduke's death was greeted in Vienna. It was felt that not only had Austria been spared a disastrous successor to Franz Josef, but that now the stage was set for a final showdown with the Serbs.

Seen against this background, it can be understood why a sensation was created amongst Kraus's admirers when, on 10 July 1914—two weeks after the assassination and three weeks before the outbreak of war, the satirist for the first time publicly revealed his sympathy for the policies and personality of the dead Archduke, 'the hope of everyone in this state who believes that an ordered society could be established in a land already given up to chaos'. The murdered Archduke 'had none of those ingratiating qualities that reassured a people of professional spectators over their set-backs and defeats': he had despised public opinion and had made no attempt to curry favour with the press by the contrived *Gemütlichkeit* which passed for statesmanship among Austrian politicans such as the Foreign Minister, Count Berchtold. The significance of the assassination and the joy with which it was greeted in Vienna symbolised the bankruptcy of the forces of genuine conservatism not merely in Austria but also in Europe:

Such affairs appear to originate only in Serbia. In reality, the line of men who stand outside their epoch has now come to an end and nationalist fanaticism is only a form of courage born out of universal cowardice. The real forces of today's world, in control in every state, are not so imbued with conservatism that they use Serbian nationalism as a motive—instead they use it as an excuse.[73]

This article marked the culmination of Kraus's support for the forces of conservatism in Austria and illustrates in a particularly striking way his mischievous desire deliberately to shock and outrage his friends on the Left. 'Politics,' the satirist commented in the course of his examination of the assassination, 'is what a man does in order to conceal what he is and what he himself does not know.' Any analysis of the crisis from a purely political standpoint would be superficial; what looked like only a demonstration in front of an embassy was really a disaster for mankind. The assassination was due not merely to a retarded adolescent inspired by Serbian nationalism: behind this action were the deeper and more dangerous forces of 'Progress' and 'Education' divorced from God. Hatred of the forces of 'Progress' was intensified in the next article of the same issue in which Kraus replied to the charges that he had deserted his friends on the Left and was showing undue enthusiasm for the admiration which he received from the aristocrats who attended his public recitals. The satirist did not attempt to deny this but refuted the claim that he was denying his radical past. Kraus pointed out that this was based on a complete misinterpretation of the *Fackel* over the previous years. His friends on the Left thought of him as a revolutionary, but he could not accept the political implications of the French Revolution, let alone of the period from 1848 to 1914: indeed, he was not sure that the power of the state should not be invoked against the decadence of peoples.[74]

Taken in conjunction with the fact that the next issue of the *Fackel* did not appear until December—when the satirist, for the first time and in terms that were somewhat veiled, announced his opposition to the war which had broken out almost five months earlier—the language used by Kraus in July 1914 was easily open to misinterpretation. It was hardly surprising that his reaction to the European crisis of 1914 was subsequently to be used by enemies of his such as the critic Alfred Kerr and the journalist Hugo Sonnenschein to show that Kraus had at first approved of the Austrian ultimatum to Serbia, despite what he said after the event. Had not the satirist in November 1913 given a public recital at the naval base of Pola in which, Sonnenschein complained, he had deplored the hatred of militarism by democratic forces? The answer which Kraus made to Sonnenschein in 1920 (when the charges were made) was that, throughout his career, his satire had been orientated towards culture and not politics defined in any narrow sense. Before 1914 he had supported the conservative forces in Austria—the Church, the aristocracy and the army—because of his hatred of those dehumanising forces of technical progress and mass democracy which he associated with the press. The satirist conceded that his trust in the moral fibre of Austrian conservatism had been misplaced: he had yielded in a weak moment to sentiment, 'A place in the sun became a battlefield. I did not want it.' (*Ich habe es nicht gewollt.*) The aristocracy and the army had plunged Austria into a war in which all those forces that were undermining the old order were given free play. Certainly he had wanted war in 1914, Kraus maintained, but it was that holy war at home which Kierkegaard had preached against journalists.[75]

What seems in fact to emerge, if the *Fackel* of July 1914 is subjected to a careful examination, is that Kraus, while yielding to the desire commonly expressed in Austria that Franz Josef should take advantage of the crisis to reassert his control over the domestic political scene and secure Austrian prestige abroad, was far from encouraging the war fever which had Vienna in its grip. The admiration which in December 1914 the satirist displayed for the moving terms of Franz Josef's war manifesto to his peoples was due far more to Kraus's appreciation of the aesthetic quality of the manifesto—a typically quixotic and misleading action on the part of the satirist—than to any impulse of chauvinism.[76] Indeed in the *Fackel* of July 1914 he had specifically aimed one of his attacks against anti-Serbian demonstrations which had taken place in front of an Austrian tuberculosis centre which employed a Serbian doctor: Kraus demanded that the 'cultivated European world', which, the Viennese press claimed, was so shocked by the assassination at Sarajevo, should also express its indignation at the great distress caused to the patients of the hospital by the demonstrations.[77]

It is also clear that the peculiar bitterness displayed by Kraus in this issue arose from the contrast between the human tragedy at Sarajevo and the barely concealed joy with which the news of the death of Franz Ferdinand was greeted in official quarters and in the press. The victim of the assassination was granted only a paltry funeral by the Emperor who had always detested him, while the war party at the Austrian court managed to prevail upon Franz Josef to sanction that war against Serbia which they had so long desired. What no one could foresee at the time, however, was that the conflict between Austria and Serbia would escalate into a major European war which would only result in either a victory of the powers of the Entente or in the domination of the European continent by Germany. Whichever way the war was going to end the values of the old Austria would be destroyed. 'We were compelled to die,' said Count Czernin, later to be Austrian Foreign Minister. 'We could choose only the manner of death and we have chosen the most terrible.' It was out of the events of the next four years that Kraus was to create *The Last Days of Mankind*.

3 The First World War: First Phase

ON 23 July 1914 the Austrian ultimatum was sent to Serbia, an ultimatum which demanded concessions so far-reaching that, had they been accepted, the latter power would have virtually become an Austrian satellite. The reply from Belgrade was conciliatory but the Serbian counterproposals were rejected in Vienna, and on 28 July Austria was at war. 'At last! At last!' were the opening words of the leading article of the Catholic *Reichspost*. Crowds surged through the streets of Vienna and demonstrated in favour of the war in front of the editorial offices of the *Neue Freie Presse*:

> 'This was no straw-fire of drunken momentary excitement,' that newspaper reported, 'no disturbing outbreak of unhealthy mass hysteria. With true manliness Vienna has accepted the fateful decision. . . . Far removed from arrogance or weakness. . . . Thousands upon thousands have surged through the streets today, arm in arm, rich and poor, old and young, the high-born and the low-born.'[1]

Even Sigmund Freud was not immune from the atmosphere that surrounded him. For the first time in thirty years, he commented, he felt himself to be Austrian. 'All my libido is given to Austria-Hungary.'[2] Viktor Adler, the Socialist leader, was deeply concerned by the outbreak of the war: after all, had not the Second International repeatedly proclaimed its opposition to war and the determination of workers in each country to call a general strike to bring any major European conflict to an end? Faced however by the support which Socialists in other countries were prepared to give to their governments and faced also by the strong movement in favour of the war to be found in the mass of the Austrian party, Adler decided it was best in the interests of party unity to follow the wishes of the majority. Although the Austrian Social Democrats had condemned the ultimatum which the imperial government had sent to Serbia, the emergence of Tsarist Russia as the champion of the Serbs inflamed left-wing opinion to the point of bellicosity. One of the ironies of the situation in Austria-Hungary in 1914 was that the outbreak of war was welcomed most vociferously by elements which prided themselves on their progressive stance towards domestic problems. The necessity for war was accepted more reluctantly by Stephen Tisza, the prime minister of Hungary.

Tisza's scepticism seemed to be borne out by the immediate course of events. The Austrian army had always been an instrument more for maintaining order within the Empire than for venturing outside its boundaries to fight the foreigner. In the course of 1914 the imperial army was to suffer two major humiliations. It was decisively repulsed from Serbia and the Empire was in turn invaded by the Serbian army: meanwhile the Russians launched a major offensive in Galicia which penetrated deep into the Carpathian mountains, the last line of defence before the Hungarian plain. Further Russian successes were only checked by the German victories to the North in the fighting at Tannenberg and the Masurian lakes in August and September of 1914.

Later in the same year however the arrival of German troops in Austria did much to stiffen the morale of the imperial armies and the next year, 1915, brought a general improvement in the Austrian situation. With considerable German help, Serbia was overrun and the Russians were expelled from Austrian territory. The one real difficulty which the Austrian army had had to face in this year was the entry of the Italians into the war on the side of the Entente, an action which made it necessary to open up a second major front in the Alps. On the other hand three factors mitigated the seriousness of this new development. Firstly, the Italian army and navy were among the few military forces which the Austrians were ever able to meet and defeat on equal terms. Secondly, the Austrian army was in a commanding position *vis à vis* the Italians throughout the duration of the war, thanks to its possession of the dominating Alpine peaks and ridges. Finally, Dalmatia was always a bone of contention between Italians and Slavs and the entry of Italy into the war tended further to enhance the loyalty to the Empire of the Catholic Slovenes and even the majority of the Croats. Already in 1914 the latter had shown by their eagerness to fight against the Serbs that the suspicions entertained in Vienna before 1914 as to the reliability of the Southern Slavs had been greatly exaggerated.

Up to 1917, then, the military position of the Habsburg Empire seemed reasonably secure: the Italians were held in check, even if they were not decisively beaten; German and Austrian troops under the command of General von Mackensen overran most of Rumania in 1916; the Brussilov offensive against Galicia in 1916 was the last major military effort of Tsarist Russia and was soon repulsed. The weakness of the Austrian position lay in the fact that none of this could be accomplished without German help and that with German military aid came increasing German control over the destinies of the Empire. This was a development which was bound to alienate the Slavs and particularly, of course, the Czechs: already in 1915 there had occurred the first of the series of mutinies and desertions which were to occur within Czech regiments fighting the Russians on the Eastern front. Furthermore by 1917 the effects of the Allied blockade were being felt in the acute food shortages which came to dominate everyday life all over the Austrian Empire outside Hungary. Time was to show that the fates of the three great Empires of Central and Eastern Europe were inextricably linked and that, although the ramshackle dominion of the Romanovs was to be the first to disintegrate under the strain and exhaustion of a prolonged war, the empire of the Habsburgs only continued to exist on borrowed time.

*　　*　　*

It was in December 1914 that Kraus predicted the atrophy of the imagination and the conscience which would result from the activities of the press and the propaganda agencies of the First World War. This was a period, he declared, in which things had happened which could not have been conceived, in which things would happen that could no longer be imagined; if they could, they would not be allowed to happen. It seemed that even the satirist was helpless against the scale and horror of events. He explained to his readers that it was only after a great effort that he could bring himself to write anything, and they must not expect anything more from him; for in the room, in which he wrote, the noise was so great and whether it came from animals, children or only from mortar batteries, he could not now decide. The crisis had made the relationship between catastrophes and editorial offices much closer but also less clear. If deeds were now stronger than words, echoes were stronger than deeds; and it was on echoes that men now lived. The war was a struggle not between nations, but between elements of the world press, the international disgrace, the profession that ruled the world not in spite of its irresponsibility but by virtue of its irresponsibility.[3]

Although several issues of the *Fackel* were to appear in 1915, it was not until October of that year that Kraus launched in earnest his offensive against the war. His relative quiescence, he had explained in February, had not been due to fear of the censor: the real reason was that he was dumb from the sheer horror of events.[4] But now in October 1915 the satirist was convinced that there was a possibility of speaking to some effect, there was a hope that something might be retrieved from the wreck of European civilisation; the chains fell off because the chains themselves showed that words were stronger than them. This indeed marked the difference between the First World War and the Nazi era. As Stefan Zweig remarked, 'words still had some significance. They had not yet been ridden to death by organised lies and propaganda.'[5]

It was true that—potentially, at least—the governments of the Central Powers possessed ample means by which they could delude their peoples. The close links between government and press in Vienna were even further tightened by Count Stürgkh, the Austrian prime minister of the first two years of the war. In Germany, too, a strict censorship was imposed and the power of the official news agency, the Wolff bureau, became paramount. While the German and Austrian War Ministries afforded facilities in the field—through the Kriegspressequartier—for reporters of individual newspapers, this was a way in which the press could be closely linked with the military authorities and prevented from publishing any information that was unpalatable to the army commanders. And finally, to supplement the censorship, the Austrian War Office and the Foreign Office possessed a number of organisations—discreetly installed in the Kriegs-fürsorgeamt (office for the welfare of military personnel) or the Kriegsarchiv—which specialised in propaganda.

And yet, despite all this, it was generally admitted in 1918 that this huge information apparatus had been woefully inefficient. The main reason for this was to be found in the degree to which control over the news had been entrusted to the army. For the army commanders were only concerned with the military situation which faced them at the front and had no understanding of the need to keep the domestic population adequately informed of the progress of the war. As a result of this situation the people of Germany and, to a lesser extent, of Austria, were kept in ignorance of any major military reverses which their armies had suffered; the check to the German advance into France at the Marne in 1914, for example, only became known in Central Europe from neutral Switzerland in the following year. The effect on civilian morale can be imagined: the shocked disbelief with which the German public greeted the news that their government was suing for peace in 1918 was to be the most striking illustration of the lack of contact that existed between the army leadership and the people whose destinies it controlled.

In Austria there were fewer illusions as to the outcome of the war, at least after 1916: the growth of German control over Austrian policy, the visibly desperate nature of the food short-

ages and domestic unrest which a demoralised government and
bureaucracy found it impossible to conceal, the summoning of
parliament in 1917 after an interval of three years—all these
played their part. In the Habsburg Empire, too, the effect of
Allied propaganda was particularly effective by 1918 in convincing the minority peoples that they could only gain if the Central
Powers lost the war. The attempts made by the German and
Austrian governments to counter this propaganda, backed as it
was by the energy and imagination of Lord Northcliffe, were
feeble in the extreme. Indeed, it was the combination, particularly to be seen in Austria, of censorship and suppression of news
on the one hand and the incompetence and inefficiency within
the whole information service on the other, which both provoked
some of Kraus's sharpest comment during the First World War
and still, at the same time, enabled him to publish *Die Fackel*
without really serious interference until 1918.

It was not difficult for the satirist to ridicule the attempts made
by the German press to invent atrocity stories. There was, for
example, the claim that on 2 August 1914, just before the outbreak of war between Germany and France, a French plane had
bombed portions of railway line near Nuremberg. In fact, no
such attack had taken place, and this was easy to establish since
the municipal authorities of Nuremberg denied the truth of the
rumour. But this did not prevent the 'incident' from being widely
reported in German newspapers and from subsequently being
repeatedly used as evidence of French responsibility for war in
1914. Kraus took every opportunity that he could to print the
truth about this matter.[6]

Another object of the satirist's attack was the practice of the
Viennese press in dwelling on the misfortunes of the enemy to
divert attention away from the problems that faced the Empire.
During the Brussilov offensive of 1916, one newspaper observed
that:

> The French now have great problems which trouble them
> sorely, problems which are only slightly alleviated by reports
> from the Russian front. But even their astonishing knowledge

of the Bukovina does not allay their anxiety over Verdun. The Bukovina is an area which, however often it falls to the Russians, can always be liberated.

If the French, Kraus commented, were not allowed to draw strength for the struggle to hold Verdun from the news of Russian successes in the East, surely it was not legitimate for the Austrian press to still fears over Czernowitz (an Austrian garrison city in the Bukovina) by news of German successes in the West.[7] Yet another variety of self-deception was to be found in the charges made repeatedly in the press of Berlin and Vienna that the public in the countries which belonged to the Entente were not informed of the true gravity of their military situation because of censorship imposed by their governments. This may have been true in the case of Tsarist Russia, but it ill became the newspapers of Vienna, gagged as they were by the government of Count Stürgkh, to accuse the French and British governments of repressive action towards the press. Even more absurd was the clumsy attempt of the German authorities to use the pernicious nature of enemy propaganda as a pretext to restrict even further the supply of news from the front. In 1916 the satirist quoted the following extract from the Berlin correspondent of one of the Viennese newspapers:

> Berlin, 13 July
> The newspapers have published a report from military headquarters which runs as follows: 'From the first day of the war, we alone of the combatant nations have published in full the communiqués of our enemies, for boundless is our trust in the steadfastness of the population at home. But our enemies have been making use of this trust. . . .'[8]

A category of the official information machine for which Kraus reserved an especial hatred was that of the war correspondents, especially the soldier and dramatist Alexander Roda Roda and Alice Schalek of the *Neue Freie Presse*. The treatment which Kraus accorded to Alice Schalek, the only woman correspondent accredited to the Kriegspressequartier,[9] was compounded out of

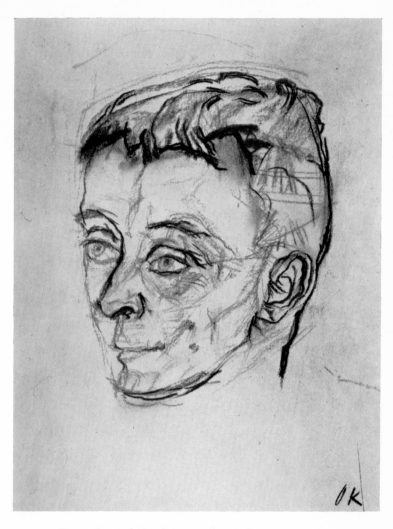

Drawing of Karl Kraus by Oskar Kokoschka

Sidonie Nadherny

amusement and hatred. On the one hand he took enormous pleasure in the contrast between the licence that was allowed to her and the scandalised attitude of the Austrian press to the way in which the English suffragettes rallied to the war effort and entered 'unfeminine' occupations.[10] And on one occasion when, on a visit to the trenches, Alice Schalek was told by the officer to duck, for the sight of even her nose might betray their position to the enemy, Kraus could not forbear the comment that her nose would betray any position. On the whole, however, Alice Schalek, peering at the war through her binoculars, was a bad joke. When she visited the ruins of Belgrade after the Austrian occupation, she commented that the architecture was bad and that there had not been anything of artistic value worth destroying, but lamented 'if only we knew that the houses which were destroyed belonged to those who had fomented nationalist fanaticism'.[11] Interviewing the commander of a submarine after the successful torpedoeing of an enemy vessel, she asked him what his feelings had been 'as he had run through the gigantic ship which had carried so many living people to a watery and silent grave'. The commander thought for a moment and then said that he had felt 'at first a mad feeling of joy'—on which her comment to her readers was, 'The Adriatic remains truly ours'.[12] On yet another occasion she rounded off a visit to the trenches by breakfasting on caviare and champagne with the commanding officer; 'crisp rolls and pretty flowers, radishes and a table cloth', she noted, 'such contrasts are only possible at the front'.[13]

For services such as these to the war effort (services which included a large number of public lectures in Vienna and Prague) Alice Schalek was honoured by the Kaiser with the award of a golden cross with the ribbon of the official medal for bravery. The satirist bitterly protested against this and was gratified when certain members of the Reichsrat asked questions about her activities.[14] So scathing were Kraus's attacks that Alice Schalek's brother challenged him to a duel. Nothing came of this and so Kraus was brought before the courts on a charge of libel. The satirist defended himself with his customary brilliance and histrionic flair, maintaining that he had never attacked her personally: the object of his attack had been the general disintegration of culture in the midst of the war; he had merely picked upon Alice Schalek as a symbol of this cultural disintegration. It says a great deal for the greater freedom of discussion that was now enjoyed in Austria after the reconvening of parliament in 1917 that it soon became clear that a judgement could not be obtained against Kraus and so the charges were withdrawn and the case dismissed.[15]

It was true of course that in all countries during the First World War the war correspondents were to come in for a great deal of criticism for misrepresenting the atrocious conditions at the front. In England there was that powerful indictment of the press published after the war by C. E. Montague, himself a journalist, in his book *Disenchantment*.[16] Sir Philip Gibbs, who wrote for the *Daily Telegraph* and the *Daily Chronicle*, was arrested five times on the orders of Lord Kitchener before he would submit to the privileges—and the disadvantages—of being an accredited war correspondent recognised by the army.[17] The gulf between life at the front and life away from the front was wide in every country during the First World War and caused terrible bitterness among the soldiers. The contrast was perhaps accentuated in Austria, however, by the peculiar unreality and frivolity of Viennese life which had existed long before 1914 and was not simply a phenomenon of the war. It found its expression in the saccharine prose which the Viennese press employed in its description of the war. At least Alice Schalek had taken the trouble to visit the front before she wrote her dispatches: some of the reporters did not bother to do even this but wrote long descriptions of trench conditions from their offices in Vienna. Many of the reporters had no military knowledge at all and, Kraus complained, were simply directed from reporting street accidents to reporting the war; in the process their style did not alter. A few even exchanged theatre columns for war dispatches: the front became the *Fronttheater*, and victories were written up as successful first nights![18]

But the transmutation of war into theatre and spectacle, while it appalled the satirist in one sense, also stimulated the sense of drama which lay at the root of his satire. Prominent among the characters of the drama that was being enacted before his eyes was, it goes without saying, the figure of Moritz Benedikt, ordering reporters to the front, exchanging cigars with Count Stürgkh, constantly urging the closest of links with Germany and proclaiming the 'troth of the Nibelungen' (Nibelungentreue) that united all German-speaking peoples. During one of the worst periods of the war from the Austrian point of view—at the height of the Russian offensive in Galicia in 1914—the *Neue Freie Presse* celebrated its fiftieth anniversary. Maximilian Harden marked the occasion by a glowing tribute to Benedikt as 'Chief of the General Staff of Culture' (Generalstabschef des Geistes). This was at a time when the *Neue Freie Presse* was completely misinforming its readers about the gravity of the situation in Galicia and was stating, quite falsely, that 'Lemberg is still in our hands'.[19] It was fitting, thought Kraus, that Benedikt should reach his apotheosis during the war by becoming a member of the Austrian House of Peers.[20] 'Still, there is a difference', the satirist commented when he juxtaposed in *Die Fackel* the photographs of Benedikt and Lord Northcliffe.[21]

Frivolity and insensitivity to the suffering of the soldiers at the front were not, of course, confined to Vienna. The *Berliner Tageblatt* reported on one occasion that a woman had called her new-born son 'Belgrade'.[22] In Munich it was reported that the police had told a woman that she was over-elaborately dressed: the newspaper adding, with unconscious irony, that 'the chief of police warned the woman that "we are not living in Carnival time".'[23] In Berlin Kraus's old enemy Max Reinhardt staged a production of Shakespeare's *Macbeth* in which, as the satirist was quick to point out, the theme of the whole production—scenery, lighting and direction—was that of blood.

And yet it seemed to Kraus that in Vienna frivolity and escapism were erected into an end in themselves. There was the macabre comedy of the attempt by the Austrians to imitate and surpass the kind of xenophobia which came much more naturally to the Germans: the Café Westminster was renamed the Café West-münster—without the Viennese apparently realising that the word 'café' was of Entente origin. Great arguments broke out among the ladies of high society, it was true, on the necessity for having distinctively Viennese fashions to free Austria from 'the yoke of Parisian modes'; but envy was mixed with indignation at reports that a new attraction in Paris was those fashion-conscious war-widows who were doing wonders with black. To the satirist this last piece of information revealed far more about the mentality of Viennese journalists than it did about the widows of Paris. His comment in the *Fackel* transmuted the incident into one of Shakespearian dimensions. '"Here's the smell of blood still: all the perfumes of Arabia will not sweeten this little hand." No, not the one that knows how to wield the pen so well.'[24]

Meanwhile the cult of Vienna by the Viennese press reached new and absurd proportions. The journalists wrote that no people could stand the strain of the war with such patience and good humour as the Viennese: no reason was advanced for this theory except that the Viennese were Viennese. The less real coffee there was actually available, the more the journalists wrote about the charm of the coffee-houses.[25] In the realm of music the operetta worked overtime to persuade people that everything was normal, as can be seen in a selection of newspaper phrases, entitled by Kraus '1916':

In the Johann-Strauss-Theater, the *Czardasfürstin* has had its 120th performance.

In the Carltheater the operetta *Fürstenliebe* has reached its fiftieth performance.

In the Bürgertheater the Strauss operetta *Liebeszauber* has been repeated for the fiftieth time.[26]

The Viennese passion for the theatre was used as a narcotic to transmute the ugliness of war into agreeable fantasy. In the Prater a trench was dug for the public to see something of the conditions at the front:

> [The trench] up to now has been visited by more than 15,000 persons. After the fabulous trench area, training exercises with searchlights are the next most interesting feature. On Sunday morning the big search-light will also go into action. The military concert has already started at 4 every afternoon. Admittance: for civilians 50 pence, for soldiers (sergeants and below) and children 20 pence.[27]

The war correspondents visited the principal cities of the Empire. The lectures of Alice Schalek were illustrated with slides of the trenches which she had visited, while Alexander Roda Roda toured Austria with a lecture entitled 'War in the present and in the future'. The composer of the *Merry Widow*, Franz Lehár, was dispatched to the Western Front to spread Viennese culture by performing *The Count of Luxembourg* before the German troops; the reports of his travels which he sent back to the Viennese press were the object of particular attention from Kraus.[28] In the Bürgertheater the widows and orphans of men who had died in Galicia were treated to a special performance of scenes from the campaign by a company composed of survivors who, at the end, thanked and saluted the enthusiastic audience.[29]

The cult of Vienna and the cult of the theatre and operetta was paralleled by the cult of Franz Josef and the imperial family. In terms of human appeal, the outwardly cold and narrow-minded Emperor—who never forgave the Archduke Franz Ferdinand for his morganatic marriage and whose remark on the latter's assassination had been 'Everything is in order again'—might seem unpromising material for such popularity. But the older the Emperor became, the more he seemed to be a symbol—perhaps the only symbol left—of the continued existence of the Empire: all disagreeable news was held back from the Emperor and it was rumoured that he only received specially edited versions of the newspapers.[30] A whole mythology was constructed about the personality of the Kaiser, full of the same phrases ('the chivalrous monarch', 'the good old man in Schönbrunn, to whom nothing has been spared') which, almost like a catechism, were reproduced on every possible occasion;[31] at the same time post-cards of Franz Josef, showing him deep in prayer, were sold throughout Central Europe. The cult of Franz Josef was extended to the innumerable Archdukes and Archduchesses of the imperial family. The Archduchesses served in the Red Cross, but these 'high-born Samaritan women', as the *Neue Freie Presse* called them, often spent only a token period of time in the hospitals and were then whisked home in their automobiles. Purchasers of the book *Our dynasty in the field* were assured, however, that their visits were anticipated with great eagerness by the chronically ill: 'It often echoed in my ear: "If only the Archduchess Zita would come once." '[32] As for the Archdukes, they were held in such esteem by their troops that each was known as 'the father of his soldiers'. In fact, many of them lived lives of luxury in their headquarters and made only ceremonial visits to the front.

Newspaper readers were continually presented with photo-graphs of the leaders of Austria-Hungary at war. Conrad von Hötzendorf was photographed studying the map of Italy, just as he had been pictured studying the map of the Balkans during the Balkan war.[33] There were smiling photographs of Count Berchtold and the Archduke Friedrich. The moustachioed Ger-man Crown Prince was nicknamed by the press 'the smiling Mosquito'. 'Ach!' cried Kraus in *The Last Days of Mankind*, 'this smiling in time of war was more appalling than tears.'[34] For behind the smile of the Archduke Friedrich there was the face of a hangman: Friedrich, a stern and brutal disciplinarian, was responsible for the shooting and hanging of thousands of men for cowardice and attempted desertion on the Eastern front. The satirist tried as far as possible to expose this and other examples of the inhumanity of military justice but, because of the censor, many of his protests had to wait until after the end of the war before they were printed.[35] To those who claimed that such incidents were exceptional and that Austria stood for the values of a tolerant and sophisticated civilisation, Kraus pointed to the execution in 1916 of Cesare Battisti, a Socialist member of the Austrian parliament and an Austrian subject from the Italian-speaking area of the South Tyrol who had collaborated with the Italians during the war. The execution of Battisti was a serious blunder by the Austrian authorities since it was bound to cause unrest amongst the Italian subjects of the Empire. But worse was to follow. Battisti was not merely hanged but the execution was photographed and a postcard was put on sale showing a smiling hangman posing with the dangling corpse for the photographer, while a group of smiling Austrians surrounded him. Exposing the corpse to this indignity, said Kraus, was like exposing the scalp of Austrian culture; the photograph was used by him as the frontispiece to *The Last Days of Mankind*.[36]

The last word on the irresponsibility of the Austrians which was so constant a theme of the *Fackel* of the war years had better come from the egregious Hermann Bahr who, in August 1914, published an open letter in the Viennese press to Hugo von Hofmannsthal, explaining that it had been necessary to publish the letter (which endorsed Austrian participation of the war in stirring terms) since he had no idea of the other's whereabouts:

I only know that you are under arms, dear Hugo, but nobody can tell me where. So I will write to you by means of the press. Perhaps the gentle wind will waft it to your campfire and convey my greetings to you.

In fact, as Kraus pointed out, the unfortunate Hofmannsthal was safely in Vienna working for the government in the Kriegsfürsorgeamt and Bahr knew this perfectly well; it was a pity that men between fifty and fifty-five were not liable for military service so that Bahr's patriotic zeal might be satisfied.[37]

It was from Germany, however, and not from Austria that there came the main threat to European civilisation. To Kraus the pernicious nature of German propaganda lay not in the efficiency of the propaganda machine but in the degree to which that machine reflected the conviction of significant elements of informed German opinion that Germany was not an aggressive power and that, even if she were, she possessed a mission to the rest of the world which justified any expansionist policies which she might adopt. In *The Last Days of Mankind*, Kraus contrasted the propaganda of Latin countries, where lies were a form of natural exuberance which were not to be taken seriously but still contained a kernel of truth, with the situation in Central Europe, where lies were venerated as a science and the war-time propaganda machines were symbolic of that insensitivity with which Germans and Austrians had, even in peace-time, deluded themselves to the realities of life.[38]

It was the prostitution of German culture in the interests of this propaganda which aroused the sharpest comment of the satirist. He was incensed, for example, by the manifesto of the ninety-three German intellectuals who in 1914 defended the German violation of Belgian neutrality and repudiated allegations of German atrocities in Belgium. What particularly infuriated him was the way in which the idea of the manifesto had occurred in the first place to a handful of people and then, sheep-like, the rest had followed. The truth of this was to be illustrated very clearly when one of the signatories, the celebrated Viennese conductor Felix Weingartner, then living in Germany, was subsequently to repudiate his signature, claiming that he had signed it in the first place without having read what the manifesto said.[39] In 1916 when rumours of the possibility of a compromise peace were circulating in Berlin, the manifesto of the ninety-three intellectuals was followed by yet another manifesto in which the Rector of Berlin University and a number of professors, including the political theorist Otto von Gierke, urged Germans to stand firm whatever the cost.[40]

When dealing with these manifestoes, Kraus was particularly concerned to point out the illogicality of the claim that Germany was fighting a 'holy war of self-defence' with the fact that the professors and intellectuals demanded that enormous annexations should be made at the expense of the Entente. Furthermore, it seemed that in order to make certain immediate acquisitions more secure, even further annexations were necessary. As, for example, Professor von Huber explained to a meeting at Munich in 1917:

A reconciliation with France through concessions is impossible. We must render France so powerless that she can never attack us again. To do this, it is necessary that our Western frontiers be pushed forward and parts of Northern France must come to us. What was formerly Belgium must not, from a military, political and economic point of view, be let out of our grip. We need a large colonial empire in Africa. In order to make this more secure, we need naval bases. A necessary condition of this is that England should be driven out of Gibraltar, Malta, Cyprus and Egypt, and her recent acquisitions in the Mediterranean.[41]

The satirist repeatedly emphasised the absurdity of the claim that a German protectorate over Belgium was freeing that country, especially Flanders, from the influence of France and England. A more realistic reason for a German annexation of Belgium was found by the Wolff bureau after Allied bombing attacks had got under way on German positions in 1918:

If the pilots of the Entente had the line of the Maas or Belgium as bases for their attacks today, then we would have to take into account that not only the west of Germany, but also the heart of the country would be open to the bombs of enemy aeroplanes.[42]

But the professors were remorseless. The ardent support which they gave to the war effort had its corollary in the enthusiasm with which they bestowed honorary degrees. The University of Graz, always a stronghold of Pan-Germanism within Austria, bestowed a degree of Doctor of Philosophy on Otto Kernstock, 'the poet of Styria', for services which included the coining of the slogan:

> All the heavenly hosts are for us
> Saint Michael is our Field Marshal.[43]

Military heroes, too, were decorated by the grateful universities. Admiral Scheer, the commander of the German fleet at the battle of Skagerrak (Jutland) was given the degree of Doctor of Philosophy by the University of Marburg[44]. It was Admiral Scheer who, in 1918, was to provoke the mutiny of the sailors at Kiel which was one of the main factors in the downfall of the monarchy; in a desperate attempt to sabotage the armistice negotiations he ordered the German High Seas Fleet to sea to attack the enemy. The resentment of the sailors had been particularly sharpened by the fact that Scheer's call to action came after a long period in which the German fleet had remained in harbour ever since the indecisive result at Jutland. During this period the attention of the German public had shifted away from the surface fleet to the successes of the navy's submarines, and once again the German universities had been in the van of public opinion. It was Kraus who coined the phrase 'submarine-professors' to describe those German academics who supported from their lecterns the policy of unrestricted U-boat warfare in 1917 and 1918: German professors, he wrote after the University of Berlin had awarded a doctorate to General von Falkenhayn, were like Austrian waiters—they addressed anyone more intelligent than themselves as 'Herr Doktor'.[45]

The situation would not have been so appalling had the German intellectuals been content simply to provide their own endorsement of the policies pursued by the Central Powers. But eminent Germans from the past were also conscripted to serve the cause. In his open letter to Hofmannsthal, Hermann Bahr had traced the spiritual roots of German militarism far back into the past:

> . . . from the Nibelungen, through the Minnesang and Meistersang, our mysticism and our German Baroque, Klopstock and Herder, Goethe and Schiller, Kant and Fichte, Bach, Beethoven and Wagner.[46]

For his part Wilhelm II constantly invoked the name of Kant and Kant's *Essay on Perpetual Peace* to demonstrate that he had not wanted the war and that he was anxious for it to come to a peaceful end. But the German Kaiser also said:

> If the enemy does not want peace, then we must bring peace to the world by destroying with an iron fist and a flaming sword the portals of those who do not want peace.[47]

Goethe suffered a fate similar to that of Kant: one of his greatest poems 'Over all the hill-tops it is still' (*Über allen Gipfeln ist Ruh'*) was adapted for the war effort to read as a panegyric of unrestricted U-boat warfare:

> Under all the waters is 'U'
> Of England's fleet you can see
> Hardly a breath.[48]

The vulgarisation of Nietzsche, too, did not begin with the Nazis but could be clearly detected at work during the First World War. German writers, like the left-wing poet and novelist Richard Dehmel, accepted Nietzsche's rejection of Western materialism but ignored his even more vehement rejection of Wilhelmine Germany for its worship of material power; they believed that German culture, although sick, could be cured of its ills by a victorious war. It was Dehmel who compared the sound of the machine-gun to the music of the spheres.[49] It was Dehmel, too, who hymned the elemental power and animal brutality of Germany at war:

> From Schleswig and Alsace, Tirol, Moravia and Carniola—
> Each man in the end wishes to be only German—
> And what sounds come from behind,
> What stamps the earth with so iron a tread
> That our hearts miss a beat?
> It was the German horses.[50]

The claims of the intellectuals who saw the war in terms of acts of heroism performed by a Nietzschean élite contrasted oddly with the grey anonymity of the trenches. 'Yes', said Kraus,

> Nietzsche would have been astonished that the 'Will to Power'

after Sedan represented, not a triumph of the spirit, but the multiplication of factory chimneys.[51]

The very idealism that underlay so much of German culture and was its glory blinded the Germans to the nature of the evil which they were committing. German intellectuals might claim that the outbreak of the First World War demonstrated that the mission of German 'Kultur' was to free Europe from the decadence of the West and the barbarism of the East but, to the satirist, it was precisely the unholy alliance of material and spiritual values by the Germans that made them the most ruthless aggressors and the most fanatical worshippers of material power. The trouble with the Germans, Kraus complained with polemical exaggeration, was not that they fired shells at the enemy but that they engraved quotations from Kant on the shells before firing them. The transition in Germany from the world of Kant to that of Krupp had been so rapid that the Germans could not see the extent to which their culture was undermined. As far as the Entente were concerned, Kraus maintained that 'The English are not idealists. For all their devotion to commerce, they would not sacrifice their whole lives to it':[52] the Russians might be fighting for reactionary Tsarism and Panslavism, but they had not yet been corrupted by the forces of capitalism and technical progress. As for Austria, it is clear that the satirist thought that her old, if now decadent, civilisation was being firmly subordinated to the German war machine: the Austrians might try to imitate the determination and energy of the Germans, but basically the fate of the Empire was no longer in their hands. It was from Germany that the main threat to traditional values came: 'No people', wrote Kraus in The Last Days of Mankind, 'have been so alienated from their language, and therefore from the source of their culture, as the Germans.' The task of the Entente in opposing the Central Powers was, perhaps, the last effort of which Christian civilisation was capable. The greatest tragedy that Kraus could imagine was that the Germans might win the war and impose their 'Kultur' on Europe: if Europe was thus 'translated into German', the only hope of rescuing civilisation would lie outside it.[53]

How had this situation come to pass? Although the satirist did not examine the problem in political but cultural terms, he clearly realised that Germany and Austria had undergone an enormous economic and social revolution without a corresponding political revolution such as had taken place in England and France. Instead, two different political, economic and cultural worlds had coexisted since the last part of the nineteenth century. The present war was not primarily one between different states, but was a bloody collision of the Old Order and the New throughout Europe. It had occurred because the Old Order was still in existence as the New developed. At the outset of the war the Old Order had apparently succeeded in mastering the new forces, but had in fact become their instrument.[54] The danger was a European one and not merely German. It could be seen in all its nakedness in Austria because Austria herself symbolised the old Europe which was succumbing to the values subscribed to by the new Germany. Because the Austrians to a large extent shared the same culture as the Germans—Kraus was always contemptuous, at least until 1933, of any attempt to talk of a distinctively Austrian culture as opposed to that of Germany— Vienna was unequalled as a vantage point for the satirist. It was the duty of the satirist to attack the evils which he knew about at first-hand; in his case, those of Central Europe. It was up to an Englishman to attack English evils. Kraus crystallised his position in one of his aphorisms, 'How can you sympathise with the English? You know absolutely no English.' 'No, but I know German.'[55]

If the distinctive feature of modern civilisation was that it elevated means into ends—if, for example, the killing of 40,000 Russians on the Eastern front now had no significance other than that the journalists would bring out an extra edition[56]— modern warfare should be sharply distinguished from that of the past. The 'militarism' of a Frederick the Great or a Bismarck had not been incompatible with a high degree of cultural achievement: the present war with the press at the helm would result in the destruction of culture. Modern militarism, too, had unlimited ends: it seemed that the First World War would last for ever for nobody seemed less able to stop it than the Austrian or German Emperors. The satirist was certainly disposed to admit that Franz Josef had been less responsible for the war than either Berchtold or the German Kaiser; but the charge which could legitimately be made against the Austrian Emperor was that of mediocrity.[57] Never before in the history of the world had such a nonentity stamped his mark on everything. On the death of Franz Josef Kraus remarked that he could believe that he had died: the difficulty lay in convincing himself that he had ever lived. Neither Franz Josef nor Wilhelm II had been tyrants: on the contrary, their mentality was characteristic of that of the masses.[58] The failure of the Emperors to stop the war, their very subservience to the demonic power of phraseology symbolised to the satirist the disintegration of the conservative tradition in which he had sought so desperately to find a haven in the years before 1914.

Profiteers were conspicuous everywhere in the great cities of Central Europe during the First World War. In Budapest it was noted that the new rich spent their time during a Shakespeare performance noisily eating salami and gherkins in their boxes at the National Theatre: 'The Will to Power' was the title which Kraus gave in the *Fackel* to this particular report.[59] There was also a noticeable breakdown of social barriers between the nobility and financiers who were doing well out of the war such as Rudolf Sieghart, the governor of the Bodenkreditanstalt bank of Vienna.[60] Count Tisza was among the leading members of the nobility who publicly welcomed the greater sense of social community which had resulted from the war. The satirist, however, was more cynical about the motives for this process of reconciliation: it perhaps reflected the bankruptcy of the conservative tradition in more senses than one.[61] Certainly the war lent itself to the making of profits by the enterprising. There were big advertising campaigns to launch ersatz products such as 'Diana War Chocolate' on the market. What, Kraus wondered, had chocolate to do with the war, the war with Diana, Diana with chocolate? Was not the slogan so remarkable an amalgamation that it outdid the *Gesamtkunstwerk* (integrated work of art) which it had been the ambition of the composer Richard Wagner to write?[62]

Throughout the war years the satirist was concerned to lay bare the incalculable amount of human suffering that existed among the poor, the weak and the helpless. There were the children in the streets happily engaged in games such as 'World War' or 'Death to the Russians'. At the Kaiser Karls Realschule in Vienna children were writing essays about the war for their teachers: Class Vb was given the choice of 'A walk during the holidays' or 'Latest methods of warfare', and Class VIa the choice 'The main characters in Goethe's *Egmont*', or 'The intensification of U-boat warfare'.[63] There was the wretched soldier in the trenches who received an illiterate scrawl from his wife who could bear loneliness no longer and had borne the child of another man:

I thought that something must have happened to you, because you had not written for three months . . . perhaps the child will die and everything will be all right.[64]

Then there was the whole suffering world of nature, which, as has been seen, the satirist regarded, together with the world of children and of woman, as a realm of innocence which was being destroyed by man's desire for mastery over his environment. A Dunkirk newspaper printed the observations of an English soldier:

The gas bombs are a fearful weapon of the Germans. The birds give us notice of an attack in a very remarkable way. Often when we have not smelt the wisps of gas, the birds have already left the branches in which they were sitting, flying in panic here and there, twittering with fear. In this way we are almost forewarned and have time to take appropriate steps. . . .[65]

The worst of the situation lay in the inability of Christianity to stop, or even alleviate, the conflict. Instead religious leaders in every country were urging the soldiers on to further slaughter. In one of his most savage comments on the war Kraus juxtaposed an account of the German bombing of Bar-le-Duc and the French bombing of Karlsruhe on Ascension Day, with the report of a speech urging support for the war by a Lutheran clergyman, Pastor Philipps:

> War is indeed the 'Ultima Ratio', the last means at God's disposal to bring the people to Him when they will not brook any other way of being governed and stray from the path . . . Therefore put more steel into your blood! German women and the mothers of fallen heroes must also not tolerate a sentimental attitude to the war.[66]

In vain did Pope Benedict condemn the brutality of unrestricted submarine warfare and the bombing of the defenceless: his voice was drowned by the exhortation of that other Benedikt, the editor of the *Neue Freie Presse*, who complimented the fishes of the Adriatic on the fine meal they were having of the French and Italian victims of Austrian torpedo-boats and submarines.[67] On the Italian front Austrian soldiers constructed a chapel with altar and altar ornaments made out of shells and shrapnel.[68] Mankind's moral sensibilities had been blunted by the war. This was the generation of the shell-shocked.

Right through the nightmare of the First World War, a nightmare in some ways worse in Vienna than actually at the front, Kraus sat through the night at his desk, trying to distil out of thousands of fleeting impressions the essence of the war and of the dangers which it represented. Periodically he visited the Engadine in Switzerland to write poetry and work on *The Last Days of Mankind* away from the censor and the turmoil of Vienna. Because of his health, the satirist had never been called for military service, although his enemies constantly said that he should have been sent to the front or, at least, imprisoned. But Kraus positively relished his unpopularity. He was used to hostility in the pursuit of his mission and quoted philosophically from Goethe:

> In every epoch, it is only individuals who have worked on behalf of knowledge, not the epoch itself. It was the epoch which murdered Socrates with poison.[69]

Not that the satirist was completely isolated during these years. Especially as the situation within the Empire grew more desperate after 1916, the intellectual youth of Vienna came increasingly under the influence of the Social Democrats and Karl Kraus, and the public recitals, which the latter—after a short break in the summer and autmun of 1914—continued to give throughout the war, were received with growing enthusiasm by large audiences. Even more important than this, however, was the contact which Kraus managed to maintain with his circle of friends—Schoenberg and Kokoschka, for example—who had been conscripted into the army but still received the *Fackel* in the trenches. The letters of Ludwig von Ficker from the Italian front were an important source of information for the satirist on conditions within the army. After one particular engagement in 1916, when the Austrians had recaptured a mountain peak in the Dolomites from the Italians at the cost of half their forces, Ficker wrote to his wife:

> Oh! I can't believe that the like of it really happened and that I didn't dream it. Please send my warmest regards to Karl Kraus. I'll write to him soon.

Ficker sent a report on the battle with an extract from the official log-book of the company which Cissy von Ficker forwarded to Kraus.[70]

Particular friends of Kraus before the First World War were the Janowitz family, father and sons, all of whom were writers and poets. When one of the sons, Franz, was killed in action in 1917, the satirist wrote a moving obituary in which he poured forth all his detestation for those responsible for the war: 'I hate them, and him I have loved.'[71] It is impossible indeed to read the letters written to Kraus from his friends without catching both the cataclysmic quality of the period and the enthusiasm, even idolatry, which the satirist inspired among so many sensitive young soldiers by the utterly uncompromising stand which he took against the war. Thus, Otto Janowitz wrote:

> On Saturday evening your October 'Fackel' arrived. I read it far into Saturday night. With the first light of dawn there was an alarm. With your magazine in my pocket, a steel helmet on my head, carrying a pistol and gasmask, I went out into the artillery fire, where I was needed. At 8 o'clock everything was over. I was able to continue my reading right through the whole day on Sunday. Today and for the last few days my thoughts have been on your work, for which I am deeply grateful. You are doing everything to save what can still be saved.[72]

Testimony such as this is of crucial importance when any attempt is made to evelute the significance of the play in which Kraus was to pass his final verdict on the First World War. *The Last Days of Mankind* was largely written between 1915 and 1917 but, although sections had been printed in the *Fackel* of the war years, it was not published in its final form until 1922 by which time the satirist, now free from the war censor, was able to incorporate into it much new material. The drama consists of a sequence of hundreds of scenes which cumulatively present a panoramic picture of the war at the front and at home through the medium of language, language which reflects the preoccupations of every level of society in Central Europe, ranging from the gross and inflated words of the German Kaiser to the Jewish dialect of Vienna. Historical incidents and figures, treated in a naturalistic style, are mixed with elements of symbolism which become dominant towards the end of the last act and in the Epilogue (The Last Night) in which scenes of slaughter, brutality and human suffering give way to the chanting of a choir of hyenas (war profiteers) whose leader (Moritz Benedikt) announces 'I am the Antichrist'. Mankind destroys itself in a hail of fire and the play ends with the voice of God using the words attributed to the German Kaiser at the beginning of the First World War: 'I did not want it' (*Ich habe es nicht gewollt*). Again language revenges itself on those who pervert it or use it idly.

'A real man of the theatre' was how Kraus was once described by Bertolt Brecht whose own *Mother Courage* and *Fear and Misery in the Third Reich* were influenced by the mixture of naturalism and symbolism, the use of an episodic technique akin to that of the cinema, and the passionate protest against war which can be found in *The Last Days of Mankind*.[73] The real significance of Kraus's play, however, is not to be found in the history of the theatre: it is basically a play for voices, in particular for the voice of Kraus himself, and although stage productions have been performed—notably at Zürich in 1945 and Vienna in 1964—its sheer length has made it impossible to be regularly performed in full.[74] The author himself claimed that it was intended only for performance on the planet Mars, for people on Earth could not bear the reality presented to them: the most fantastic events and speeches that were recorded in the play were things which had really happened, the most horrifying episodes were only quotations. It is the essential realism of the play which is responsible for both the 'dated' character of *The Last Days of Mankind* to modern audiences and the fascination which that play can exert if it is seen against the background of Kraus's society during the First World War. As the veteran German pacifist Alfred H. Fried commented, just before his death:

> Kraus does not show us life at the front so brilliantly as Barbusse or Latzko. He shows us the war at home. . . . In his *The Last Days of Mankind* Kraus shows us for the first time *all* aspects of the war.[75]

It is true, of course, that the satirist can give only a one-sided view of events. Marxists like Otto Bauer, while approving the spirit in which *The Last Days of Mankind* was written, were to criticise Kraus for ignoring the economic background of the war. Other critics have pointed out that, in his pathological hatred for Moritz Benedikt and the *Neue Freie Presse*, Kraus failed to mention the fact that, despite heavy pressure from Germany, Benedikt's newspaper was urging throughout 1918 that a compromise peace was necessary if the Habsburg Empire was to be saved.[76] A further objection can be made to the historical accuracy of *The Last Days of Mankind*: dramatic necessity was sometimes responsible for events being transposed in time and place. Take, for example, Kraus's treatment of the outrageous behaviour of the German Kaiser in tipping champagne over the heads of his courtiers and throwing caviare toast at them while they bowed low and chanted, 'If it pleases Your Majesty'. This incident, although based on fact, took place *not* during the First World War—as depicted by Kraus—but in 1901.[77]

But these are only pedantic objections. It was only through the distorting medium of polemic and satire that Kraus could fully realise the deep forces of evil at work in the world; the truth for which he sought, he said, was not mathematical but apocalyptic.[78] Who is to say that, in the middle of the First World War, an apocalyptic view of history was in no sense justified—especially amidst the icy wastes of the Eastern front? As Hans Reimann, a soldier writing from Galicia, put it, excusing himself for not having written to Kraus for a long period:

> The frightening thing about you is that you know *everything*, and have read everything without having to read it.[79]

4 *The First World War: Final Phase*

A S the war entered its third year, the suffering and disillusionment of the soldiers at the front now began to communicate itself to the civilian population at home. Whereas in Russia the process led to revolution, in 1917 in Austria the makings of a revolutionary situation were overshadowed by the fact that the imperial government was coming increasingly under the domination of Germany and ceased, at length, to have an independent policy. In Germany itself the successes of the army on the Eastern front in the autumn and winter of 1917 did much to reassure a public opinion which showed growing signs of restlessness. At the same time, however, civilian government now yielded to that of the military: in the summer of 1917 Bethmann-Hollweg, the Chancellor, was dismissed at the instigation of the army which now assumed effective control over many aspects of German life. 'You are right,' remarked Wilhelm II to the chauvinist poet Max Bewer from the *Lokalanzeiger* newspaper, 'Hindenburg is our Wotan and Ludendorff is the Siegfried of our times.'[1]

'The enthusiastic young soldiers who set out singing,' reported the German press, 'have now become men of grim determination.' This was symbolised by the introduction of steel helmets and grey uniforms, 'much more attractive than the previous coloured battledress. . . . . It is as if there was a giant from the time of the Frundberge before one. . . .' 'Valhalla with export department' was the title which Kraus rightly gave to this report.[2] For on the whole the glorification of the romantic spirit of war, epitomised by the slogan 'Be proud to be a barbarian!',[3] contrasted sharply with the prosecution of war with all the modern weapons for mass destruction. Hindenburg was aware of this, although he blamed it on the Entente. Talking to the Viennese writer Raoul Auernheimer, he commented on the use of tanks by the English:

> It is always a bad sign when an army tries through technical innovations to find a substitute for the spirit. That is irreplaceable.[4]

Increasing savagery on the land was paralleled in the air and on the sea. The technique of bombing from the air was still extremely primitive compared with that evolved during the Second World War, and the horror felt by Kraus and his contemporaries at this phenomenon was due to the fact that it was an innovation which marked the end of the distinction, hitherto made in wartime, between soldiers and civilians. The satirist deplored the failure of the Hague Conference of 1907 to outlaw the bombing of houses, hospitals and schools, but realised that the reason why the proposal to do this was rejected was due to the conviction that if large-scale exceptions were made, it would be impossible to conduct any effective bombing at all; the result would only have been that combatants would have ignored the ruling.[5] This did not in his view, however, excuse the activities of the press which found it easier to glamorise the bomber and fighter pilots, who carried out their tasks alone, than the anonymous millions who struggled against each other on the land. The public was always anxious to read the personal accounts of pilots who had returned from bombing raids:

> 'It was an extraordinary feeling for me,' said a German pilot after returning from a raid over Verdun, 'loaded with bombs I felt like a king. . . . I dropped all my bombs right on target and saw them explode on impact! . . . Never in my life have I experienced anything so wonderful! Above all earthly things flying in safety and peace, I thought myself to be a God.'[6]

There was the hero-worship of Richthofen and his flying circus which was later captained by Hermann Goering. From Richthofen

himself came a comparison between the English and German
pilots:

> With the English you can still detect in them something of
> their Teutonic blood. They are also great sportsmen, but they
> carry this too far. . . . That may be right for the Johannis-
> thaler Sports Week, but the trenches do not constitute so
> appreciative an audience. More is needed than entertainment.
> The blood of English pilots will always rain down from the
> skies.[7]

On the sea, the successes of submarine warfare had already
in the first half of the war resulted in a stream of reassuring
communiqués:

> Berlin, 22 September.
> The Wolff bureau reports: One of our U-boats hit in the
> Mediterranean on 17 September a packed enemy troopship.
> The ship sank within 43 seconds.

Kraus entitled this report 'With watch in hand'.[8] A film was
made of the sinking of the *Lusitania* and shown in Berlin with
the billing:

> The sinking of the Lusitania
> True to life.
>
> At this point in the programme smoking is permitted.[9]

The unrestricted use of submarines and the bombing of
undefended targets was justified as reprisals against the economic
blockade of the Central Powers by the British fleet, a blockade
which led to serious food shortages in 1916 and 1917, especially
in Austria which was so dependent on the grain of Hungary.
That these reprisals should be regarded as equivalent to the
economic consequences of the blockade was, to Kraus, simply a
reflection on the difference in the approach to the war by the
Entente and the Central Powers, especially when the press and
governments of Austria and Germany claimed that the food
shortage was non-existent, and that the whole affair was a
propaganda trick by the Entente.[10] This claim could be refuted

by merely looking at other pages within the same newspapers which were so vehement in their denials. For example, during a production at the Burgtheater in Vienna, real bread was used on the stage:

> At this point the noise of whispering filled the packed house. So much so, that the action of the play was halted and the actors could not conceal their smiles. [11]

When the food shortage was openly admitted in the press, its gravity was minimised by the kind of argument which Kraus crystallised in one of his aphorisms, 'Father, bread!', 'Children, France is starving!' [12]

It was no accident, therefore, that during the war Vienna should have been a city of rumours. In 1917 there were rumours that the new Emperor, Karl, who had succeeded to the throne on the death of Franz Josef in November 1916, was trying to make peace with the allies. It will be seen later that these rumours had some foundation in fact, but the Austrian government was naturally obliged to deny that they were true and claimed that the rumours originated from an enemy source. Kraus was sceptical about the denial and pointed out that the government had only itself to blame for the rumours because it did not tell the truth to the people: the lies of the Entente were less dangerous than the 'truth' put out by the Central Powers who had mobilised the moral and spiritual reserves of their culture for propaganda purposes to a far greater degree than the Entente. Furthermore, the propaganda of the Entente had a disconcerting habit of being based on the truth, such as their prediction that Conrad von Hötzendorf would resign his post as Chief of Staff of the Austrian army in February 1917, after criticisms of the stalemate on the Italian front in 1916. [13]

The fundamental insecurity of the position of Austria was strikingly demonstrated to the satirist by the precipitate haste with which the government claimed military victories. This had occurred over the Isonzo campaign in 1916, and Hötzendorf was, somewhat unfairly, blamed afterwards for the failure of the Austrian army to exploit its initial successes. Certainly at Caporetto in October 1917 the Austrians *did* achieve a great victory which pushed the Italians back beyond the Tagliamento river to the line of the Piave. But at the beginning of the last offensive of the Austrians at the Piave in June 1918 the Viennese press was somewhat premature in hailing the early successes of the Austrians as a portent of total victory:

> We see in the words of the Kriegspressequartier the imprint of history. The enemy has tried everything to defeat us. . . . Now they will cry for American help, that will o' the wisp of the Entente, which leads them even deeper into the marshes of difficulty and defeat.[14]

After being repulsed with the loss of 100,000 men, the Austrians were more chastened. A minister explained to the Reichsrat the difficulties which the army were facing:

> Against the large number of prisoners that were reported, I must confess . . . that our casualties were very high. In view of this, the number of prisoners cannot be claimed to be very large.[15]

The minister went on to claim, however, that, despite the heavy losses, the Austrian offensive had prevented the Italians from sending troops to the Western front. Kraus compared this explanation with one of the standard propaganda slogans of the Central Powers, 'France is being bled to death by England'.[16]

Great play was made by the Central Powers of the perfidy of France and England in bringing America into the war in April 1917 to counterbalance the effects of the Russian Revolution of March 1917. Hertling, the puppet chancellor of the German High Command, traced this latest example of the French desire for revenge and the greed of British imperialism back to the encirclement policies of Edward VII.[17] Meanwhile Ludendorff had decided that the Western Powers must be crushed in a major offensive before the Americans arrived in numbers sufficient to affect the balance of power. Paul Goldmann, the Berlin correspondent of the *Neue Freie Presse*, on his fourth visit to Hindenburg and Ludendorff on behalf of that newspaper, assured his readers that both generals sincerely desired peace. But it was clear from the interview that neither contemplated any concessions to the Allies but intended to inflict on them a great military defeat. Hindenburg's parting words to Goldmann were sufficiently ambiguous to admit either interpretation of the interview: 'You have seen us here today for perhaps the last time.'[18] It was hoped in Berlin and Vienna that the release of prisoners of war from Russia would make the decisive difference to the outcome of the spring offensive in the West in 1918. 'Let us reflect', wrote one newspaper 'that perhaps a million or more prisoners have returned from Russia, most of them young men with experience of war, hardened in the climate of Siberia.'[19] The press denied that Bolshevik propaganda against the war had had considerable influence on the prisoners. It failed to point out however either that the army had been so concerned about this problem that it had on 1 April 1918 set up a special department of propaganda at General Headquarters to combat revolutionary opinions among the returning soldiers, or that as soon as the prisoners crossed over into the Empire they were sent to camps where they were thoroughly screened.[20] Instead, the newspapers concentrated their attention on how strong and healthy the prisoners were, how they had laughed at Bolshevik attempts at indoctrination, and how much the prisoners would enjoy their four weeks' leave before rejoining their regiments.[21]

All this, and much more besides, was documented by Kraus in the pages of *Die Fackel*. The satirist saw in the last years of the war the culminating process of that displacement of human values by those of the machine which he had feared and foreseen for so long. This process was mirrored in the language of war. Men were no longer men but units of 'manpower'—the German word 'Menschenmaterial' is even more expressive—manpower which it was the object of the enemy to 'wipe out' and then 'mop up' (*abtrocknen*); the thing to do was to 'stand fast' (*durchhalten*), to 'do one's bit' (*sein Scherflein beisteuern*).[22] The war itself had become a machine in which the expense of human

lives was no object. The feverish calculations made in Berlin and
Vienna in the early months of 1918 as to the balance of forces in
the coming offensive, had had their parallels at the beginning
of 1915, of 1916 and of 1917. If the war had become one of
exhaustion in which neither side could inflict a decisive defeat
on the other, then victory must ultimately lie in the superiority
of numbers and equipment. It was clear that, in the last analysis,
equipment was more important than men. As the *Neue Freie
Presse* had written at the beginning of 1917:

> The process of disintegration has already begun and it will
> end with the destruction of English influence. When this
> point is reached then the war will come to an end, too. Nobody
> believes that it could be ended by a lack of men, but lack of
> war materials would certainly accelerate the end of the war.[23]

Kraus could hardly believe his eyes when he reflected on the
implications of a statement such as this.

Perhaps the most brilliant of the campaigns which Kraus
fought during the First World War was the attack which he
levelled at Berchtold's successor at the Foreign Office, Count
Czernin, although the attack could not, for censorship reasons,
appear in the *Fackel* until after the latter's dismissal.

Soon after his succession the new Emperor, Karl, realising that
a prolongation of the war could only result either in an Austrian
defeat or in the subordination of the Empire to the status of a
German satellite, initiated secret negotiations with the French
for a compromise peace. A well-intentioned but in many ways
foolish person—at a critical point during the war, for example,
he publicly celebrated his hundredth visit to the cinema[24]—
Karl did not inform Czernin correctly about his intentions:
whereas Czernin understood that the Emperor was merely
exploring the possibilities of a peaceful settlement, Karl was in
fact trying to seek a basis for a separate peace for Austria-
Hungary. In retrospect, it is easy to see that such an attempt was
doomed to failure, irrespective of the methods which were

employed. Had there been any serious prospect of a separate peace treaty—and Karl was even willing to countenance the French claims to Alsace-Lorraine as the price for such a treaty— the Habsburg Empire would have been immediately occupied by German troops, troops which had, after all, been propping up the Austrians on the Eastern Front ever since 1915. Czernin himself realised that Austria needed peace: indeed in a memorandum to the Austrian Emperor in April 1917 he predicted that the Empire would collapse if the war continued for another winter. Where the Austrian Foreign Minister differed from Karl, however, was in the methods which should be employed to gain this end. Czernin believed that the only way in which Austria could influence Germany in favour of peace was in close alliance with her. In October 1917, therefore, he signed a secret agreement with Kühlmann, the German Foreign Minister, which involved a greater co-ordination of effort between Germany and Austria at every level—diplomatic, military and economic. This agreement foreshadowed the Spa Treaty of May 1918, although by that time Czernin had been succeeded as Foreign Minister by Burián.

Kraus did not of course know of these secret arrangements. Nevertheless he was justified in believing that the guarded welcome which Czernin gave in a speech at Budapest in February 1918 to Wilson's proclamation of the Fourteen Points a month earlier conflicted with Austria's commitment to the German cause and in particular with Czernin's support for the major spring offensive in the West which Hindenburg and Ludendorff were planning. In this speech Czernin on the one hand avowed his wish for peace and a permanent system of international arbitration: on the other, he admitted that, although Austria wanted a peace without annexations, if the conflict did not end within a stated time and if the military position of the Central Powers had improved in the meantime, then Austria and Germany would feel free to alter the peace terms to their own advantage. The logical inconsistency in such a policy was shown a few days later when Czernin attempted to 'clarify' the points in his speech, stating that, although Wilson's proposals represented an important step nearer to the Austro-German position, he must make it clear that Austria would stand by her commitments to Germany over the possession of Belgium and over the maintenance of the Turkish Empire.[25] Austrian opinion which had been full of rumours about the imminence of peace was deeply disappointed. The maze of contradictions into which Czernin had drawn himself and the public was reflected in the initially friendly and then violently hostile treatment which Wilson's proposals received in the government-inspired press of Vienna as the chances of a settlement waned.

To Kraus, Czernin had bungled the one major opportunity for Austria to make peace: the whole episode was 'a new and most intriguing case study in the belles lettres of diplomacy'. Czernin, this 'word-artist' had spoken with all the clichés and non sequiturs of the leader-writer.[26] His speeches proclaimed high principles of international arbitration and the renunciation of annexations, but they set a time limit on the implementation of these principles and clearly hinted that certainly Germany, if not Austria, would increase her territory.[27] What were the Entente to make of Czernin's proposals, asked the satirist, especially when that statesman increased the confusion further by assuring the Versailles war council through the official *Fremdenblatt* that he had in his speech 'in the clearest and most unmistakable way' proclaimed a peace without annexations?[28] No wonder the Allies rejected the Austrian proposal, especially since Czernin blandly talked elsewhere of an Austrian hegemony over Serbia.[29]

The *Arbeiter Zeitung* might see in Czernin a combination of Metternich and Wilson, but Kraus preferred to see his policy as an impossible combination of Machiavelli and Kant.[30] The satirist, as usual, was interested, not in the exigencies of the political situation in which Czernin found himself, but in moral absolutes: nor was he concerned so much with the activities of politicians considered in isolation; what Kraus *was* concerned about was how the politicians and the press explained matters to the public. Far worse than Czernin's insincerities was the impression given to the public by the press that he was a competent politican to whom they might entrust the destinies of an Empire which was visibly falling apart in the early months of 1918:

> Count Czernin is a personality who will not stand for slackness and *laissez-faire*. He was obliged to translate the gospel of President Wilson into the language of diplomacy; it was a gospel that would have brought not peace but war. . . . A diplomat needs such principles as ideals, but there is also the reality of daily life to be considered.

On which the comment of Kraus was 'Daily life, daily death!'[31]

The impotence of Czernin and Austria in the face of German intransigence was clearly demonstrated in the negotiations which led to the peace of Brest-Litovsk with Soviet Russia, a peace which finally gave the lie to all talk of a peace without annexations. Although Czernin tried to cut a figure at the negotiations, arguing with Trotsky about the applicability to Austria-Hungary of the principles of self-determination, the reality of power lay with the German army who were determined to impose a dictated peace. When the representative of the German High Command, General Hoffmann, made this brutally clear to the Russian delegates who were trying to spin out the negotiations in the hope that the situation might change in Russia's favour, Czernin explained Hoffman's conduct to the Austrian public by saying that the affair was simply 'a storm in a tea-cup', a slogan which Kraus lovingly quoted as an imperishable monument to the power of phraseology.[32] For the connoisseur of diplomatic double-talk there was also the explanations which Czernin offered regarding the erection of a Ukrianian republic which was to make a separate peace with the Central Powers and was to be, in fact, their satellite: 'The conclusion of peace with the Ukraine', said Czernin, 'must not be regarded as an unfriendly act against the Russian government. The Ukraine has become through this treaty not an ally of the Central Powers but a neutral state.'[33]

All that Czernin was really interested in was to plunder this 'neutral' state of its grain for the hungry people of Austria. But, asked Kraus, were not the people of the Ukraine hungry too? When it was reported that a 'commission' was leaving Vienna to 'buy' grain in the Ukraine, Kraus commented:

> No one knows which grain commission is superfluous. No one knows if the peasants of the Ukraine will quickly sell their grain. . . . No one knows who has defeated whom in the Ukraine. . . . The only thing one knows is that the Ukraine is known to be rich in grain.[34]

The fact was that, although Czernin welcomed the opportunity to plunder the Ukraine of its grain, the establishment of Ukrainian independence was a diplomatic defeat for Austria-Hungary because it was bound to alienate the Poles who ruled over a large Ukrainian population in the East of Poland and who had, hitherto, been one of the most dependable props of an Empire whose tutelage they preferred to domination by either the Germans or the Russians. Kraus was also quick to point out the hypocrisy with which the Austrian Prime Minister, Seidler, invoked Wilson's principle of self-determination to justify the cession to the Ukraine of the district of Cholm, although its western part was Polish.[35] It was clear that the Austrian government had agreed to this cession, as indeed to the whole policy of creating an independent Ukraine, only under strong German pressure.

But by the logic of his policy of maintaining the closest links with Germany Czernin was forced not only to sanction the Treaty of Brest-Litovsk but also to stake the future of Austria on the spring offensive in the West in 1918 which was to be the German High Command's last bid for a victorious conclusion to the war. 'In our foreign policy we are, thank God, steering the German course,' was Czernin's latest cry, the corollary of which was the negotiations which were initiated for strengthening the Austro-German alliance.[36] These negotiations were to reach their final form in the Spa Treaty of May 1918 which, by reducing

Austria completely to the status of a German satellite, alienated the Slav minorities within the Empire and made the dismemberment of Austria-Hungary imperative for the Allies. Czernin's successor, Burián, tried to conceal the appalling implications of the treaty for Austria by issuing a communiqué in which the phrase 'extension and deepening of the alliance' was constantly used as if to batter the public into a dazed acceptance. Kraus quoted this document at length in the *Fackel* and juxtaposed beside it the communiqué issued by the Japanese after their victory over China in the war of 1895, a communiqué concerning the Sino-Japanese military convention which was intended to give Japan virtually complete control over Chinese policy: 'In one word', said Kraus of the Japanese document, 'the alliance between Japan and China has been extended and deepened.'[37] When people objected to Burián that Austria had been subordinated to Germany the Austrian Foreign Minister quoted the proverb 'Only the most stupid calves choose their own slaughterers'.[38]

By the time the Spa treaty was signed, Czernin was out of office as a result of his unfortunate speech to the Vienna city council on 2 April, in which he had hoped to boost hopes that France would crumble under the impact of the German offensive by revealing that peace feelers had been put forward by the French. Infuriated and embarrassed, Clemenceau revealed to the world the fact that the Austrian Emperor had been trying to negotiate a separate peace for Austria-Hungary. In a press release on 11 April, Czernin implied that the letter of the Emperor which Clemenceau had quoted was a forgery. But on 13 April, under the full impact of the revelations of the French Prime Minister, Czernin was forced to admit to the authenticity of the letter—except for the passage referring to French claims to Alsace-Lorraine. Most observers came to the conclusion that this was a flagrant contradiction and that the whole letter was genuine, as indeed proved to be the case. Czernin's action thus brought nothing but discredit upon himself and the Habsburg Monarchy. To Kraus he was simply a journalist manqué: whereas Bismarck had been a genius, Czernin was merely a man

Alice Schalek on the Italian front

Postcard showing the corpse of Cesare Battisti

of talent, and this was worse than having no talent at all.[39] After
the war the satirist impatiently dismissed the apologies which
Czernin put forward for his conduct. The latter claimed that he
had wanted peace at the beginning of 1918 but that Ludendorff
had vetoed this. Why then did he not make a separate peace with
the Entente? Because, said Czernin, he feared a German
invasion of Austria similar to the German invasion of Rumania
after that nation had come into the war against Germany in
1916.[40] Kraus was convinced that, in such an eventuality, the
Entente would have supported Austria against Germany,
especially since the latter, on Czernin's own admission, was not
in a position to continue the war if Austria withdrew.[41]

It is true that Czernin, like Burián and the Austrian prime
minister Seidler (a bureaucrat and amateur dramatist by whose
honesty and talent Kraus was not impressed)[42] was nothing more
than a mediocrity. It was also true that, instead of revealing the
facts of the desperate situation of Austria, Czernin and Burián had
encouraged the press to talk about 'the rejuvenated Austria'
which, in the fourth year of the war, was to emerge from a
strengthening of the alliance with Germany. And yet it is
difficult to see that the separate peace demanded by Kraus,
Professor Lammasch and others inside Austria, was ever a
practical proposition, even if the negotiations for such a peace
had been handled more expertly on the part of the Emperor and
had they not been sabotaged by Czernin.[43] The fact was that, in
the last years of the war, effective power rested with the German
army and not with Vienna. Furthermore soon after his accession
to the throne Karl had discovered that he would not be allowed
his coronation in Budapest unless he gave a solemn oath to
uphold the privileges of Hungary. Both Karl and Czernin came
to realise that no peace terms offered by the Emperor to the
Western powers could overcome the opposition of the Hungarian
magnates to any major concessions being made to the Slav
elements within the Empire. The power of Budapest was further
strengthened by the bad harvest of 1917 and the hunger in
Vienna in that year and in 1918, for the Hungarians controlled

the main wheat-growing area of the Habsburg Empire. As Kraus himself remarked after the whole business was over, what had been performed in Vienna during the First World War was a 'dance operetta with text from Berlin and melody from Budapest'.[44]

It has already been seen that the events of 1914 had presented the Social Democrats of Germany and Austria with the necessity to make a difficult and cruel decision. On the one hand, they had for years worked through the Second International in an attempt to prevent a war breaking out which would involve the workers of the various countries fighting against each other: on the other hand, they were convinced that the real threat to peace in 1914 came from the expansionist designs of Tsarist Russia which, to Marx and Engels, had been the symbol of the dark forces of reaction against which all Socialists must fight. The fact that Russia had been the first power to mobilise her forces in the crisis of July 1914 weighed very heavily in Social Democrat circles in Berlin and Vienna. A war against Russia, therefore, seemed to be both right and necessary. But what about the struggle with France and Britain? These, after all, were democratic countries with powerful labour movements, and one of the main objects of the Second International had been to prevent a war between Germany and France. Here was a problem which upset the peace of mind of many Socialists.

Nevertheless, the widespread belief that the war would last for only a few months helped to salve a number of consciences. Furthermore it might be argued that the outbreak of war would bring certain political advantages for the Left: war, after all, has often been the harbinger of social change. Majority opinion within the Austrian party in 1914 sided with Karl Renner who held that the war would facilitate that natural alliance between the dynasty and the peoples of the Empire, an alliance for social progress which had been temporarily established during the campaign for universal suffrage in 1906 and 1907 but had been upset in later years by the forces of nationalism and particularism. Renner's arguments were all the more potent because the voice of Otto Bauer was, for the time being, stilled: Bauer was absent from Vienna, having been conscripted into the army and then subsequently taken prisoner by the Russians in Galicia in December 1914. The small group of radicals who collected around Friedrich Adler, the son of the leader of the party, to assert their outright opposition to the war, were no substitute for the big battalions of Social Democratic strength which supported Renner. Viktor Adler himself, although anxious to maintain contact with all the groups within the party, felt compelled to give the war his reluctant blessing.

The mixed feelings of the Austrian party about the war by 1915 were, however, clearly to be seen in the pages of the *Arbeiter Zeitung*. In some ways the war could be described as a school of good Social Democrat virtues. Conscription, rationing and the organisation of a war economy admitted the socialist principle of equality: 'Europe is full of heroes. . . . And then this perfection of organisation. . . . Man is powerful.'[45] But when this enthusiasm was accompanied by both humanitarian scruples and a due respect for the censor, then a rich source of satire was exposed to the editor of *Die Fackel*. When for example the Social Democrat newspaper criticised the glee with which the Viennese press had hailed the bombing of the city of Milan but then itself deemed the action to be a 'tragic necessity', Kraus replied that it was all very well for the *Arbeiter Zeitung* to exculpate the bombing of fortified towns but it never mentioned the bombing of cities that were unfortified and completely defenceless.[46] The satirist mocked at the industry with which Social Democrats assembled collections of documents to prove that neither Austria nor Germany had been responsible for the war.[47] To Kraus such activities only underlined the impotence of the Socialist parties: they were following events and not attempting to control them. The war had brought out into the open the degree to which the Social Democrats of Austria and Germany had become revisionists in practice, even though they retained the superstructure of a Marxist ideology.

No amount of revolutionary phraseology, Kraus lamented, could conceal the inherent conservatism of the party bureaucracy. He was not surprised, therefore, that determined opposition to the war within the ranks of Social Democracy was confined before 1917 to a small minority of courageous individuals. In Germany there was Rosa Luxemburg and the group around her who suffered imprisonment rather than cease to preach the need for a revolution to end the war.[48] In Austria one frail and nervous intellectual went further: in October 1916 Friedrich Adler caused a sensation by assassinating the prime minister, Count Stürgkh. At his trial Adler defended his action in a speech that was to be one of the most poignant testaments to come out of the final years of the Habsburg Empire, an electrifying indictment not merely of the Austrian government but also of the opportunistic policies of the section of the Social Democratic party led by Karl Renner, whom Adler described as the Lueger of Austrian Social Democracy. The assassin declared that he bore no personal animosity towards Stürgkh but that he had felt impelled towards committing the crime of murder because Stürgkh was a symbol of the system of oppression and authoritarianism which was destroying Austria. This evoked the deepest sympathy from Kraus, although he was not allowed by the censor to manifest this sympathy until the next year, when the death sentence on Adler had been commuted to 18 years' imprisonment with hard labour—the Austrian government had not dared in the end to exact the supreme penalty in the circumstances of 1917.[49]

Adler's trial certainly hastened the movement of opinion within the Austrian party against the war, a process that was further accelerated by the Russian revolution and the downfall of the Tsarist régime, an event which seemed to remove the primary justification for the conflict. But even after the downfall of Tsarism in Russia, the *Arbeiter Zeitung* clung to the idea that, in 1914 if not in 1917, the war had been a defensive one as far as Austria was concerned. It was in nostalgic terms that the Social Democratic newspaper of Vienna lamented the sordid nature of the war in the West in 1917:

In the fighters of today there flickers hardly a flame of that spiritual quality which the war possessed, a quality which reached its highest peak in history in the deeds of a Hindenburg and a Mackensen on Russian and Rumanian soil.[50]

In Germany, too, the Left had to be galvanised into opposition to the war by the operation of external forces. The Reichstag Peace Resolution of July 1917 (which declared that Germany would seek a peace without annexations) owed more to the Catholic leader Matthias Erzberger than to the Majority Socialists. The latter indeed threatened that if the German Chancellor did not accept 'completely and without reservations' the terms of the resolution, they would . . . but what? Go into opposition! The contrast between the assertive self-confidence of their slogans and the feebleness of their actions was what Kraus was concerned to emphasise.[51] Even this was not the end of the story. Worried by the situation created by the Peace Resolution, the German army sent the Crown Prince to Berlin to discuss with the political parties the possibility of removing Bethmann-Hollweg (whose weakness and irresolution made him increasingly unpopular with both the army and the politicians) with their consent. Erzberger hoped that, by removing Bethmann-Hollweg, a new Chancellor —preferably Bülow—would be installed who would be better able to control the army: and to this end he also hoped that the Majority Socialists would join a strong government coalition in the Reichstag. The Socialists, quite naturally, were deeply divided over this issue and, at the interview with the Crown Prince, their representative Edward David was obliged to return a non-committal answer. The unhappy position in which the Social Democrats found themselves was emphasised, however, when the party leadership sought to justify their acceptance of the invitation in terms of Marxist ideology. The result was grotesque. Their acceptance of the invitation had been:

. . . no infringement of basic Social Democrat principles. Comrade David was correct in accepting the invitation of the Crown Prince. The Social Democrat party is a revolutionary party. Because of this, when conditions are favourable, it must revolutionise its own supporters and break with old traditions.[52]

The upshot of the affair was that, under Erzberger's tutelage, the Social Democrats gave general support to the government. Bülow was not appointed, but instead the nonentity Michaelis, who was shortly followed by Hertling; and both these chancellors were full of evasions about the implementations of the Reichstag Peace Resolution. Hindenburg and Ludendorff were satisfied that the Reichstag could be kept quiet. But what, implied Kraus, had become of the revolution that the Social Democrats claimed they were making?

Still, both in Germany and Austria, the year 1917 saw a marked movement against the war within the ranks of Social Democracy. The return of Otto Bauer from a prisoner-of-war camp in Russia in September 1917 did much to swing the Austrian party away from the policies associated with Karl Renner. Bauer demanded an end to the tactical alliance between the Socialists and the dynasty: the subject nationalities of the Empire should be given their independence and the Austrian Germans must seek union with a new democratic Germany. Increasing pressure coming from below, from the hunger of the workers, finally led the party to endorse the strikes of January 1918 which for a time paralysed Vienna and other industrial centres. By this action, however, the Social Democrats were brought face to face with certain harsh facts of the situation: Viktor Adler quickly realised that if the strikes were prolonged, the authorities could still rely on the imperial army to intervene and crush the workers' organisations. After fierce opposition from the radicals within the party, the strikes were called off. It was not until November 1918 when the army was in complete disintegration and the threat of external intervention had been eliminated by the collapse of German power that the Austrian 'revolution' occurred. Even then it was only through the persistence of Bauer that Renner was prepared to agree that the Habsburgs must be removed and a republic proclaimed.

But although Kraus was in January 1919 to announce his public support of the republic and the Social Democrats, it was not a Social Democrat but a Catholic and a conservative whom the satirist honoured most for his opposition to the First World War. Kraus had admired Professor Heinrich Lammasch long before 1914: as early as the first year of the *Fackel* Kraus had expressed his support for the efforts of Lammasch to institute reforms in the Austrian penal code; the latter had responded by congratulating the satirist for his attacks on the irresponsibility of the Viennese press in matters affecting the legal system. A member of the Upper House of the Austrian parliament, Lammasch had had a distinguished legal career, including a period as legal adviser to the Austrian delegation to the Hague Peace Conference of 1907; on several occasions he had served as a judge in the International Court.[53] As a firm believer in the principles of international arbitration, he had opposed the war from the start. He was allowed to indulge in literary activity directed against the war, but was allowed to undertake no direct political involvement; only the personal intervention of Franz Josef saved him from arrest and imprisonment. It was one of his articles in the *Arbeiter Zeitung* in 1916, calling for some form of international arbitration to make wars impossible in the future and attacking the action of the German government in deliberately wrecking the Peace Conference of 1907, which brought forth unstinted praise from Kraus who called him one of the few honourable men in Austria.[54] Later on, the satirist was quick to defend Lammasch against the attacks of Professor Friedjung who wanted a continuation of the war in close alliance with Germany[55] and as late as 1918 was urging that Serbia, already conquered, must now be formally annexed by Austria.[56] Lammasch, on the contrary, was one of those who believed— somewhat naïvely it must be admitted—that the Habsburg Empire could be saved by the conclusion of an immediate and separate peace. It was his tragedy that when in October 1918 he and his friends like Ignaz Seipel, together with the Liberal politician Professor Redlich, were summoned by Kaiser Karl to form a government, the Empire had virtually ceased to exist. His administration was in office for only three weeks and could do little more than prepare for the abdication of the Emperor. Lammasch died shortly afterwards.

The importance of Lammasch for the student of Kraus, however, goes beyond the immediate issues of 1917 and 1918. Lammasch represented that type of Christian and conservative to whom the satirist instinctively responded. It is significant that, although Kraus was later in the course of the 1920s to attack the policies of Seipel who was a colleague of Lammasch in the latter's brief and ill-fated administration, the final political position of the satirist was one of support for Dollfuss; and it was in Dollfuss that he claimed to find the same combination of qualities which he had admired in Lammasch. Still the fact remained that, with the honourable exception of Lammasch, the forces of Christianity and conservatism in Austria had been less conspicuous than those of the Left in the struggle to bring the war to an end. Indeed, claimed Kraus, by their actions during that war the Christians had crucified Christ again. Where, then, were the real Christians? When the war ended in the collapse of the Habsburg Monarchy, the Catholic *Reichspost* put the blame for the defeat on the Jews, the Freemasons, the Czechs and the Social Democrats. 'Were Hötzendorf and Berchtold Jews?' asked the German pacifist Friedrich Wilhelm Förster, whom Kraus quoted with approval.[57] When Friedrich Funder, the editor of the *Reichspost*, attempted to identify Lammasch with the Christian Socialist party, Kraus pointed out that it was Funder who had resisted many attempts by Lammasch to express his views in the *Reichspost*.[58] The satirist also recalled a meeting during the war with Lammasch at his home in Salzburg where the latter expressed his detestation of Funder.[59] The attitude of the Austrian Catholics to the First World War was one of a number of reasons which provoked Kraus into leaving the Catholic Church in 1922.

The conservative tradition he was convinced was exhausted both religiously and politically: it had sold out to the forces of materialism and capitalism. In the long and important 'Retro-spect' (*Nachruf*) on the war, which Kraus published in January 1919, he announced his support for the republic and the Social Democrats who had established the republic:

> The coexistence of thrones and telephones has led to the use of mustard gas grenades to maintain the thrones. They (the thrones) must disappear to make the forces of science of service to life. The question of a republic or a monarchy is no longer to be solved according to the political preference of the individual. The epoch has already decided in favour of the former. A long while ago the problem ceased to exist.

The support which Kraus gave to the Social Democrats was, thus, both reluctant and conditional; it was rather in the nature of a protest vote against the other side. The conservative ideal seemed lost for ever. The monarchy, and with it the Empire—'this union of jovial executioners, this stepfather whose authority shamed the world, who kept his family together at the cost of thwarting the national feeling of its peoples'—had to be reluc-tantly cast aside. Both had been guilty of such evil that it was just that they should disappear: 'It was all a dream. . . . It ended like a film, full of waltzes and bloodshed.'[60] The individual, having lost his focus of loyalty in the traditional order, was now forced back to a dependence on God alone. The satirist explained that he did not expect men to behave better under the republic than they did before; but at least they could not longer evade the problems of life by seeking refuge in a political order that was rotten. Now, at least, there would be nothing to obscure man's perception of his basic isolation in this world: not only Vienna, but mankind also, must shed its illusions and face the future with courage.[61]

And so on 2 February 1919, in one of his public recitals in Vienna, Kraus appealed to his audience to vote for the Social Democrats in the coming elections, elections in which the Social Democrats were, in fact, returned as the largest single party.[62] Again in the elections of 1920, Kraus urged support for the Social

Democrats although this time the number of votes which they received was exceeded by that of the various groups of Christian Socialists, a party which played in its propaganda on the myth that the war had been a defensive war and that the Austrians were guiltless of responsibility for it.[63] The Social Democrats with all their faults, declared the editor of *Die Fackel*, were closer to the spirit of Christianity than the professed Christians. It was in terms more reminiscent of Kierkegaard than of the hard world of politics that Kraus regarded the new republic.

No account of Kraus's activities during the war would be complete without some reference to the acrid and often wearisome polemics with which he castigated the activities of many German and Austrian writers during this period. There was often some justification for his attacks. The German humorous magazine *Simplicissimus* amused itself with the following poem which celebrated the fact that the ship carrying Lord Kitchener on a mission to Russia was torpedoed in the North Sea:

> It is frustrating and dismaying:
> Herr Kitchener is certainly now drowned—
> But Grey? There is much to hope for yet.[64]

The German poet Ernst Lissauer was awarded the Order of the Red Eagle by the German Kaiser for his notorious 'Hymn of Hate':

> Hate by water and hate by land
> Hate of heart and hate of the hand
> We love as one and hate as one;
> We have but one foe alone—England.

For many years in the 1920s Kraus pursued a long vendetta with the left-wing film and theatre critic Alfred Kerr of Berlin, accusing him of the authorship of poetry that was abusive towards the Rumanians and sadistic in the pleasure which it expressed at the fate of Russian soldiers drowning in the Masurian lakes during the battles of 1914.[65]

It was during the 1920s, too, that *Die Fackel* was constantly to remind its readers of the war-time activities of the famous Socialist dramatist Gerhart Hauptmann who had signed the manifesto of the ninety-three intellectuals justifying the German violation of Belgian neutrality and had written propaganda for the German war-effort. After the war Hauptmann was widely regarded as one of the ornaments of the Weimar republic. But the period of his most creative work was now over. He was now more concerned to enjoy his position as a distinguished literary personality and to fulfil his social aspirations; he mixed easily with the millionaires of the inflation period. In 1921 Hauptmann was to be awarded an honorary doctorate by the German University at Prague, although Kraus was suspicious of the motives behind this award. In the citation for the degree the Dean of the University proclaimed:

> Gerhart Hauptmann is an intellectual commander in chief of the German people: through him Germany won and still wins her most striking victories.

Upon which Kraus, who had been an admirer and supporter of his early work, commented that whether the victories won by the work of Hauptmann would be more enduring than those of Ludendorff remained an open question.[66]

Sometimes, of course, Kraus was guilty of a virulent personal animus in his comments on other writers. The fact that both Kerr and Lissauer were Jewish is not without significance in this respect. Lissauer, in particular, was an attractive and tragic personality, an idealist who was driven to write his war-poetry by the need to compensate for the fact that he had been rejected for military service in 1914. In 1933, by contrast, he was to be a refugee from Germany after the advent of Hitler to power. Stefan Zweig vividly described the irony inherent in Lissauer's career. 'No one was more familiar with German poetry and no one was more enraptured by the German language; like so many Jews whose families had entered German culture late, he had more faith in Germany than the most devoted Germans.'[67]

Alfred Kerr, also a refugee from Germany after 1933, was, it was true, a less sympathetic figure than Lissauer: Kraus's long and bitter fight with Kerr had its origin in a controversy that dated back long before 1914, to the period when Kerr was editor of the magazine *Pan* and Kraus had attacked him for posing as an enemy of all forms of corruption while at the same time attempting to destroy the reputation of the police president of Berlin by claiming that the latter had made advances to his (i.e. Kerr's) wife.[68] Even so, many of Kraus's admirers were to point out that Kerr was not a sufficiently important figure to bear the weight of the ridicule and invective which was heaped on him over the years by *Die Fackel*.

Even more distressing for the satirist's admirers was the hatred with which Kraus pursued such naïvely well-intentioned individuals as Franz Werfel and Stefan Zweig, perhaps the two most quintessentially Viennese of all modern Austrian writers. Werfel had been an early friend of the satirist and yet their friendship was destroyed by a literary squabble which was followed by a series of polemics in which Kraus attacked Werfel's work at the Kriegspressequartier during the war. Werfel counter attacked by pointing out the very real moral difficulty that many writers faced after they had been conscripted: if they wished to have leisure to get on with their writing, they had far greater opportunities to do so in such organisations as the Kriegspressequartier than if they remained outside; on the other hand, by working for the government or the army they were compelled, often against their own inclination, to write propaganda for the war-effort.[69] The case of Stefan Zweig, who was also a favourite object of Kraus's attack, was somewhat similar.[70] Both Werfel and Zweig were genuinely opposed to the war and made this quite clear in the work which they were able to publish in Switzerland during the war. Indeed they were both able to profit from the fact that by 1917 the Austrian government was concerned that its willingness for peace should be known in neutral Europe. Both Werfel and Zweig were sent out to Switzerland to further this cause, and this gave them the opportunity to make contacts with other intellectuals who were opposed to the war, such as the French writer Romain Rolland. Kraus, however, refused to be impressed by all this. When Rolland praised the Zürich performance in 1918 of Zweig's anti-war play *Jeremiah*, the satirist mocked at his claim that, by writing this work, Zweig had shown great courage: Rolland, he remarked, had certainly never heard of the *Fackel* which attacked the war from behind the lines of the enemy.[71]

Indeed it is clear that in 1918 and 1919 Kraus's attack on his fellow writers, far from diminishing with the conclusion of peace, now acquired an even sharper edge. The satirist was obsessed with the fact that many of those writers who, willingly or unwillingly, had collaborated with the governments of Berlin and Vienna during the war, now sought salvation in supporting the Bolshevik experiment in Russia. All sorts of ideological combinations seemed possible in 1918: Werfel and Franz Blei proclaimed that they sought a synthesis between Communism and Catholicism and harangued crowds in the streets of Vienna in favour of the Austrian revolution; at one point a mob, led by the Prague journalist Egon Erwin Kisch (later to be extremely influential in the left-wing press in the 1930s) occupied the offices of the *Neue Freie Presse* in an attempt to spark off a Communist uprising. To Kraus it was like exchanging one nightmare for another. Although he himself had by 1918 moved to an extremely radical position in politics, he was a consistent opponent of violence and saw in Russian Communism a terrible perversion of the humanitarian element within socialism. Bolshevism, he was convinced, was a product of the brutality of the First World War and must be opposed.[72] The fact that many of the intellectuals who were attracted to Bolshevism were also the literary exponents of Expressionism only increased the vehemence of his repudiation of the latter movement.

In typical fashion Kraus followed up his attack on intellectuals who had been involved in the official propaganda and information services during the First World War and then openly avowed their revolutionary sympathies once the war was ended by playing a cruel joke on them. In 1919 a telegram was sent anonymously to Munich appealing for the reprieve of the poet and dramatist, Ernst Toller, who was under sentence of death for his part in the brief Communist régime which had seized power in Bavaria in the chaos at the end of the war. The protest was signed by many famous political and literary figures in Central Europe, without their consent having been sought previously. A group of the people thus compromised (including Werfel and Rolland) issued a statement to the press declaring that, although their names had been used without their permission, they were happy to give their assent to such an appeal. A few days later, on 18 June 1919, a broadsheet appeared in Vienna in which these very same people declared their abhorrence of the violence being committed in Hungary by the Communist régime which had seized power under Béla Kun, but explaining that they had not protested against the brutality of the First World War and would have had to disavow any anonymous person who had done it on their behalf then. It was the *Arbeiter Zeitung* which pointed out the similarity between the style of the broadsheet and that of Karl Kraus.[73]

It would be an understatement of the gravity of the situation to say that the Austrian Republic needed all the support it could get in the difficult years between 1918 and 1920. Faced as they were with the short-lived Communist régimes in Hungary and Bavaria, and faced also with the radicalisation of the near-starving Viennese working class, the Social Democrats discovered that their main problem was to uphold democratic freedoms in a political and social context that favoured revolution. In order to do this they joined a coalition government with the Christian Socialists, an administration which maintained an uneasy existence until 1920. Karl Renner became first Chancellor of the Austrian Republic and Viktor Adler its first Foreign Minister, a post which passed on his death almost immediately afterwards to Otto Bauer. At the War Office the Social Democrat Julius Deutsch was responsible for the delicate operation of disbanding the remnants of the Imperial army and maintaining order throughout the country by means of a new defence force, the Volkswehr or people's army, which he created in collaboration with General Körner, one of the high-ranking officers of the old régime.

One of Deutsch's main problems was to prevent Communist infiltration into this force and to restrain the radical elements already within it from resorting to violent measures to resolve the many difficult controversies that arose. His task was made much easier than it might have been by the traditional discipline and unity which had characterised the Austrian Social Democrats for so long. The creation in 1918 of a separate Austrian Communist party had indeed presented a serious potential threat to the Socialist position; but both Bauer and Deutsch were very concerned to prevent their party from ever moving so far to the Right that a substantial part of the Austrian working class should desert it for the extreme Left. This was one of the reasons behind the withdrawal of the Social Democrats into opposition in 1920, a move that Renner, for example, was reluctant to take but was finally driven to sanction in the interest of party unity. A further blow for those who hoped for a split within the Austrian Socialists was the refusal of Friedrich Adler, on his release from prison in November 1918, to accept the leadership of the Communist party. In this way, the quite unique respect which Adler enjoyed within the Austrian Left as a result of his courageous stand during the First World War was denied to the Communists who remained a tiny and insignificant group until the tragic collapse of the Social Democrats in 1934.

As far as Kraus was concerned he was, of course, a vigorous opponent of Bolshevism and a supporter of the Social Democrats. On the other hand he was a constant critic of the caution which the latter displayed during their period within the coalition government. Thus when Karl Seitz, Social Democrat Mayor of Vienna and first President of the Austrian Republic, delivered a public testimonial to the satirist in 1919, thanking him for his efforts during the war to 'exorcise the ghosts of the past', Kraus took the opportunity to point out to Seitz that these 'ghosts' were still very much alive.[74] When the First World War had broken out, Kraus had maintained that it was merely the realisation of the status quo. The corollary of this was that, as far as he was concerned, the end of the war had settled nothing. True, the monarchy had been removed, but there remained the tremendous task of breathing life into republican institutions which were born of defeat and despair. Kraus, therefore, did not relax his efforts when peace was concluded: on the contrary, they were redoubled in an attempt to combat the understandable desire of people to forget the past and concentrate on the present. Nothing could be achieved unless the wicked were punished and the lesson of the past was properly learned.

The satirist dismissed the excuses which were made after the war by generals and politicians as well as writers: 'It was war-time', 'You cannot generalise', 'I was not to blame, I was only acting under orders'. It seemed, then, that no one was to blame: 'They were all anonymous', exclaimed Kraus, 'even the leading personalities. The Chief of Staff was only his own deputy.'[75] It was scandalous that a man like Conrad von Hötzendorf, responsible for incalculable bloodshed, should be allowed to write memoirs exculpating himself from any guilt for the war: 'What! Must we now have rivers of ink as well?'[76] There must be punishment of all those beribboned generals who amused themselves in brothels and in champagne parties at military headquarters while millions of wretches died in the trenches. Militarism must be rooted out and the army abolished.[77] A special day in the year must be set aside on which those journalists and intellectuals who had glorified the war should be driven in front of platforms on which war-invalids were sitting: they should then be publicly whipped.[78] Krupp, Skoda and Manfred Weiss should be forced into church to seek expiation for their crimes: if the profits of the munition kings were distributed to war-invalids, then the satirist would renounce his dearest wish—to see Wilhelm II and all his sons put into a cage in that goose-step position in which they were pictured in so many photographs on the walls of Prussian hotels.[79]

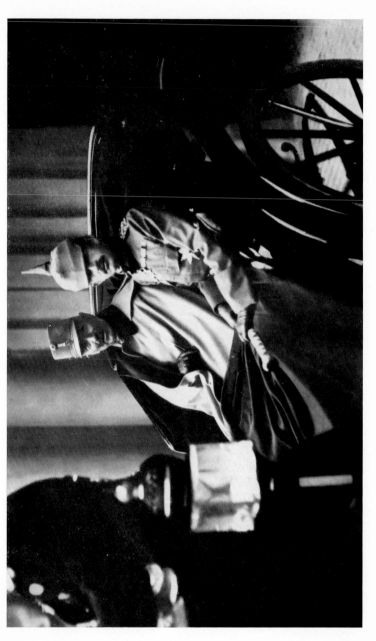

The two Kaisers — Wilhelm of Germany and Karl of Austria.
Each is wearing the uniform of the other's army

Social Democrats sing the Internationale on May Day in Vienna

Social Democratic election campaign. Note the Marxist answer to the Virgin and Child imagery of the Christian Socialists

The Heimwehr

It would be wrong, of course, to interpret everything which Kraus wrote on the subject of the First World War and the birth of the Austrian Republic with complete literalness. Although he took his material from real speeches and newspaper accounts, it was the satirist who shaped the material into a final picture. It was inevitable that, in the process, the relentless and neurotic logic of the satirist should have ignored the complexities of human behaviour and the conditions which govern that behaviour. As the critic Werner Kraft has commented on *The Last Days of Mankind*:

> Neither Wilhelm II, nor Moritz Benedikt, the proprietor of the *Neue Freie Presse* spoke like this all the time, although Kraus put their own words into their mouths.[80]

The same comment might be applied to the picture which over the years Kraus built up of himself. At the very least the extremism of his attacks on others demands that the position of the satirist himself should be examined with the same ruthlessness.

It is easy, in fact, for a present-day reader of *The Last Days of Mankind* and the *Fackel* of the First World War to mistake the real significance of Kraus's achievement. With the benefit of hindsight it is easy to read into his polemic and satire an astonishing premonition of the events that were to occur in Central Europe after the war. Kraus, after all, demonstrated in a uniquely vivid way the extent to which the traditional values of Central European civilisation, already undermined before 1914, perished of the brutality and barbarism of the war. Even the victors were themselves infected by the spirit of mistaken idealism and militarism which it had been their object to destroy. The savagery of the German military machine had called forth the savagery of the terms of the peace settlement at Versailles:

> Whither fled the Holy Spirit when the opponents departed from the scene of battle unreconciled? . . . In order to destroy Prussian values and to prevent them from reviving for another fifty years, Europe has had to Prussianise herself,

so that Prague is now the capital of Austria-Hungary and Paris that of Germany. . . . The flouting of national feeling has only moved its headquarters and the curse of militarism has exchanged its home.[81]

The brutality of war had also given rise to Communism which sought to better the lot of mankind by the methods of the war. The violence of Communism had further brutalised those who had been responsible for the crushing of the Communist uprisings in Central Europe in 1919. Rosa Luxemburg, who had detested the barbarism of war and had detested the cruelty of the Bolsheviks, had herself, after the failure of the Spartacist revolt in Berlin in February 1919, been murdered by troops nominally in the service of the new German republic.

The bitterness of the Germans and the Austrians at the terms of the peace treaties led to a revulsion not only against Wilson, whom at the end of the war they had compared to Gustavus Adolphus:[82] the hypocrisy of the Allies, on top of the lies which the Central Powers had fed their peoples during the course of the war, could only give currency to the story that the defeat of the Central Powers had been due to the 'stab in the back' by the Social Democrats and the Jews. Already in 1919, as has been seen, the *Reichspost* was subscribing to this notion. Among no section of the population did Kraus fear more the effect of such lies than among the soldiers returning from the trenches. In the very first act of *The Last Days of Mankind* there was a most terrifying prophecy of the reign of violence and nihilism that would begin after the war:

> The returning soldiers will break into the hinterland and begin the war there. They will grasp at those victories which were denied to them, and the spiritual content of the war —murder, plunder and desecration—will be child's play compared with the outbreak of peace. . . . Freed from the trenches, led no more by commanders, a frightful form of activity will reach for satisfaction and for weapons. More death and sickness will come into the world than was ever hinted at during the war.[83]

Erich Heller has indeed written of *The Last Days of Mankind*:

> It was Karl Kraus who discovered to what satanic heights
> inferiority may rise. He anticipated Hitler long before anyone
> knew his name.[84]

And yet the political and intellectual climate of Austria-
Hungary between 1914 and 1918 was not that of Germany in
1933. The fact that Kraus had been able to continue with his
work during the war was due to his awareness that, even by
1915, the word was stronger than the forces by which it was
menaced. It was also a tribute to the freedom that still existed in
Vienna. If Battisti had been hanged, Friedrich Adler had been
spared. Particularly after the murder of Count Stürgkh and
the reconvening of the Reichsrat in 1917 there was greater
freedom of discussion in Austria than in Germany or, for that
matter, in France following Clemenceau's accession to power.
Doubtless Kraus faced many difficulties and dangers during the
war. His magazine was subjected to frequent but haphazard
mutilation by a censor: but it was a censor who was possessed of
the Viennese tolerance for an artist (especially if he was witty),
and a censor who in any case found it difficult to deal with a
magazine which was ostensibly concerned with the cultural and
not the political implications of the war.[85] Well might the satirist
look back in 1933 to the old Habsburg censor 'who was still a man
of culture'.

It is true that Kraus showed great courage in exposing the
cruelties of military justice committed against the occupied Serbs
and the civilian population living in the frontiers of the Empire
where martial law had been proclaimed. In this campaign, however, his rôle was less significant than that of the editor of the
Arbeiter Zeitung, Friedrich Austerlitz, with whom the satirist
established a personal friendship that lasted until the former's
death. Often during the First World War Kraus would spend
hours in the offices of that newspaper urging Austerlitz, who from
1916 was personally opposed to the war, openly to commit the
newspaper against a continuation of the struggle. The difficulties

of the position of Austerlitz in relation to a party that did not come out wholeheartedly against the war until the early months of 1918 must be taken into account when the strictures of Kraus on the Socialist newspaper are considered.

It must in any case be remembered that the *Arbeiter Zeitung* and the Social Democrats supported the satirist when in 1918 he came into serious difficulties with the War Office. Towards the end of the war the young people of Vienna used every opportunity to show their opposition to the war; any large gathering—at a concert or at the theatre—was likely to be used for a demonstration in favour of immediate peace.[86] The authorities were anxious therefore lest Kraus's public recitals might lead to some form of public disturbance: the army forbade military personnel to attend them, claiming, falsely, that at these recitals the satirist deliberately incited soldiers to mutiny. This was the first step in a campaign of persecution which the army was determined should end in the imprisonment of Kraus whom it described as 'the leading defeatist in Austria'. Pressure was brought to bear by the army on the witnesses which Kraus brought forward to testify that he had not spoken the words attributed to him. A typical Viennese charade ensued in which the police and the army quarrelled over the evidence. Letters and memoranda flew to and fro until the collapse of the Empire put an end to the affair.[87] After reading the *Fackel* of the war years a detached observer might wonder why no attempt was made to shut the satirist's mouth until the final desperate year of 1918.

The fact was that, as Kraus was himself to appreciate in later years, the evils which had to be endured during the First World War were more the result of accident and incompetence than of sinister intent. As Erich Heller has himself pointed out, Kraus was primarily interested in the realisation of immediate dangers: his apocalypticism was not projected on the future. Despite the enormous loss of human life, despite the collapse of the Empire and the reduction of Vienna to the status of a provincial city, he looked forward to the future in 1919 with hope, hope that is discernible in his writings and was apparent to his friends. It was during the period immediately after the First World War that Kraus turned away from politics and concentrated his main creative energies on his poetry, the bulk of which was written during these years. It was not until 1932 that the satirist fully awoke to the dangers of Nazism, an evil which surprised and overwhelmed him.

Still, the reader of Kraus cannot but be influenced by the fact that it is in the First World War and its immediate aftermath that the historian must look in order to understand the formative influences which led to the triumph of Nazism in Central Europe. Disguised by the trappings of the past—by princes and Kaisers, by censors who were still men of culture—forces were at work which were to astonish even the satirist who described them. Hitler combined bitter experience of the disintegrating world of the Habsburg Empire with all the resentments of the trenches of the war: both were themes with which the polemic of Kraus was concerned. The frightful atrocities—the slaughtering of prisoners, children and animals—which Kraus depicted in terms of symbolism at the end of *The Last Days of Mankind* were in many ways merely an abstraction from the chaos inside Austria-Hungary in the last weeks before the end of the war. And yet, when the play was performed in Zürich in 1945, the *Tages Anzeiger* could quite legitimately compare the events of the epilogue, *The Last Night*, with the reality of a devastated Europe after the defeat of Hitler's Germany.[88] Already in 1914 the satirist had prophesied that language would revenge itself on those who perverted it: the hideous distortions of the propaganda machines during the First World War would one day become living reality. Referring to Allied propaganda on German atrocities in Belgium, propaganda in which he himself always maintained that there was an element of truth, Kraus commented:

If the reporter has poisoned our imagination by his version of the truth, he brings us back to reality by his lies. His imagination is the most frightful substitute for what we formerly possessed. For if over there he reports that women and children are being killed here, they believe it over there and put his lies into actual practice.[89]

In the very last year of the war, the desperate propaganda of the Entente and the Central Powers, both of which claimed that the other side was producing fat and oil from human bodies, foreshadowed the realities of the future—at least in Central Europe.[90] Pushed to its furthest conclusion, even the cruelty of satire was inadequate to describe what one day was going to be done by Man to Man.

5 Republican Interlude

I N a very real sense the years after 1919 present a melancholy, if fascinating and lengthy, postscript to the career of Karl Kraus. The world which he knew—that of Vienna under the Habsburgs —collapsed catastrophically at the end of the First World War. Vienna, once the leading city of an Empire of fifty millions, now found herself the capital of a small Alpine state of just over six million people, of whom over a third were concentrated within her own boundaries. In 1919 the Austrians had voted for *Anschluss* with Germany: but this had been denied to them by the Allies. The provinces were discontented with rule from Vienna and there was constant talk of secession in areas such as the Tyrol in the early 1920s. However terrible the plight of Germany might have seemed after the Treaty of Versailles, she still remained potentially a powerful nation with a future. The whole *raison d'être* of Austria, by contrast, seemed to have been irrevocably destroyed.

If England and France would not allow the Austrians to find a new identity in union with Germany, might there not be a possibility that the Entente would at least allow the Habsburgs to return to Vienna? This was an idea that was sedulously fostered by the Christian Socialists and especially by the *Reichspost*. Kraus attacked this propaganda with characteristic pertinacity. The failure of the monarchists, he maintained, was the failure to distinguish between the personality of a man and the nature of an institution. Monarchy as an institution was doomed, since it had capitulated during the last war to the forces of 'Progress': any attempt to bring it back would merely restore the former unsatisfactory state of affairs in which the trappings of Spanish ceremonial (a legacy which the court of Vienna maintained from the time of the Emperor Charles V right down to 1918) had disguised the true forces at work in the world. In any case, the return of the monarchy was impossible for other reasons: it would drive the Social Democrats into a position of extreme intransigence, and the Entente would not agree to a restoration which might serve as a focus for *revanchiste* sentiment in Austria and Hungary.[1]

Austria was so divided internally and so dependent on foreign credit that she was forced to obey the dictates of Britain, France and Czechoslovakia. But what of Hungary? To the Communists there had succeeded the right-wing government of Admiral Horthy and the reassertion of the power of the old ruling class. It was on Horthy, the self-styled Regent of Hungary, that the monarchists pinned most of their hopes for an early restoration. In April 1921 Kaiser Karl suddenly returned to Hungary in an attempt to recover his throne. 'I was so homesick', he declared, a phrase which Kraus lovingly added to the collection of clichés for which the house of Habsburg had been responsible in the past. Karl's return was fruitless. After he had been easily outmanoeuvred by a Regent who subscribed to the sentiment but not to the reality of a monarchist restoration, the former Emperor was driven to more extreme measures: in October of the same year he returned again and attempted a putsch, which failed miserably. When, a few months later, there were rumours in Budapest concerning the formation of a Karl-Brigade for yet another royalist coup, the newspaper *Ungarische Rundschau* was quick to point to the reality of the situation:

It appears that the entire Brigade was composed of twelve young boys who under the leadership of the nineteen-year-old film writer Zoltan Petrovitch, wished to organise a putsch on behalf of Karl. They took an oath on a six-point programme. The programme insisted first of all on the return of the king and a solution of the Jewish question. Most important of all, however, were the rewards expected by the members of the Brigade. Their leader had reserved for himself the rank and title of a Prince of Ragusa.[2]

The ex-Emperor died broken-hearted in Madeira in 1922. He was only thirty-five.

Meanwhile in Germany the failure of the Spartacist rebellion in Berlin and the Communist régime in Munich had been followed by a period in which political murders of republican notabilities became common. The Catholic leader Erzberger, who was particularly hated for his responsibility for accepting the terms of the treaty of Versailles, was murdered in 1921. Walther Rathenau, the sensitive and cultured Jewish industrialist who had largely been responsible for the mobilisation of the German economy during the First World War, was murdered in 1922. That old enemy of Kraus, Maximilian Harden, had been an ardent advocate of German military and colonial expansion before 1914 and had greeted the outbreak of the First World War with a violent enthusiasm. But as early as the end of 1914 Harden's bellicosity had cooled and he was to support the idea of a compromise peace with the Entente. As a result of the unstinted support which Harden gave to the new republic in 1918, a régime in which he unsuccessfully attempted to gain public office, he was the object of an assassination attempt in 1922; although Harden was not killed, he was so severely wounded that he was forced in the next year to suspend publication of *Die Zukunft*. He died of his injuries in 1927.

The danger from the extreme Right in German politics was underlined by Hitler's Munich putsch of 1923 and the earlier Kapp putsch of 1920, which occurred while Kraus was in Berlin giving recitals from *The Last Days of Mankind*. Although the Kapp putsch was defeated by a general strike of the workers and although the army leaders had refused to give positive support to the conspirators, the fact remained that the army refused to take the initiative in putting down the revolt. This contrasted markedly with the attitude of the army towards the Spartacist revolt of 1919. The magazine *Freiheit* of the Independent

Socialists, which greatly praised Kraus's Berlin recitals of 1920, was not perhaps exaggerating too much when it claimed that, had Kraus been born a German, he would have been arrested long ago, driven away in an army lorry, and never heard of again.[3]

As it was, the fact that Kraus, like so many Jewish intellectuals in Central Europe, was by now a sympathiser with the forces of the Left, made his recitals into a standing provocation for the nationalist and anti-semitic reaction which gathered strength after 1919. The *Fackel* was banned in Hungary because of the fierce attacks by Kraus on the Horthy régime: people found with the magazine in their possession were arrested.[4] The satirist's attempt to give public recitals from *The Last Days of Mankind* in Prague in 1923 was defeated by nationalist pressure being brought to bear on the theatre management to cancel the engagement, a decision that was hastened by the threats of German students to wreck the theatre if the performance went ahead.[5] At one of his earlier recitals in Prague in 1920, Kraus, who always proclaimed that he was not Viennese but that his native land was Bohemia, had appealed to the German-speaking citizens of the new state of Czechoslovakia to forget the past, to work for a rapprochement with the Czechs and learn their language. He coupled this with an attack on the intolerance of the Czechs themselves towards the German minority.[6] The events of 1923 demonstrated that the conflict between Teuton and Slav in Bohemia, a conflict which had plagued the last years of the Empire, still survived in an even more exacerbated form.

The nationalist onslaught on Kraus was not confined to areas outside Austria, however. In February 1920 the satirist was forced to abandon a series of recitals from *The Last Days of Mankind* which he had planned to give in Innsbruck. Admittedly, he could not have been more deliberately provocative: at his first recital he read the scene entitled 'William and his generals', the scene in which the German Kaiser is displayed tipping caviare and champagne over his courtiers. Several people were so scandalised by this attack that they left the hall, but otherwise there was no disturbance. Nevertheless, to the Viennese press this seemed to be the opportunity for which they had so long been waiting to humiliate their most dangerous opponent. The *Neues Wiener Journal* took the lead in a campaign to magnify the disturbance out of all proportion by reporting that there had been cries of protest and cat-calling from the gallery which had forced the satirist to break off his recital. False as it was, the report gave an opportunity for opposition groups in Innsbruck to mobilise; and Innsbruck, still at this period unreconciled to the Austrian Republic and with a strong body of opinion in favour of a union between the Tyrol and Bavaria, was a promising field for trouble-makers.

The main source of opposition to Kraus in Innsbruck was to come from the 'Association of Tyrolean Anti-semites' whose supporters at the University sent letters to the local newspapers threatening to break up any further meetings which the satirist might be holding in the future. After schoolchildren had broken the windows of a bookshop and destroyed copies of Italian books attacking Wilhelm II, the police stepped in and informed Kraus that his remaining recitals must be cancelled. The local Social Democrats supported the satirist and forced a debate in the Town Council on the action of the police; but the Left were in a minority in Innsbruck and nothing came of this. The same story was repeated in the Reichstag when Friedrich Austerlitz and other Social Democratic deputies interpellated the Minister of the Interior. The whole affair, in fact, was a perfect illustration of the tragi-comic nature of Austrian political debate. The *Tiroler Bauernzeitung* of 20 February was headlined: 'Jewish insult to the German Volk in Innsbruck. The Tyrol Socialists come to the aid of the Jews'. The *Allgemeiner Tiroler Anzeiger* of 23 February reported a meeting of the 'Association of Tyrolean Anti-semites' which had been called on the previous day to express the concern of Christian völkisch groups at the danger of Jewish influence. The main business of the meeting was a speech by Professor Edgar Meyer who warned of the pernicious influence of Jewish Vienna on the health of provincial life. He then reassured the Jews of Austria that they would not be maltreated (at which point there was thunderous applause) and praised Kraus for his attacks on the Jewish press. The meeting then resolved to put pressure on the local authorities to get rid of the satirist.[7]

In addition to the political chaos that followed the First World War, there was also acute economic distress in Europe East of the Rhine. Millions starved to death in the prostrate Russia that was left after the civil war between the Red and White armies. In Central Europe, also, hunger and disease were widespread in 1919 and 1920. Profiteers from the war and the inflation years might be able to pay 60,000 crowns for portions of caviare in the Hotel Bristol in Vienna but, asked Kraus, had the mass of the Austrian and German people got rid of the Habsburgs and Hohenzollerns only to die instead of tuberculosis?[8]

The situation was particularly desperate in Vienna with its overconcentration of bureaucrats and officials of every kind left over after the wreck of the empire. And yet even in these circumstances, the press still attempted to remind the rest of the world of the 'Austrian Mission'. The singers of the Volksoper, having visited Copenhagen where they were wined and dined luxuriously (in stark contrast to conditions at home), were greeted by the press on their return with a *Gemütlichkeit* born of desperation: 'You are back . . . in your beloved Vienna, which you carry in your heart and can never forsake'.[9] Meanwhile singers collapsed of malnutrition at rehearsals in the State Opera and Anton Wildgans, the director of the Burgtheater, was forced to journey to Paris to plead with the Comédie Française to give money so that the Viennese theatre could survive. Austria, Kraus lamented, was economically and culturally bankrupt; all that was left to her was the tourist industry and the operetta.

The satirist was scandalised by the failure of the wealthy Viennese to help the efforts of the Friends' Mission (sponsored by the English and American Quakers) to alleviate the condition of tubercular children. Only the *Arbeiter Zeitung* would print the

public appeals for money made by the Mission: and when, after
repeated appeals from politicians of all parties, the other Viennese
newspapers *did* consent to publish these appeals, they carefully
excluded from the appeals any mention of Kraus's forthcoming
recitals in Vienna, the proceeds of which were to be devoted
entirely to the relief of tuberculosis.[10] It was because of this
policy that the satirist felt justified in publishing in the *Fackel*
details of his work for charity, including the letters of gratitude
which he received from various charitable organisations. In 1919,
too, he was involved in a widespread controversy as to the
priority of culture over the necessities of life. So desperate was the
financial situation of the Austrian republic that it was proposed to
sell many works of art abroad in order to save money to pay off
the huge state debts incurred during the war. At once a great
debate arose, turning in the main around a proposal to sell the
famous Gobelins tapestries in the imperial palace at Schönbrunn.
Kraus angrily rejected the arguments of individuals such as the
Rector of the University of Vienna who claimed that man's need
for Art was greater than his need for bread: after what the Germans and the Austrians had done to their *Kultur* during the
war, how dare they mouth phrases about the sanctity of Art? Life
was more important than Art. When it was claimed that one
statue of Phidias had done more to enshrine the glories of
Greece in the memory of mankind than all the victories of
Alexander the Great, the satirist replied that during the war all
the statues of Phidias had done less to preserve Austrian culture
than the *Neue Freie Presse* had done in one year to destroy it.
The intellectuals who raised their hands in pious horror and
talked of the sanctity of Art could not distinguish one of Goethe's
last poems from an early one of Hofmannsthal.[11]

Kraus employed many of the same arguments in his attack on
Richard Strauss and Max Reinhardt for their association with the
opening of the Salzburg Festival in the years immediately after
the war had ended. The satirist's dislike for Richard Strauss
was due to several factors; the composer's indifference towards
political and social issues which did not impinge on himself or his

own immediate circle of friends; Strauss' cheerful philistinism and occasional vulgarity when it came to furthering the popularity and financial success of his work. As has been pointed out previously, the foundation of the Salzburg Festival by so many of his enemies and, in particular, the financial negotiations between Max Reinhardt and the Archbishop of Salzburg was to be one of the main reasons behind Kraus's spectacular departure from the Catholic Church in 1922. 'Thank God', Kraus had written in 1920, 'that I am responsible to a higher power than the Jews of the spirit and the Christians of money.'[12] In 1924, on the tenth anniversary of the outbreak of the First World War, he was to call for a 'mass exodus out of the Church towards God'.[13] Having cut his final links with the traditional order in Austria, the satirist was now to be the enfant terrible of the left-wing writers and artists of Vienna.

If, after the break-up of the post-war coalition in 1920, the great achievement of the Christian Socialist party was to have largely overcome the worst effects of the inflation years by 1924, the Social Democrats, too, had much to show for the undivided attention which they had been able to bring to the task of administering Vienna. It was a remarkable tribute to the spirit of this city that, in spite of the difficult economic situation of Austria, the decade after the end of the First World War should have been an era of great municipal reform. Vast new housing schemes were put into operation, resulting in the creation of the famous workers' flats which drew admiring visitors from all over the world. Hospitals were built, and important educational experiments took place under the influence of the psychologist Alfred Adler and his disciples. In order to stem the emigration of artistic talent to Berlin, the municipality gave large subsidies to Viennese orchestras and theatres. That all these imaginative schemes were made possible without unduly straining the finances of the city was largely due to the taxation policies associated with the name of the Social Democratic financial expert Hugo Breitner, who ensured that the main burden of increased taxation should fall on the shoulders of those who were most able to sustain it.

Meanwhile a number of Viennese intellectuals were honoured at last after years of official neglect. Freud, for example, was given the freedom of the city in 1924, although he was still subjected to the disapproval of the University authorities. In other directions, too, there was a deliberate cultivation of the talent of the avant-garde. Alban Berg lectured on his music to proletarian audiences, and pupils of the Vienna Circle taught philosophy at the various institutes for further education which the municipality organised for workers. The activities of the cultural department of the Social Democratic party, the Kunststelle, were expanded under the directorship of one of Schoenberg's disciples, the philosopher and musicologist David Bach, a man of wide personal culture who, in addition to all his other interests, had links with the circle around Freud. Kraus himself gave a large number of public recitals under the auspices of Bach's organisation—performing plays by Nestroy, reading sections of *The Last Days of Mankind* and singing his satirical version of the old Imperial anthem at the May Day celebrations of the party and on the anniversaries of the founding of the republic.

And yet, despite all this, the satirist was constantly critical of the Socialist party. He demanded from the Social Democrats a more radical policy than that which could be achieved by waiting for the citadels of capitalism to collapse of their own internal contradictions. Kraus was also deeply concerned with the steep decline in artistic standards in Vienna despite all the efforts of the municipality to halt this decline. In particular he was obsessed by the condition of the press, which was deteriorating despite the attempts made by the Social Democrats to legislate against the worst instances of press corruption. Far from getting better, however, the standard of the press declined sharply in the era of the inflation. The new Austrian republic had indeed enacted that newspapers should make it clear which advertisements and notices in the newspapers had been paid for by outside bodies. To

Kraus this was not sufficient: it merely amounted to the regulation of this form of corruption and not its abolition. The *Neue Freie Presse* and the other newspapers refused to obey even this simple regulation. The *Neue Freie Presse* declared in an obscure reference on an inside page that, in future, insertions which had been paid for would be marked by a small cross. It was clear that the intention of the newspaper was dishonest: many people would not see the reference or would not understand what it meant; furthermore, the newspaper did not mark items individually with a cross but let one cross suffice for a whole string of advertisements. This practice was challenged and brought before the courts to test the new press laws (although Kraus, for once, was not responsible for this). Despite the fact that the practice of the *Neue Freie Presse* was clearly against the spirit of the law, the newspaper was acquitted. After its triumph in the courts, the *Neue Freie Presse* waxed even bolder and frequently omitted to mark its advertisements with even one cross: and when it apologised for such omissions, Kraus found its apologies insolent.[14] Once again the *Neue Freie Presse* was brought before the courts but the republican authorities were frightened to take action against the press because they feared its political power and its ability to play on the weakness of a régime so dependent on foreign goodwill. The newspapers, for their part, attacked the press law because it had been inspired by the Social Democrats in general and by Friedrich Austerlitz, editor of the *Arbeiter Zeitung*, in particular.

The main object of Kraus's attack during this period was, however, no longer the *Neue Freie Presse* nor even the *Neues Wiener Journal*, but more recent newspapers such as the *8 Uhr Blatt*, the *Neuer Tag* and the *Abend*. The first two were anti-communist and the last was pro-communist. But ideological differences always hung lightly on these papers: greater than the differences between them was the common bond which united them, a bond comprised of complete disregard for the principles of objective reporting, financial corruption and scandal-mongering. The new post-war sensationalist newspapers, unlike the

Neue Freie Presse and its contemporaries, were not content with accepting large sums from advertisers and financial groups: they took the process one stage further and blackmailed wealthy individuals and companies with the threat that, unless they paid substantial sums of money, details of their private lives and sources of income would be exposed. This was a particularly lucrative business in the Vienna of the early 1920s when inflation was rife and the city was full of every kind of financial adventurer and hard-faced man who had done well out of the war.

The new press was itself the product of the dislocation of society and morality produced by the war. Much of its personnel and techniques had first seen the light of day in the propaganda machine of the Béla Kun régime in Hungary: with the collapse of that government, many of these journalists (mostly Jewish) had sought refuge in Austria. The most brilliant of these Hungarian Jewish adventurers, Imre Bekessy, the proprietor of the notorious *Stunde*, whose peculiar brand of 'radicalism' enabled him to flirt with both Left and Right, will be discussed in greater detail in subsequent pages. Let it suffice, for the moment, to look at the kind of petty blackmail which the *8 Uhr Blatt* exercised in its column called 'Self-Help', by means of which it terrorised theatre managements and restaurant proprietors into submission:

> (The Three Bells restaurant) in the Gartenstrasse is a place for shameless extortion. Beef with vegetables there costs 18,000 crowns, a piece of toast 3,000 crowns.
> (The farce *Fritzi gets into the bath*) in the Residenztheater is a foolish piece of work. The leading lady is at least 50 years old.

This kind of thing, said Kraus, was the reality that existed behind the façade of Seipel's régime.[15]

Nor did the Social Democratic press escape the satirist's adverse comment. Although the general standard of honesty of most of the journalists who wrote for the official organs of the party was immeasurably higher than some of those who wrote for the popular press, the demands of mass circulation coupled with the dullness which has seemed to afflict all Socialist newspapers throughout Europe meant that certain changes had to be made if the party press was to survive. This did not, of course, meet with Kraus's approval: the growing recourse to advertisements (sometimes of an extremely dubious nature) and the serialisation of cheap romantic novels by the *Arbeiter Zeitung* was, he claimed, a symptom of the ethical and intellectual decline of the party since the days of Viktor Adler.

When he made these charges, the satirist was aware that an internal battle was taking place within the Socialist newspaper on the very issues that he had raised. Friedrich Austerlitz, editor of the *Arbeiter Zeitung* from its foundation in 1895 to his death in 1931, did not approve of the changes that were being made. He belonged to the older generation of the party who looked with disfavour on the growing signs that Austrian Social Democracy was becoming more concerned with quantity rather than quality. Oskar Pollak, his successor, was of the younger school, a personality with all the virtues and the faults that characterised the era of bureaucratic control. Pollak's influence grew within the party newspaper in the 1920s as the ageing Austerlitz was forced, with the utmost reluctance, to delegate more and more of his responsibilities. The temperamental clash between Austerlitz and Pollak during these years was revealed by a running controversy which they carried on in the Socialist theoretical monthly *Der Kampf* on the party's attitude towards Karl Kraus.

Not only was Austerlitz one of the latter's closest friends, the first editor of the *Arbeiter Zeitung* resembled the satirist in many ways. As Julius Braunthal, editor of *Der Kampf*, has written:

> He regarded the careful cultivation of the language as the supreme task of a journalist. . . . A trivial phrase, or a wrong comma, would evoke his white hot rage; he would burst into the cubicle of the careless writer and would passionately

dissect the wrongly applied expression, often revealing a new meaning of words and phrases which had become petrified by their thoughtless use . . . this man, with an intense ardour for things noble, was of an incredible ruthlessness in his intercourse with his fellows. He possessed a highly refined taste in literature, often beautifully reflected in his restrained style; he was capable of the most genuine emotions; and yet he was coarse and even violent in his manner. This intractable feature of his temper had its root, I believe, in his voracious insatiability. . . . It may appear curious to an English journalist to learn that an editor in chief should himself write and edit nearly half the paper and should personally dictate most of the editorial letters which left the office. Austerlitz, literally, did. Every day he wrote one and sometimes two leading articles; he sub-edited the daily flow of political material; he wrote half a dozen political notes; he read the proofs of everything concerned with policy; he made the lay-out of the paper; he answered almost every letter the paper received. This was his day's work in addition to reading scores of papers. He was a bachelor with no private life. . . .[16]

With all his faults, however, Austerlitz was old enough to remember the days when the party had ungrudgingly welcomed all helpers to the Social Democrat cause, whether they were card-carrying members or not. As a self-educated man of very humble origins, he was certainly over-sensitive to any intended or unintended personal slight. He could be extremely jealous of intellectuals such as Otto Bauer who possessed an easy familiarity with philosophical and theoretical subjects which he himself had learned to understand only after a painful struggle. But towards the personality of Kraus Austerlitz displayed an especial tolerance and respect, a respect which had been born out of the struggle which the two men had fought together against the cruelties of military justice during the First World War. Pollak, by contrast, was infuriated by the satirist's constant carping at the deficiences of the party—and this from a man who was not even a party member! In 1923 *Der Kampf* published the first of Pollak's full-scale polemics against Kraus. It attacked the satirist for his distrust of the forces of technical progress and the dialectics of materialism: in his hatred of materialism, Kraus showed himself to be an idealist; in his repudiation of the dialectic he branded himself as a pessimist. Certainly Social Democrats ought to be grateful for the services which the satirist had rendered to their party by his exposure of the rottenness of the ancien régime and the bourgeoisie in Austria: but Marxists were better equipped intellectually than he was to implement positive reforms. They did not criticise affairs negatively from the standpoint of aestheticism.[17]

It is interesting that, in his reply, Kraus did not attack Pollak so much for the crudity of this analysis but took issue upon the charge that his recitals were not popular with the proletariat but only with the *jeunesse dorée* of the middle class who, Pollak claimed, simply enjoyed the comedy of the satirist's attack on the *Neue Freie Presse* which stood for the opinions of their fathers. This charge was perhaps the most telling which Pollak had made, and it cannot be pretended that Kraus's own answer to this charge was convincing, nor the reply to Pollak in the next issue of *Der Kampf* by David Bach, director of the Kunststelle.[18] It was no good simply detailing the number of recitals which the satirist had given to audiences of workers, nor the numbers which had listened to him at the May Day celebrations of the party. The most damaging point which Pollak made was that in his concern for the nuances of language and style, Kraus was talking above the head of his proletarian audience, and that his attempts to establish contact with them had not been completely successful. It is not necessary, of course, to accept the extreme Marxist position that in the last analysis the achievements of Kraus and other Viennese intellectuals like Freud and Schönberg were expressions of the decadence of the bourgeois order. But certainly the atmosphere of Kraus's thought and achievement was far removed from that of the workers of Vienna: not surprisingly the satirist's views on sexual freedom, for example, were received in shocked silence by the serried ranks of middle-aged party workers at his recitals. The significant point is that the vehemence of Kraus's reply to Pollak showed that the latter had touched a most sensitive spot in the position of the satirist. Kraus might continually declare that the penalty for his mission was isolation from his society; but he felt terribly wounded and dismayed when this penalty was exacted in practice.

The most notorious of the group of Budapest Jewish journalists who arrived in Vienna after the First World War was undoubtedly the proprietor of the daily *Stunde* and the weekly *Börse* and *Bühne*—Imre Bekessy. In Hungary Bekessy had, during his varied career, worked in one of the great Budapest banks where he acquainted himself with all aspects of financial operations before launching himself into the newspaper business where his speciality was a kind of left-wing popular journalism which attacked and denounced the financial corruption of large companies and banks in order to obtain enormous sums of money from these organisations in return for dropping his campaigns. Bekessy had a long criminal record with the Budapest police for blackmail and attempted blackmail.

He was undoubtedly a talented journalist, with a lively style and a gift for attracting clever young writers to work for him. Ample use was made in his newspapers of photographs, which had hitherto been used only sparingly in the Viennese press. The lay-out was also attractive: technically his newspapers were very well produced and greatly superior to the old popular press symbolised by the *Neues Wiener Journal*. Bekessy, too, was a character of extraordinary facility and charm who was able to accommodate himself to any situation that might arise. Before the outbreak of the Béla Kun revolution he had persuaded the banks of Budapest to give him large amounts of money in order that he might use his influence against the Communist danger. When the revolution broke out, he announced his support of the new régime and urged all his fellow journalists to do likewise: he became a prominent propagandist on behalf of the new régime and undertook to produce cheap editions of Marx's works in return for a large sum of money. But even during this time of upheaval, Bekessy's cynicism did not desert him. As the Hungarian newspaper *Hétföi Napló* later reported:

> In the editorial offices he scorned and ridiculed the Communist leaders and was anxious that the salaries of his staff should be paid in 'blue' (i.e. non-Communist) money.[19]

More sinister was the rumour that Bekessy had denounced some of his former associates after the fall of the Béla Kun régime and even in Vienna maintained links with the government of Admiral Horthy.

Arriving in Vienna, Bekessy found a lucrative field for his talents in a city where very large elements of the population were suffering from the after-effects of the war and the inflation, while a small class of financiers and industrialists who had done well out of the war continued to make money in many of the speculative enterprises which accompanied the inflation. Among the latter were such men as Camillo Castiglioni (who had made a fortune out of rubber and automobiles) and Siegmund Bosel, President of the Union Bank. Already in 1923 Kraus had protested against the fawning attitude which the press had taken towards those men who had grown richer while the rest of the population had grown poorer.[20] These men were accorded the attention formerly given to Monarchy: they were held up as models for emulation by the young. Their 'human' qualities were commented upon at great length—the fact that Castiglioni gave large sums of money to the blind and that Bosel was good to his relatives. The new rich were careful to establish relations with both major political parties, both of which were to be tainted by the financial corruption which surrounded such people. This corruption was publicly revealed when first Castiglioni and then Bosel suffered heavily by the collapse of their speculations; the latter indeed was imprisoned for fraud. Several years before that collapse, the politicians had constantly accused each other of being in the pay of the war millionaires. The particularly close connection between Bosel and the Styrian group of Christian Socialists such as Rintelen and Ahrer disgusted Kraus. Long before the extent of their relationship to Bosel was exposed in 1926, Kraus satirised the alliance between Jewish finance and antisemitic provincial politicians.[21]

Bekessy was quick to establish a position of ascendancy over both Castiglioni and Bosel. He obtained knowledge of their businesses and the nature of their relations with leading members of the Christian Socialist party and threatened to publish details of this unless large sums of money were advanced to him. Even the payment of Bekessy did not mean that he kept his mouth shut completely and attacks upon the new rich were frequent in his newspapers. Companies and banks were forced to pay heavily for their advertisements in his newspapers or else were denounced as fraudulent (as many of them were, although this did not prevent Bekessy from accepting their advertisements). Great use was made of sexual scandals, either for publication or, preferably, to form yet another source of blackmail.

It was true, of course, that the elements of the older Viennese newspapers had been guilty to a lesser degree of such corruption. One of the differences between them and the new press lay, however, in the extent to which the latter openly admitted the most damaging details about its activities. This was well brought out in 1923 when Bekessy issued a writ of libel against Dr. Gustav Stolper, the distinguished editor of the economic journal the *Oesterreichischer Volkswirt*.[22] Stolper as an economic expert had been appalled by the corruption which was endemic in the higher reaches of the Austrian economy and by the use made of this corruption by Bekessy. In the issue of the magazine of 7 July 1923, Stolper declared Bekessy to be 'a politically shameless and characterless subject', in the hope of bringing him into a legal suit that would discredit him for ever.[23] The extraordinary feature of the case that ensued was the frankness with which Bekessy admitted the fact that he had received enormous sums of money from Castiglioni, although he attempted to avoid the charge of blackmail by referring to the number of occasions upon which he had attacked Castiglioni in his newspapers.

On the central issue, however, Bekessy made no attempt at evasion:

> A newspaper . . . is not an institution of morality. . . . I also believe that a newspaper is a business that must be conducted on the one side with clean hands and on the other with unclean hands.[24]

So damaging was Bekessy's own evidence and the evidence which was produced about his previous record of blackmail in Hungary that he was in great danger of losing his case completely. He avoided this by withdrawing his suit against Stolper, but not before the Austrian police had testified that Bekessy regarded his victims in the same light that a doctor regarded his patients.

It was the frankness of Bekessy's position which drew Kraus into the struggle. For the first time the hypocrisy and pretence of the press had been torn away and the inherent evil of its activity had been admitted openly: this had been made possible by the collapse of standards brought about by the war and the inflation. The press now did not pay even lip-service to ideas of morality or cultural worth; its power now regarded no form of traditional restraint. Bekessy and the *Stunde* were symbolic of the state of post-war Central Europe, a mixture of Jazz and the Czárdas, of murder, sport and crossword puzzles. Here was an enemy who was indeed worthy of attention. As Kraus wrote after the fall of Bekessy:

> Truly I have never in my life felt so much an artist, so free. . . . I smelt the atmosphere and realised: this is my type. How he rejuvenated me![25]

After the failure of Stolper to destroy Bekessy, the Buda Pest as Kraus called him, the satirist turned his main energies for the next two years towards encompassing his fall. Now instead of generalised invective against the failure of the republic to clean up the press and the scandal of the law concerning advertisements, Kraus had something concrete to attack.

It was both difficult and dangerous to attack Bekessy, however, because of the disarming frankness with which the latter admitted the ambivalence of his work.

> My temperament (confided Bekessy in the *Börse*), my situation and my attitude to life attract me towards compromise, and so newspapers develop that seem full of contradictions, which carry the stamp of a man who sees through the activity of the capitalist world and who wishes to unmask this activity without becoming a revolutionary or an ascetic. To conceal this contradiction by resort to hypocrisy was not given to me.[26]

The Bekessy press was indeed full of contradictions. There were revelations of sexual scandals which made Jakob Lippowitz, proprietor of the *Neues Wiener Journal* look like an amateur. And yet Bekessy found it quite compatible to combine this with a 'crusade' against the police for their harrying of prostitutes and their interference in the private life of citizens. He had, furthermore, the audacity to claim as justification for his campaign against the police the views on state interference in private morality which Kraus had expressed in writings such as *Sittlichkeit und Kriminalität*. Here, indeed, the satirist had met his match.

Bekessy possessed all the arts of the great adventurer: if his charm failed to work, he could become ruthlessly vindictive. Thus when it became apparent that Kraus could neither be appeased nor flattered by the use of conciliatory tactics, Bekessy instigated an enormous press campaign against him. The *Stunde* renewed all the standard charges which had been made against the satirist by his enemies, many of whom were now glad to find in the Bekessy press yet another vehicle for their attacks. Needless to say, the *Stunde* supported Max Reinhardt and Alfred Kerr in their controversies with Kraus. Once again it was claimed that Kraus had only founded the *Fackel* because of personal spite against the *Neue Freie Presse*. Once again it was claimed that the satirist had supported the First World War in its earliest stages and had only opposed it later because of a desire for personal notoriety. Typical of the *Stunde* attack was the public onslaught in a lecture on Kraus delivered by the left-wing writer Anton Kuh, an old enemy of the satirist who now worked for Bekessy: Kraus was a neurotic and a retarded adolescent; Kraus was an out-dated remnant of the liberal bourgeois tradition; he was an historical curiosity whose reputation depended not on the admiration of the Viennese but on the pious liberal politicians of the succession states of the Habsburg monarchy. At the point in the address when Kuh compared Kraus to Hitler there was tumultuous applause and noisy counter-demonstrations in the hall.[27]

The *Stunde* next published photographs of Kraus, copied from Leopold Liegler's study of the satirist *Karl Kraus und sein Werk*, but altered and distorted to make Kraus look ridiculous (as, for example, by enlarging his ears). When the satirist protested against this, the *Stunde* replied that the practice of altering photographs was one that Kraus himself had pioneered. This was not true: Kraus had certainly printed photographs of the victims of his satire, often in ridiculous poses, (such as Hermann Bahr in bathing robe and beard), but he had never tampered with the originals. Alternatively, the *Stunde* pleaded that the whole affair was a joke and that Kraus was, as usual, making a mountain out of a mole-hill. The newspaper also attempted to poke fun at Kraus by entitling the article which admitted the falsification of the Liegler photographs, 'Was Karl Kraus a pretty child?', accusing him of Jewish self-hatred; his dislike of mankind was due to the fact that he had not been born with blond hair and blue eyes.[28] The next object of Bekessy's attack was the bookseller Richard Lanyi, the manager of Kraus's recitals, who was trying to organise a petition against Bekessy: in revenge the latter revealed the fact that Lanyi had been prosecuted for the sale of obscene books. Lanyi was also accused of being the centre of a circle of homosexuals. The implication, as far as Kraus was concerned, was obvious.

In numerous issues of the *Fackel*, the satirist denounced every aspect of Bekessy's moral and financial blackmail. But it was extremely difficult to bring Bekessy to justice. He could not be deported because the Social Democrats who had been in the coalition government in 1920 had extended to him, as to many other refugees from Hungary, the protection of Austrian citizenship. It was also difficult to accuse Bekessy personally of libel because one of the weaknesses of the press laws of the Austrian republic was that the proprietor of a newspaper could hide behind the fiction that the editorial policy of his newspapers was completely independent of the proprietor; furthermore, the so-called responsible editor of a newspaper could plead in a libel suit that he had not read the particular material in question. It was equally difficult to force Bekessy to issue writs of libel against Kraus; the drawbacks in this procedure had been shown in the abortive outcome of Stolper's attack on the *Stunde*. And even if Bekessy *could* be got into court, it would be difficult to broaden the basis of the dispute from the simple issue of libel to a wider examination of Bekessy's activities which would lead to official intervention by the State Prosecutor.

As a result of this situation, from the beginning of the satirist's fight in earnest against Bekessy early in 1925 until the latter's flight from Vienna in the summer of 1926, Kraus and his lawyer, Dr. Samek, were condemned to spend between fourteen and sixteen hours each day in collecting evidence of Bekessy's activities that could be used against him in court. Lanyi was instructed to get to work with a petition to the President of the Republic asking for the removal of the proprietor of *Die Stunde* from Vienna. At the same time Kraus pursued such employees of Bekessy as Anton Kuh through the courts on charges of libel. The ramifications of Kraus's campaign against Bekessy were so vast that it is not possible to deal with them in full, but the result of the labours of Kraus and his lawyers can be seen in the vast pile of documents relating to the campaign against Bekessy to be found in Dr. Samek's papers, which have been deposited since his death in the Kraus-Archiv of the Stadtbibliothek. And the satirist succeeded in his fight—a fight which was in many ways the most successful of his career. For once, Kraus felt, a single individual had been able to do something positive to rid the world of the evil which was destroying it.

Of course the satirist had had some good fortune. Primarily there was the fact that it was in 1926 that the Central Bank of Vienna collapsed. One of the reasons for the failure of this bank lay in the fact that it and Bosel's Union Bank had unwisely taken over control of a number of provincial banks that had themselves been on the verge of failure; it was more than ironical that many of these provincial banks had been established after the war with the precise aim of 'freeing' the peasantry from control by the Jewish bankers of Vienna. The reason why the Viennese banks were prepared to take over these tottering concerns was that they were promised by the provincial politicians, powerful within the Christian Socialist party, that means would be found to recompense them for their trouble. In order to bolster up the Central Bank and the Union Bank, therefore, large sums of money had been made available to them by the government-controlled Post Office Savings Bank. The collapse of the Central Bank in 1926, despite all these precautionary measures, now brought all these unsavoury transactions to light. This was the beginning of the end for Siegmund Bosel, one of Bekessy's most powerful backers. Furthermore, this scandal eventually brought down the Ramek government and there followed another administration led by Seipel who was intent on cleaning up the sources of corruption.[29]

But although the revelation of this corruption was fortunate for Kraus in his struggle against Bekessy, the fall of the Ramek government did not take place until several months after the flight of the proprietor of *Die Stunde* from Vienna. Of more immediate use to the satirist was the information which he received from Hungarian opponents of Bekessy on the latter's activities before 1920. Kraus and Dr. Samek were also lucky in being able to utilise the material placed at their disposal by a young journalist, named Schmidl, who was appalled at the nature and extent of Bekessy's power. When Schmidl was attacked by Bekessy in the *Stunde* the former immediately issued a writ of libel. This was the opportunity for which Kraus and Samek were waiting. They had already secured promises from the office of the State Prosecutor that he would take action if any of Bekessy's blackmailing activities were revealed at the trial; and by now Kraus and Samek had assembled a large amount of such material. To demonstrate their confidence, they subpoenaed a large number of individuals to appear as witnesses, including Castiglioni and Bosel. Bekessy's nerve failed at this and he fled first to Paris and then to Hungary. 'The scoundrel is out!' Kraus could confidently claim in August 1926.[30]

In Kraus's view, the problem of the Bekessy press, in contradiction to that of the older newspapers, had been not that of the editors and journalists but of the readers. The only people who did not believe what these newspapers contained were the people who wrote them: Liebstöckl, the editor of the *Stunde*, was reported once to have described his newspaper as 'pure gangster journalism'.[31] And what about 'the right of self determination' of the editors of which Bekessy had boasted during the Stolper trial, a right which he described as 'that which the peoples of Europe do not possess . . . . my editors can write what they wish'? In fact, the editors were largely Bekessy's puppets whom he made and broke with astonishing rapidity. The 'freedom' which the editors possessed was only the right to print anything which would boost circulation: everything that was written in the newspapers was written in the same style—that of the proprietor. But Bekessy disclaimed responsibility. Where then did the responsibility lie? Despite the vices of the older Viennese press its great strength had lain in the fact that its editors stood for a point of view, even if it was only that of the economic and political interests of financial groups behind the newspaper. But Bekessy felt himself responsible to nobody, except to the categorical imperative that more and more circulation must be built up, and more power must be accumulated for the proprietor. The fundamental nihilism of the Bekessy press was mirrored in its ambivalent attitude to the capitalist class—a source alike of denunciation and blackmail. There was a parallel here with the policies of the Nazis, a parallel which Kraus did not fail to draw, even though

Bekessy had constantly attacked the Nazis. In the hands of the satirist, the personality of Bekessy was inflated into the dimensions of a satanic spirit that held Vienna in its spell for over two years, a devil that was only exorcised by the courageous action of a handful of individuals. When in 1933 Kraus was to confront the phenomenon of Nazism he did not hesitate to claim that in Bekessy there was a spiritual ancestor of Dr. Goebbels.

In order to form any idea of the accuracy of the satirist's estimate of the significance of the career of Bekessy, it is necessary to look at the degree to which the *Stunde* did indeed in the years 1925 and 1926 come to occupy an extremely powerful position in the world of Viennese politics and the press. In the first place, the majority of the Viennese newspapers gave tacit support to Bekessy in his dispute with Kraus by not printing a word about the latter's campaign. The press had suffered so long from the satirist's attacks that they took enormous pleasure in seeing him fight alone against heavy odds: occasionally they would attack Kraus in bitter terms, but their attacks never mentioned Bekessy; mostly however they stuck to their traditional policy of ignoring Kraus altogether.[32] But this conspiracy of silence was not due entirely to a desire to see Kraus in trouble: it was also due to a fear of Bekessy who was quite capable of attacking the rest of the press for their connections with financial groups. Very often the respectable newspapers such as the *Reichspost* and the *Neue Freie Presse* denounced Bekessy's methods and operations but did not go as far as denouncing him by name. As Kraus remarked, the only person courageous enough to talk of Bekessy's blackmail was Bekessy himself.[33]

Worse than the failure of the press, however, was the failure of the political parties to take effective action against Bekessy. This was partly due to the indolence characteristic of the Austrian scene; it was also due to more sinister reasons. Powerful groups within the Christian Socialist party were linked to Bosel and Castiglioni and therefore to Bekessy who entertained his political friends at lavish staff parties and campaigned on their behalf at election times.[34] Successive finance ministers like Ahrer and Kollmann belonged to this group. When the scandal of the Post Office Savings Bank broke, Ahrer fled to Cuba and was succeeded as finance minister by Kollmann, who remained in that post until the final fall of the Ramek government in October 1926. When Ahrer eventually returned to Vienna from Cuba in 1927, Kraus juxtaposed the report of his return with reports of the centennial celebrations of the death of Beethoven.[35] Behind Ahrer and Kollmann there was the enigmatic figure of the 'Black Knight of Styria', Anton Rintelen, who had played on Styrian separatism to create in that province a powerful political machine independent of the Christian Socialist organisation. He drove the central party to a hard series of bargains in which he gave the support of his machine to Vienna in return for concessions to the Styrian group of deputies. Later on in the 1920s Rintelen was to be a prominent member of the Heimwehr movement and his intrigues with the Nazis were to be one of the main features behind the attempted Nazi putsch of 1934. But even more shocking and depressing to Kraus than the action of a section of the Christian Socialist party was the attitude of the Social Democrat party which until about the last minute before Bekessy's flight from Vienna refused to come out openly in Kraus's support.[36] The attitude taken by the Social Democrats to the Bekessy Affair marked the beginning of the break between Kraus and that party, a break which was finally sealed in 1932.

The reason why the Social Democrats did not aid the satirist was quite simple. After fleeing from Vienna, Bekessy wrote an article which was published in the *Neues Wiener Journal* accusing the Socialists of having betrayed him by breaking an earlier promise which they had given to Bosel that they would not involve themselves in the campaign against the proprietor of the *Stunde*. There was an element of truth in Bekessy's charge. Several years earlier Bosel had earned the gratitude of certain sections of the Social Democratic party close to Karl Renner by buying shares in and ultimately taking over completely the Hammerbrotwerke, the Socialist owned bakery in Vienna, an organisation which had been coming under increasing attack from various members of the party's co-operative movement because its management seemed to be both inefficient and corrupt. It was largely due to this favour which Bosel had rendered their party in relieving them of a responsibility which seemed increasingly embarrassing that the Social Democrats did not involve themselves in the Bekessy Affair.[37] Neither did they press vigorously in the Austrian parliament for a wide-ranging inquiry into the Post Office Savings Bank scandal until December 1926, by which time the Ramek government had fallen. Indeed, the party leadership seem to have negotiated a deal with Seipel, the leader of the new government, to the effect that, in exchange for not exploiting the situation created by the financial scandals, the wishes of the Social Democrats would be respected in the drafting of new laws for old-age and disability pensions for salaried employees and manual workers.[38]

There was, however, a group of Social Democrats, of which Friedrich Austerlitz was a member, who were opposed to this policy of opportunism. For over a year a battle took place within the party over its attitude towards Bekessy until finally Austerlitz was permitted to come out openly against him in the *Arbeiter Zeitung* in July 1926, a few weeks before the former's flight. Even so, it has already been seen that the party did not attack the government in earnest over the Post Office Savings Bank scandal until months later; and it only did so then when Seipel broke his word over the implementation of generous social insurance schemes. That the Social Democrats were still afraid of further revelations that Bekessy might make after his flight was demonstrated by the fact that when, in the Spring of 1927, Kraus printed a placard attacking Bekessy, a placard which was to be posted on the public hoardings of Vienna, the Socialist-controlled municipal authorities refused to allow the poster to be displayed and the satirist was obliged to distribute the placards through bookshops.[39]

Before his enforced departure from Vienna, Bekessy had, of course, been quick to exploit the differences within the Social Democratic party. Whenever it seemed that the Austerlitz group was gaining the upper hand, Bekessy pointed to the Fascist danger and urged a combination of all left-wing newspapers (including his own) against this. He also played on the fact that many of the party functionaries were suspicious of Kraus and his refusal to be completely committed to the party cause. In the struggle within the Social Democratic organisation over the attitude to be adopted towards Bekessy, the controversy between Austerlitz and Oskar Pollak over Kraus and the policy of the Kunststelle in involving itself in work that was neither ideologically sound nor of immediate practical use to the party, a controversy which had been started in *Der Kampf* in 1923, now sprang to fresh life. Pollak again attacked the satirist for his exclusive concern with cultural problems and his ignorance of economics: Kraus had portrayed Bekessy purely as a figure of evil and not in the context of the social and economic conditions of the post-war inflation, conditions which marked the decadence of the capitalist system. The nub of Pollak's objection to the satirist was, however, that the latter refused to join the party but criticised it from the outside. To criticise the party effectively one must be on the inside: it was easy to point out the mistakes of the party, but only those who were prepared to listen to old comrades talking of the difficulties which the party had faced in the heroic period of its beginnings were fitted to criticise it. Great as was his contribution towards the attack on bourgeois values, Kraus was too individualistic to belong to the party; and it was to the party that the future belonged. [40]

Austerlitz replied in the next issue of *Der Kampf*, defending the validity of Kraus's work in general terms, but even he had to admit that the satirist was 'certainly not a comfortable travelling companion'. [41] In his reply to Austerlitz, Pollak seized upon this admission and explained that he had not been attacking the artistic merit of the work of Kraus, but the efficacy of any political activity performed by an individual outside the organisation and discipline of the party. Furthermore, Pollak, in the same article, played cleverly on the abhorrence of the party for any cult of the individual such as that which it seemed was practised by a writer who indulged his vanity by his constant intellectual posturing.[42] The controversy over Kraus in *Der Kampf* appeared in print just before Bekessy's flight from Vienna, but everyone had known since 1923 that there was considerable disagreement within the Social Democratic party over the attitude to be adopted towards the satirist. The latter, as usual, did no good to his own cause by refusing to give any further public recitals under the auspices of the party and by mounting a massive onslaught on the policies of the Kunststelle in subsidising the performances of worthless operettas and all sorts of dramatic *kitsch* instead of concentrating on helping the work of first-rate writers. In this instance—as in so many of Kraus's encounters with the Social Democratic party—he was firing on his own troops: it has already been seen that the director of the Kunststelle was one of his admirers and the unfortunate man was under constant pressure from different sections of the party as to the policies which he should follow and for which tastes he should cater. The satirist's popularity with the party at large was not increased by the continual appeals which he made to the audiences at his public recitals in 1925 and 1926 to use their influence within the party to put pressure on the party functionaries to change their policy towards Bekessy. The actions of the party leadership, Kraus complained, were a betrayal of the principles laid down for Social Democrats by Ferdinand Lassalle and Wilhelm Liebknecht, both of whom had been deeply concerned over the evils of the Central European press. The satirist took this opportunity to print in the *Fackel* letters written to him privately by Wilhelm Liebknecht in 1899 and 1900 bitterly criticising the failings of the Social Democratic party and press. The idealism and dedication of the early days of Social Democracy had been lost, Kraus proclaimed: Liebknecht had voluntarily incurred poverty for the sake of his party, but now the bureaucracy had taken over control and Renner and Karl Seitz, the Burgermeister of Vienna, were more interested in the security of their comfortable positions and in dancing the 'Shimmy' at the Rathaus.[43]

Given the hostility which the satirist provoked in wide sections of the party by attacks such as these and given also the opportunistic policies which were in fact being followed by that party in 1925 and 1926 (despite all Pollak's rhetoric and assurances to the contrary), why was it that Austerlitz was permitted to come out openly against Bekessy in the *Arbeiter Zeitung* of July 1926? The answer was simple: Bekessy over-reached himself. In an attempt to discredit that section of the party which wanted a frontal attack on *Die Stunde*, Bekessy accused Friedrich Austerlitz of sexual crimes which included that of corrupting young children. The monstrosity of such a charge against one of the most respected men within the Social Democratic organisation had, of course, the opposite effect to that which was intended: the party now closed its ranks and came out against Bekessy openly. At the very last moment the satirist received that support from the Left for which he had been appealing for the past two years.

It is possible to argue that Kraus inflated the significance of the Bekessy affair far beyond its real importance. The years of the satirist's struggle with Bekessy were, after all, years of comparative peace and prosperity for the Austrian republic. It may also be relevant that none of the standard histories or autobiographies that deal with this period of Austrian history make anything more than a passing reference to the Bekessy Affair. And yet the whole episode throws light upon the extraordinary laxity and lack of moral fibre in Austrian society, a deficiency that was to have disastrous results when that society was faced with the challenge of a militant Germany under Hitler. The lesson of the affair was, said Kraus, that the readers of the Viennese press would not be unduly disturbed the next morning, if, overnight, the newspapers had come into the hands of the Nazis; if Vienna could tolerate Bekessy, she could tolerate anything.[44] In what other city would the career of this man have been possible? Even when it was clear that Bekessy's days were numbered, the authorities had failed to deal properly with the situation. Certainly the State Prosecutor had promised that he would take cognizance of the evidence of Bekessy's blackmailing activities which Kraus and Dr. Samek intended to present at the libel case between Schmidl and Bekessy. On the other hand, the State Police had not co-operated in bringing Bekessy to justice. Indeed, there was evidence to suggest that the police had been instrumental in helping him to evade that justice: when Bekessy's fall was inevitable and the State Prosecutor was preparing for his arrest and trial on charges of blackmail, it seems that someone within the police organisation warned Bekessy that his arrest was imminent with the result that the latter was able to flee to Paris. As will be seen subsequently, this was one of the main charges which Kraus was to make against the police chief, Schober, in 1927.

In any case the story would not be complete without some reference to the later career of Bekessy himself. Even after his flight from Vienna, the *Stunde* continued to be published, still very much under Bekessy's influence even though he had sold his shares in it and was in exile. It continued to vilify Kraus. In 1928 there appeared a volume in praise of Bekessy entitled *Bekessy's Panoptikum* with contributions from such enemies of Kraus as Stefan Grossmann, Franz Blei and Anton Kuh. Bekessy was portrayed as the innocent victim of the satirist's malice: instead of attacking Mussolini and Hitler, Kraus had concentrated on attacking the friend of the downtrodden—Imre Bekessy. Subsequent attempts by the former proprietor of *Die Stunde* to secure an anullment of his Austrian nationality to escape the charges against him were quashed as a result of the efforts of Dr. Samek, acting on Kraus's behalf. Eventually, when it became clear that Bekessy would not return to Austria, the charges against him were dropped, much to the satirist's indignation.

During the 1930s Bekessy was active in Hungary as an economic expert, still living in that strange political and journalistic underworld which he had manipulated so successfully in Vienna. Faced in 1940 with the growing menace of Nazism throughout Europe, Bekessy went to the United States. He took with him the manuscript of a novel which was to be published in New York in 1946 under the title of *Barabbas: A novel of the Time of Jesus*, a book which shocked the reviewer of the Jewish magazine *Commentary* because of the author's overt hatred of the Jewish people. This hatred was particularly expressed in passages such as Pontius Pilate's tirade against the people who were compelling him to have Christ crucified, 'Don't you think that some day the world will lose patience with you and exterminate the whole pack of you?' It seemed, then, that the book had originally been intended for publication in Hitler's Europe! And the author of this book was himself Jewish! The reviewer was particularly scandalised by the fact that this novel was selected by the Religious Book Club of America as one of its recommended choices.[45] Despite this evidence that Bekessy in America still retained that capacity for deluding the innocent and the gullible which he had displayed so outrageously during his years in Vienna, the fact remains that he found it difficult to come to terms with his wartime exile and on several occasions threatened to take his own life. After the war he returned to Budapest where in 1951 he and his wife committed suicide, terrified, it seems, by the outcome of the Rajk trial which marked the culmination of the Stalinist oppression within Hungary.[46]

It is not difficult to see why in the years between 1920 and the burning down of the Palace of Justice in Vienna in 1927 the influence of Monsignor Seipel was dominant within Austrian politics. He was a man of courage and of finesse. Furthermore he was possessed of a remarkable capacity for concentration on the hard routine of administration, a quality which sharply distinguished him from most other Austrian politicians, both of the Right and, with the exception of Renner, of the Left. And yet, with all his gifts, Seipel repelled more than he attracted: he was an austere intellectual who despised the trappings of power, a single-minded servant of the Church who, even when Chancellor, never lived in his official apartments on the Ballhausplatz, but returned every night to his cell in the convent of the Sacred

Heart of Jesus. His dream was the creation of a regenerated Catholic Austria which could act as a source of inspiration to the suffering and tormented peoples of post-war Central Europe. It was a noble dream, but not only did Seipel demand from his fellow Christian Socialists more than they were capable of offering, the fulfilment of his ideal would of necessity entail considerable difficulties in a political situation in which both the Social Democrats and the Christian Socialists received roughly equal shares of the popular vote and neither party could, by itself, win an overall majority within the parliament.

In order to solve this problem Seipel devoted his considerable powers of intrigue and persuasion to build up an anti-Marxist coalition which would preserve supreme political power in the hands of the Christian Socialists. Whenever the rivalries within the Christian Socialist party and its allies made it expedient, Seipel was perfectly willing to practise self-effacement and relinquish office for a period so that this coalition would be enabled to continue. But he never quite succeeded in his plan to bring all the non-Socialist groups into the same camp: although one section or other of the Christian Socialists was represented in every Austrian government during this period, it was always difficult to secure to a priest like Seipel the loyalty of the Pan-Germans who shared with the Social Democrats a basic anticlericalism as well as a desire for *Anschluss* with Germany. Meanwhile, in the elections of 1924 and 1927 the strength of the Social Democrats, far from decreasing as Seipel had hoped, moved steadily upwards; even in the elections of 1920 when the Left lost support, the loss was slight (only 20,000 votes) and was easily compensated by the fact that the Social Democrats emerged once again as the strongest single force within the Austrian parliament. It was due partly to the incomplete nature of his success in building up a stable government coalition to keep the Social Democrats in permanent subjection and partly as a response to the violence which increasingly intruded into Austrian politics towards the end of the 1920s, that Seipel despaired of working a democratic system in Austria. Before his death in 1932, he was moving very rapidly towards favouring that ideal of the Catholic authoritarian state which Dollfuss attempted to put into practice after 1933.

It was one of the major tragedies of the Austrian Republic that its politics should have been dominated by two idealists of the intellectual and spiritual calibre of Seipel and Otto Bauer and that the mutual respect and admiration which these two men displayed in their private friendship was not reflected in their clashes within the Austrian parliament. The son of a wealthy Jewish textile manufacturer from Bohemia, Bauer brought to the services of the Socialist cause an ardent and romantic spirit. Certainly in human terms he was a more sympathetic personality than Seipel: the arrogance and the stinging scorn which he displayed towards his opponents was combined in Bauer's case with an intense devotion and generosity towards his disciples. Julius Braunthal has summed up the feelings of many of those who came into contact with him:

> We felt that to him life would not be worth living, and even learning would perhaps appear meaningless, if there were not the perception of a new world to come. . . . Though he derived his Socialist conception from a sober analysis of the dynamics of modern economy, with its social, material and psychological implications, it appeared (at least to me) in a Messianic hue.[47]

Lenin's description of him was much less favourable—'an educated fool'.

The basic paradox at the heart of Bauer's career stemmed from his inability to decide which it was most important for him to be, a practical politician or an ideological theoretician of the Left. It had largely been because both he and Friedrich Adler were repelled by both the revisionism of the socialist parties of Western Europe and the brutality of the Marxist-Leninism proclaimed from the Soviet Union that the Austrian Social Democrats had attempted between 1921 and 1923 to reunite the world of international socialism, divided since the end of the war between the organisation of the Western parties, centred on Berne and Geneva, and the Third International, based in Moscow. The subsequent failure of the so-called 'Two and a Half International' of Vienna may be seen as a portent of the eventual failure of the policies of Otto Bauer within Austria itself. For whereas Adler henceforth devoted his life to the reconstituted Socialist International in Brussels, Bauer's position in Vienna was a difficult one. The fact was that his policies fell completely between two stools. The Right wing of the Austrian party under Renner constantly advocated a whole-hearted acceptance of the new political situation which had arisen after 1918 and the necessity for the party to enter into coalitions with non-Socialist groups so that it should be able to return to office. On the Left there was an unwillingness to betray the principles of the party by any concessions to the forces of the bourgeoisie and a determination that the political revolution of November 1918 should be accompanied by sweeping social and economic changes.

Bauer could never quite make up his mind which policy he supported. Certainly his heart was with the Left; the decision of the party to leave the post-war coalition in 1920 was partly due to his insistence and had aroused opposition from Renner. Bauer argued that if the Social Democrats were to remain in office they would be forced into tactical compromises which would not merely destroy the ideological cohesion of the party but also force radical elements into the arms of the Communists. Whilst maintaining a genuine and profound faith in the democratic system, Bauer insisted that the party should consolidate its position in opposition and extend its influence to other sections of the Austrian electorate—notably, of course, the peasants—which had hitherto resisted the appeal of socialism. Once the party secured an overall victory at the polls (the magic figure of 51 per cent of the electorate was often mentioned in party speeches) then the stage was set for the ushering in of the socialist millennium.

However, despite the theory, the party never did go in for a consistent policy of opposition towards the forces of the bourgeoisie. The advantages of using the considerable power of the party to extract concessions from the government or from such individuals as Siegmund Bosel were too attractive to be ignored both by Renner and even by Bauer himself, and several instances of the politics of compromise practised by the Social Democrats during the 1920s have already been noted. Given this situation, the high-sounding principles that were continually proclaimed by Bauer could only serve to accentuate the contrast between the party's theoretical stance, which was one of a sophisticated Marxism, and its actual policies, which were at times crudely opportunistic in character. Bauer was not of course consciously hypocritical, but the party which he led was profoundly Viennese: an approach to life that was doctrinaire in theory but infinitely more elastic in practice was an approach which the party easily absorbed from the social context in which it was placed. So, too, was the civilised irresolution which marked the deliberations of the Social Democrats. Advocates of extreme measures were confined to a minority of the rank-and-file membership after the years of post-war economic and political crisis had come to an end. Bauer believed that time was on the side of the Socialists and that ultimately their cause would triumph without recourse to a determined effort of the will: the ideological extremism which he displayed in his speeches was a form of psychological overcompensation for the fact that neither he nor his party really believed that they needed to be ruthless in order to achieve their aims.

But although their support increased steadily throughout the 1920s, the Social Democratic party did not in fact win that overall victory at the polls which Otto Bauer needed in order that his policies should be justified. It was not merely that Bauer's party was faced in this decade by the considerable efforts being made by Seipel to break the deadlock in Austrian politics and build up his cherished anti-Marxist coalition: behind Seipel there was the growing influence of the para-military forces of the Right, the Heimwehr and Frontkämpfer. Admittedly these forces had their origins in the necessity for policing the provinces in the early years of the Republic when there were constant frontier incidents with Italians, Czechs and Yugoslavs. The trouble was, however, that even after the frontiers had been stabilised, the political armies remained in being and came increasingly to be seen as a counterpoise to the power of the police and the army, both of which had been largely remodelled by the Social Democrats in the period between 1918 and 1920 and which contained many sympathisers with the Left. Faced with growing provocation from the Heimwehr in particular, the Social Democrats formed in 1923 their own force—the Republikanische Schutzbund— which was intended to defend the party against right-wing violence. In this way the stage was set for the troubles of the late 1920s.

Already by the middle of the decade there was continual talk of a counter-revolution by the forces of the Austrian Right against the political system that had been created in 1918. The contradictions within Bauer's position on this question were revealed at the Linz Congress of the Social Democratic party in 1926. On the one hand the party affirmed its basic belief in democracy and expressly repudiated the use of violence by the workers' movement as a means of attaining political power: on the other hand the one situation in which force would be justified was that in which the forces of capitalism attempted a counter-revolution. It was from this inability to come to terms with the facts of the situation in which they found themselves that there flowed many of the troubles which plagued the Social Democrats in the years after 1926. It can be quite clearly seen that the great majority of the leadership—Bauer and his group included—were deeply averse to an extremist policy: and yet not only did the ideology of the party demand that it should be free to use force in certain special circumstances, the opposition to a policy of whole-hearted collaboration with non-Socialist elements could only mean that, when the Social Democrats were faced with the necessity for taking direct action, they would be completely isolated from the rest of Austrian society. Defeat, in these circumstances, seemed almost inevitable.

Nobody thought in 1926 that the situation would deteriorate to the point where the resolutions of the Linz Congress would have to be put into practice. The whole point of the exercise was to preserve the unity of the party by arriving at compromise solutions which would enable it to obtain the best of both worlds. Looked at from the point of view of the leadership the Linz resolutions seemed a masterpiece of sophisticated compromise. Insufficient attention was paid, however, to the increasing remoteness of the leadership from the mass membership, a development which was largely the result of the growth in strength of the party organisation but a development which was disguised by the illusory intimacy between the various echelons of the party which seemed to persist from earlier days. It was only when violence did break out that the gulf between the leadership and the radical minority of the rank and file was clearly revealed.

On 15 July 1927 a crowd of Viennese Social Democrats rioted after a demonstration which they had organised was challenged by the police. The crowd set fire to the Palace of Justice and prevented fire engines from putting the blaze out, even though Bürgermeister Seitz appealed to them to let the engines through. Finally Dr. Schober, the chief of police, was compelled to quell the riot forcibly with a total loss of eighty-nine lives, including four policemen. The riot had its origins in the hostility that existed between the Heimwehr and the Schutzbund; a court in Vienna had just acquitted a group of Heimwehr men who six months previously had killed two members of the Schutzbund. The verdict of the court appeared to be only one of a number of instances in which it seemed that the judiciary was hostile to the Left. In order to prevent violence but at the same time to allow their members the right to protest against this verdict, the Social Democrats had organised a peaceful demonstration through the streets of Vienna. Demonstrations like this had often occurred in the past and it had always been agreed between Seitz and Schober that the police should not make an appearance so that no incitement to violence could be given; the arrangement always was that detachments of the Schutzbund should act as a kind of voluntary police force to maintain order during the demonstration.

Two factors were responsible, however, for the violence of 15 July: the police arrangements were muddled with the result that detachments of the police came in contact with the demonstrators, and, by another piece of *Schlamperei*, the Social Democrats had not arranged for the Schutzbund to accompany the procession.

To Karl Kraus the burning of the Palace of Justice and the bloodshed that ensued in the streets of Vienna was symbolic of the future of the republic. His article on the episode. The Protection of the Republic, was one of the most powerful pieces which he ever wrote.[48] It opened with a long series of newspaper quotations contrasting the horror of events with what people said about the events. Seipel's praise of the restraint displayed by the police was juxtaposed with the statement of Otto Bauer, who claimed that the police had shot members of the retreating crowd in the back. Different estimates were given of the number of people killed, estimates on which the Vice-Chancellor of the Republic said, 'Do not lie always about a hundred deaths, when it was twenty-five.' The leader writer of the *Neues Wiener Journal* declared that the number of dead was only a trifle to pay for the restoration of order. Kraus contrasted the headline of the *Wiener Mittagszeitung* with its advertisements at the top of the page:

> Tabarin
> Weihburg Bar
> 99 Deaths so far.

The *Neue Freie Presse* pointed out that the events of 15 July had a relevance that extended beyond the immediate circumstances of Austria. Even in the most unexpected quarters emphasis was laid on the European significance of the riot:

> The Grand Hotel states: we attach great importance to our announcement that the very regrettable incidents which have happened here, as in other countries at the instigation of the Communists, have not affected the safety and comfort of the foreign guests in the hotel.

The *Frankfurter Zeitung* reported that the Social Democratic leaders had failed to control their followers but that it was clear that the police had been guilty of unnecessary brutality. A reader of the *Reichspost* and a supporter of the Christian Socialist party wrote to the *Arbeiter Zeitung* to say that he had seen a policeman shoot at a passer-by and severely wound a woman with a child in the Rathauspark. The *Berliner Tageblatt* of 31 July contained a letter from a German police expert who criticised the Viennese police for allowing the situation to get out of hand and then firing indiscriminately to cause unnecessary bloodshed: particularly reprehensible was the fact that the police had been issued with ammunition the effects of which were similar to those of Dum Dum bullets.

But the most interesting document which Kraus printed in this long preamble to his article was the text of his own placard which was posted up everywhere in Vienna between the 17th and 19th of September and had subsequently been ripped down by the police:

> To the police president of Vienna, Johannes Schober.
>   I demand that you resign.
>
> Karl Kraus
Publisher of *Die Fackel*.

Johannes Schober, president of the Vienna police force since the summer of 1918, was an old imperial official, trained to deal with men as they are, able to use every means—from conciliatory tactics to the threat of force—to achieve some kind of practical agreement in a situation that was potentially chaotic. Like a number of such bureaucrats he came to the conclusion after the collapse of the Empire that the only future for Austria lay in *Anschluss* with Germany: the loyalty which he had given to the Habsburgs was now to be given to yet another 'mission' which transcended the narrow confines of Austrian patriotism. Since the possibility of *Anschluss* had, however, been ruled out by the terms of the peace treaties, Schober devoted himself to his police duties, duties in which he had distinguished himself until the events of 1927 by being on good terms with both major parties in Austria. He himself was most sympathetic, of course, to the aims of the Pan-German party although their racialist chatter was repugnant to him and he was never actually a party member. In the final analysis Schober despised all professional politicians and saw himself as the servant of an imperial idea which must maintain itself above all parties. Already in 1922 he had been Chancellor of the republic, heading a government composed of Pan-Germans and sections of the Christian Socialist party, demonstrating, incidentally, that the rôle of the bureaucrats in holding the administration together had not disappeared with the end of the Empire.

It was a typical Viennese irony that Schober's mishandling of the riots of July 1927 should have made him into a popular hero with all sections of political opinion outside the camp of Social Democrats. The Heimwehr were particularly attracted towards him by the fact that he so obviously did not belong to the devious and often corrupt politicians within the Christian Socialist party; and when Schober again became Chancellor in 1929 it was with Heimwehr support. The latter soon discovered, however, that although Schober wanted a more centralised and authoritarian government which would reduce the dependence of the executive on the parties, he was so convinced a bureaucrat and so pedantically concerned to do his duty as an honourable man that he would not stomach that violent overthrow of constitutional government which the Heimwehr demanded. A piquant feature of his second period as Chancellor was the fact that, in order to thwart the Heimwehr, he came increasingly to rely on the support of the Social Democrats, by whom he had been so execrated in 1927. This, as will be seen, did not endear the Social Democrats to Karl Kraus. But in order to understand the peculiar hatred which Schober inspired in the editor of *Die Fackel* already in 1927 it is important to note that Kraus was concerned to attack Schober not so much for his suppression of the riots of that year but for his earlier weakness and prevarication in allowing Bekessy to escape from Austria. It was typical of the satirist that at a time when Schober was being praised as the 'strong man' of Austria, Kraus should come out into the open to pay off an earlier score.

The whole issue revolved around the question of the record of Bekessy's previous convictions in Hungary for blackmail and extortion. This had been produced by the police in evidence during the libel case between Stolper and Bekessy in 1923. In 1925 when Kraus and Samek were trying to assemble material to bring Bekessy to justice, they appealed to Schober to co-operate in securing evidence from the police in Budapest. Schober promised to do so. But when Kraus's protégé, Schmidl, had brought Bekessy to court on a charge of libel and the State Prosecutor had agreed to take note of any evidence brought against Bekessy with a view to prosecuting him, the police produced a new record sheet which left out or falsified many of the convictions detailed in that of 1923 which, to start off with, had not been a complete record. The police, then, had performed a complete volte-face and had come down on the side of Bekessy who had consistently denied the accuracy of the 1923 record sheet. Why had Schober and the police changed their attitude? Kraus himself thought it was probably due to pressure from Bekessy who had been carrying out a furious campaign against police persecution of prostitutes and police regulation of night-clubs and had offered to drop this campaign if Schober agreed not to co-operate with Kraus in securing material with which to destroy him. An even stronger reason, perhaps, was the influence of Bosel with his contacts in the Christian Socialist party who put pressure on the police to drop the case. Bosel himself acted under the threat of blackmail from Bekessy who theatened to reveal full details of his financial activities. These seem to be the salient points of the situation, but the whole affair (like most scandals in history) remains, for obvious reasons, shrouded in mystery to this very day. Kraus thought that Bekessy had found sexual misdemeanours a more potent source of blackmail than financial corruption and reported the rumour that, after Bekessy's flight, a file was found in his desk containing details concerning the private lives of bank directors and politicians. If this file existed, the police saw to it that it was suppressed.

Kraus did not claim that Schober was being blackmailed in a personal capacity—the chief of police, had, after all, rendered the satirist considerable services when he was in difficulty with the army authorities in 1918—but that he simply gave in to the pressure of politicians. Similarly Kraus did not at first accuse Schober in person of warning Bekessy about his impending arrest in 1926, but it seemed that someone in a position of authority near to him had done so and that Schober was protecting him from the consequences of this action. It will never be possible accurately to determine Schober's share of guilt in this affair, but two incidents suggest that Schober himself did not have a clear conscience. In the first place Kraus revealed that after he had first attacked the failure of the police during the Bekessy Affair (in general terms and *before* the events of July 1927) a police official had telephoned him in the spring of 1927 to explain that Schober wanted to clear up the 'misunderstanding' between himself and the satirist. The latter replied that the only way to do this would be to dismiss the guilty officials: in answer the voice at the other end of the line sighed and spoke of 'difficulties'. In the second place Bekessy himself wrote to Kraus denying most of the latter's charges against him, but in such a way that much was revealed that was damaging to Schober: he accused Schober of trickery in that the chief of police had been in contact with Kraus at the same time that he (Bekessy) and Schober were arranging an agreement.[49] Schober dealt with Bekessy through the head of the Political Police, Hofrat Pollak, who, it seems probable, was the person responsible for warning Bekessy of his impending arrest. It is virtually certain that Pollak did not do this without Schober's knowledge.

As it happens the usefulness of Pollak to Schober can be corroborated from a source quite independent of the satirist. It will be remembered that one of the main charges against the police for their part in the events of 15 July was that through criminal carelessness they had been supplied with Dum Dum

The satirist at one of his public recitals

The coffin of Dollfuss leaves the Chancellery

bullets to use against the rioters; and it is a well known fact that
the wounds inflicted by this type of bullet, which splinters on
impact, are far worse than those caused by many other varieties.
Julius Braunthal ferretted out this information and published it
in *Der Kampf*. He was answered by a flat denial from the police
that any such bullets had been used. The situation became more
complicated, however, when the English journalist G. E. R.
Gedye, then *Daily Express* correspondent for Austria and the
Balkans, managed to obtain a private admission from Hofrat
Pollak, a genial and expansive personality by all accounts, that,
in the excitement of the moment, Dum Dum bullets had in fact
been issued to the police on 15 July. The *Arbeiter Zeitung* seized
on this information and printed it. The police issued yet another
denial. Pollak sent for Gedye and tried at first to persuade him
that the use of such ammunition was really humane because it
had less penetrating power. When this approach failed, Pollak
then said, 'What harm would it do you in England, Mr. Gedye,
if I denied—only in the Austrian press—something you had
written in England? But by denying my démenti, you put a
senior police officer in a very awkward position.'[50]

There was some point in Pollak's exasperation. It was a
damning comment on the whole Austrian political system in the
1920s that the police should have been drawn into the centre of
the political struggle and that Schober, a man of personal decency
and sensitivity, should have been so deeply involved in a squalid
scandal. Interesting, too, is the reaction of Kraus. Although he
repeatedly denied that such was his ambition, he genuinely felt
that, by his action in exposing the links between Schober and
Bekessy, he would have the same success in getting rid of the
former as he had had with the latter. In this, however, he was to
be disappointed. Throughout the summer of 1927 the reputation
of Schober had never been higher. The Viennese press, with the
exception of the *Arbeiter Zeitung*, ignored the charges of Schober's
complicity in the Bekessy Affair. The chief of police issued a public statement denying the truth of Kraus's allegations and in February 1928 yet another statement which attacked the malicious

gossip about him. This was a veiled reference to Kraus. The
satirist brought an action for slander against Schober but the case
was dismissed as not being sufficiently specific. When people
objected that Kraus ought to have taken legal action against
Schober as early as 1926 and that Kraus was open to the accusation that he had deliberately waited until after the events of
July 1927 to blacken the name of the police president, the satirist
replied that it was impossible to invoke the organs of justice
against the corruption of justice. But this was an attempt to
explain away the failure of his attempt to drive Schober from
office.

Instead, Kraus had to content himself with the arrangements
for the production of his play *Die Unüberwindlichen* (The
Invincibles) which he had written as a dramatisation of his
struggle against Bekessy and Schober. The play had a certain
amount of success when it was performed in Berlin.[51] Indeed in
the years between 1927 and 1932 Kraus often toyed with the
idea of moving to Berlin where, with friends such as Brecht and
Weill, he felt his work to be appreciated. He was, however,
repelled as well as attracted by the German capital, 'that Babylon'
as he called it, then at the high point of its feverish artistic
brilliance before the collapse of the Weimar Republic. The theme
of *Die Unüberwindlichen*, like that of the later Brecht/Weill
Threepenny Opera, dealt with the corruption of justice. It was
a theme which seemed particularly apposite in Berlin where in
1929 there was to be bitter criticism by the radical left-wing
intellectuals of the action of the Social Democrat police president,
Zörgiebel, in ordering police to fire on a demonstration of Communist workers. This action led to street fighting in the German
capital which lasted several days. Over thirty people were killed.

Many consequences flowed from the events of 15 July 1927 in
Austria. The illusions of so many Viennese that it would somehow be possible to muddle through, despite the deep differences
that separated the two major parties, were rudely shattered. On
the Left the action of the courts in ignoring evidence of police

brutality and in indiscriminately convicting a large number of people for complicity in the riots alienated many besides Kraus; after Seipel had invoked the gratitude of God for the devotion of the police there was a steep rise in the numbers of those who withdrew from the Catholic Church. Meanwhile, on the other side of the barricades, the violence displayed by militant elements within the workers' movement alarmed many sections of the Christian Socialists who had hitherto been sceptical of Siepel's attempt to isolate the Social Democrats. Friedrich Funder forcefully expressed this mood after an attempt had been made on 15 July to burn down the offices of the *Reichspost*:

> We stand firm! They have tried to knock us down—we stand erect. They have tried to burn down in Vienna the stronghold of the press of the Christian people of Austria. . . .[52]

Alarmed by what seemed to mark a return by the Social Democrats to the principles of violent revolution, Seipel and the Christian Socialists decided greatly to increase the strength of the Heimwehr—a step with fateful consequences for the future of the Austrian republic.

Within the ranks of Austrian Social Democracy consternation reigned after the events of 1927. The party had indeed suffered a notable defeat in that year. In the first place the belief which the party had hitherto possessed that the police and the army were so thoroughly infiltrated by left-wing sympathisers that they would not move against the workers, was utterly destroyed. Furthermore, it had been shown that the party could in certain circumstances lose control over the radical minority within its rank-and-file membership and that the one weapon which the party had always believed in as the one alternative to a trial of military strength—the general strike—was useless: after the brutal suppression of the riots the party had declared a general strike throughout Austria as a measure of protest; this had to be called off in humiliating circumstances after the Heimwehr used methods of intimidation to break the strike in some of the provincial centres.

Even more serious than this, however, were the repercussions which the affair was bound to have on matters of policy. When the party met for its annual conference in the summer of 1927, Bauer and his group came under heavy fire from two quite different directions. The extreme left-wingers demanded a more violent policy to meet the challenge of the Heimwehr: Renner and the Right wing argued that, since the party was in no position to embark on reprisals for the injuries done in July, the best solution was to jettison the negative and sterile policy of opposition and instead to follow the implications of revisionism to their logical conclusion and collaborate with other parties to form coalition administrations, a policy which would undermine Seipel's leading rôle within the Christian Socialist party. Although no vote was taken at the conference on this issue compromise resolutions were passed which barely concealed the fact that Renner's arguments had carried the day. Although the party retained the proviso that violence might be justified as a last alternative if counter-revolution was threatened, it went on record as saying that Social Democrats were not opposed completely to the idea of entering coalition administrations. Furthermore, the violence employed by the workers on 15 July was condemned and great care was to be taken to see that nothing like this happened again; to this end the Schutzbund was to be strengthened. With something for everybody in this new policy, the party now closed its ranks in the name of unity. As Otto Bauer said, 'It is a hundred times better to go the wrong way united—for errors can be corrected—than to split in search of the right way.'[53]

This change of emphasis in the party line tended to underline the growing estrangement between Kraus and the Social Democrats. The satirist was still obsessed with the Bekessy Affair and the failure of the party to support him until almost the very last moment of his campaign. The split was widened by the growing influence of his enemy Oskar Pollak within the organisation of the *Arbeiter Zeitung*. The Socialist newspaper now followed a policy of ignoring Kraus and his activities: the Vienna production of *Die Unüberwindlichen*, for example, was not reviewed; that it was mentioned at all was due to Kraus's action in paying for an advertisement in the newspaper.[54] The satirist retaliated by subjecting the *Arbeiter Zeitung* to his most corrosive ridicule, attacking in particular the policy of that newspaper in accepting the advertisements of Julius Krupnik, the owner of a large department store in Vienna. To an English reader this might not seem particularly damaging: and yet, given the traditions of Austrian Social Democracy, this was a development which would never have occurred in the heyday of Austerlitz's editorship. The appearance of such advertisements seemed to Kraus to be conclusive evidence of the bourgeois spirit with which the party had become infected, so that, on the day the Social Democrats marched through the streets of Vienna in a demonstration against Fascism and Nazism, an advertisement appeared in black type in the party newspaper: 'Let it go! Krupnik is making a total clearance of his stock. Everything must go!' The satirist was also scandalised by yet another advertisement in the *Arbeiter Zeitung* which featured Franz Lehár explaining that he had his best ideas whilst shaving with a certain type of razor-blade.[55]

But these were small matters compared with the fact that, in 1929 following the new policy of flexibility, there occurred a rapprochement between the Social Democrats and Kraus's arch enemy—Johannes Schober. In September 1929 Schober again became Chancellor of Austria, leading a coalition between Pan-Germans and Heimwehr. The Social Democrats were anxious not to push Schober into too close a dependence on the Heimwehr, who were talking wildly of abolishing the constitution. Schober's brief government of one year did, in fact, accomplish some useful measures. Against a background of a mounting economic crisis which followed the failure in 1929 of the Boden Kredit Anstalt bank in Vienna, the Chancellor visited The Hague where he secured the cancellation of Austria's responsibility for the payment of war reparations. Furthermore the Chancellor managed to put through the Reichstag a revision of the constitution which involved a centralisation of the security forces. The Heimwehr increasingly felt that they had been duped by Schober who had, in fact, strengthened and not eliminated the constitution. Elements of the Heimwehr therefore attempted a half-hearted putsch in 1930 which was easily put down by the government with a handful of arrests. Thanks to the support of the Social Democrats, the Chancellor had been able to uphold legality and defy the extremists on whose support his administration had rested. A few days after the revision of the constitution Otto Bauer told a conference of workers that, 'We have won a defensive battle. . . . This was the Battle of the Marne for Austrian Fascism!'[56]

But these considerations did not excuse the conduct of the Social Democrats to Kraus, so single-minded was he in his hostility to Schober. The final rupture between Kraus and the Social Democrats occurred after a ceremony of reconciliation between the Schober régime and the Social Democrats on the third anniversary of the riots of July 1927, when President Miklas laid a wreath at the cemetery where the victims of the riots were buried. The satirist accused the party of going the way of their German comrades who, by their collaboration with the forces of the Right, had driven their radical elements into the arms of the Communists. Within the Socialist ranks themselves there was a section of youthful left-wingers which was distressed at the alienation of the satirist from the party. As early as 1928 a group of his admirers had formed the 'Sozialdemokratische Vereinigung Karl Kraus' to protest against the failure of the party to support Kraus against Bekessy and the policy of the *Arbeiter Zeitung* in lowering itself to sensational journalism and accepting advertisements from such people as Krupnik. The group produced a news-sheet which attempted to break the conspiracy of silence in the Socialist press surrounding the satirist's activities by printing notices of Kraus's books and recitals: it also demanded free and open discussion of all cultural problems in the party press without dictation from the party apparatus.

The history of this group was short and unhappy. Its membership was small (an average of fifty people attended its meetings) and confined almost exclusively to intellectuals.[57] Not altogether surprisingly, the party leadership turned down its demands for such things as a boycott of the capitalist theatre on the grounds that the political and economic difficulties facing Austria were so vast that it would be a waste of vital energy to pursue such issues.[58] In any case the group was killed by Kraus himself, who although he had always sympathised with its aims, had stood aloof from its operations within the party. In 1930, however, he went further and now urged his followers not to work within the party at all but to break with it completely: he did not wish, he said, to participate in the tragic conflict which had opened up between his followers and the party leadership. This was an impossible demand. His followers replied in terms which reveal just how tragic this conflict was for them:

> We realise that the party and Karl Kraus stand together as the church does to religion. But we are determined to hold firm to our faith and not to leave the church.[59]

His admirers refused in fact to do what the satirist had done in 1922 when he had stormed out of the Catholic Church. Amid internal dissensions and dwindling membership the group passed out of existence.

Meanwhile Kraus continued his campaign against Schober. He made great play with the contrast between Schober's handling of the riots of July 1927 and the gentle words of rebuke which the Chancellor employed after the failure of the Heimwehr putsch of 1930. Kraus suspected, with some justification, that Schober was so deeply implicated with the Heimwehr in its authoritarian tendencies that he dare not proceed against them.[60] Prince Starhemberg, the leader of the Heimwehr, later accused Schober of double-crossing him by agreeing at first to radical alterations in the constitution and then suddenly switching to the Social Democrats for support to crush the Heimwehr putsch. Starhemberg tried to take Schober to court over this, but the case came to nothing because the court decided that the affair was exclusively political in the issues which it raised. Certainly Schober had wanted to go further in strengthening the executive than he had achieved in the revision of the constitution in 1929, but he was never the man to support illegal methods on the scale which Starhemberg had wanted. From the start the Chancellor's coalition with the Heimwehr had been very much a marriage of convenience. His supporters amongst the Pan-Germans agreed with the Heimwehr that closer links were desirable with Germany and that Seipel's influence must be reduced. On the other hand Schober had been genuinely distressed by the hatred which he had aroused on the Left following the events of July 1927: and this reluctance to follow the extreme policies of the Heimwehr, which would have ended in civil war, was confirmed by the rapidly deteriorating economic situation of Austria following the failure of the Boden Kredit Anstalt Bank.

The break between Schober and the Heimwehr was Seipel's opportunity. In September 1930 Schober's government was replaced by a coalition between the Heimwehr and the Christian Socialists, with Starhemberg as Minister of the Interior and Seipel at the Foreign Office. Everything seemed set for yet another Heimwehr putsch. But the groups represented in this government soon disagreed amongst themselves over the spoils of office and, to crown everything, the Socialist and Pan-German opposition polled more votes than the government parties in the elections of November. The government fell after being in office for only two months and another administration was formed out of Pan-Germans and Christian Socialists. The Heimwehr withdrew into sulky opposition, their distrust of professional politicians only intensified by their experience over the previous year.

It had indeed looked at one time as if they would refuse to allow themselves to be displaced from office, but their leaders were rent with personal rivalries and with disputes over the relative attractions of Hitler or Mussolini. Starhemberg had taken part in the Munich putsch of 1923 but in the next decade he was to move closer towards Italian Fascism in opposition to German designs on Austria. The Heimwehr, in fact, were hopelessly confused in matters of policy and ideology. Even their antisemitism was profoundly Austrian; one of the movement's most strident supporters was the *Neues Wiener Journal*; most of its arms were supplied by Fritz Mandl, the Austrian industrialist and munitions king, who was a Jew; and much of its finance was derived from a small section of the wealthy Jewish bourgeoisie of Vienna. Starhemberg himself was only an antisemite in so far as he disliked those Jews who supported the Social Democrats. A hedonist and a political dilettante with a flair for demagogy, the prince in any case was not of the stuff out of which dictators are made. On one occasion he denounced Hugo Breitner, the Socialist financial expert, and declared that 'the head of that Asiatic would have to roll in the dust'. The next day he repudiated this outburst, claiming that he had not wished to hurt anyone's feelings.[61]

Mention has been made of the collapse of the Boden Kredit Anstalt Bank in 1929. This collapse was due partly to the financial war of attrition which Rudolf Sieghart, the governor of that bank, had waged on Bosel's Union Bank (which at last came under the former's control in the spring of 1927) and partly to the large subventions which both Bosel and Sieghart had been giving to the Heimwehr. Faced with the failure of Sieghart's bank, Schober as Chancellor had been forced to resort to desperate measures: he had virtually forced Baron Louis Rothschild, governor of the other major bank of Vienna, the Credit Anstalt, to take over responsibility for Sieghart's commitments. This overstraining of the resources of Rothschild's bank was largely responsible for its collapse in 1931, an event which not only did tremendous damage to the Austrian economy but also set in motion that progressive decline in financial confidence which resulted in the world economic crisis of that year. This crisis had grave political consequences, especially in Germany where, in the elections of 1932, the Nazis emerged as the largest single party within the Reichstag.

Already before the collapse of the Credit Anstalt, Schober

(now Foreign Minister) had pressed forward with a project for a customs union between Austria and Germany. This scheme seemed particularly attractive to Schober: not merely would it perhaps help to solve Austria's economic problems, it was also the first step towards *Anschluss* with Germany. The Austrian republic was, however, so desperately in need of foreign loans that it had to agree to the demands of the French that, in return for financial assistance, the customs union project should be dropped and that under no circumstances would Austria seek *Anschluss* with Germany. Several months of internal political crisis followed the failure of Schober's policies. On two occasions, once from Seipel and a second time from the Chancellor, Karl Buresch, the Christian Socialists made overtures for a coalition with the Social Democrats. These were rejected, the latter party believing that, if it waited only a little longer in opposition, the growing economic crisis would bring them to power on their own terms and not those of Seipel. In any case they had reason to distrust Seipel intensely.

In May 1932 a new administration was formed under Dollfuss, a government that depended on support from the Heimwehr. Both Dollfuss and the Social Democrats realised that the problems which faced Austria were now so overwhelming that some sort of coalition was sooner or later inevitable; but in the meantime both sides were jockeying for political advantage and both sides thought that the time was not yet ripe for a radical reversal of previous policies. Time, however, was running out. Dollfuss was under heavy pressure from the Heimwehr to have a final showdown with the Social Democrats: and the Socialist leadership was divided over the possibility of a coalition with Dollfuss; Renner was in favour of such a move while Bauer, fearing the reaction from the radicals within the party, was lukewarm. Unable to come to terms with Dollfuss, the Social Democrats found themselves in opposition to his government in the company of the Pan-Germans. This was a strange alliance: apart from moderates such as Schober, the latter party was a curious mixture of extreme German nationalists and anti-semites, segments of the provincial middle class and a number of Viennese Jewish bankers. With the death of Schober in 1932 the Pan-Germans lost their most respected spokesman and in the succeeding months this party rapidly lost support to the Nazis and virtually disappeared from the Austrian political scene.

The fate of the Pan-Germans is illustrative of the fact that, under the impact of the economic crisis and the enormous growth in the strength of the Nazi party in Germany in 1932, the traditional party alignments inside Austria were becoming increasingly irrelevant. The growing air of unreality which surrounded Austrian politics was strikingly demonstrated by the scenes within the parliament in the summer of 1932. Christian Socialists and Social Democrats conducted a shrill campaign of synthetic hatred against the other. The former accused the latter of being agents of international communism, a charge which was demonstrably false. For their part the Social Democrats made capital out of the humiliation involved for Austria in the further ban which had been placed by France on the question of *Anschluss* and accused the Christian Socialists of selling out Austrian interests to the forces of French imperialism; Otto Bauer comparing the condition of the Austrian people with that of the oppressed negroes of French Africa.[62]

All the time, of course, Bauer and the Social Democrats were aware that they did not really want *Anschluss* with a Germany where by 1932 democracy was in a far more desperate condition than it was in Austria. Neither the Social Democrats nor the Christian Socialists really believed in the charges which they flung at each other in the parliamentary debates of 1932: the important thing was which party would gain most advantage from the situation. Meanwhile the strength of the Christian Socialists in the country as a whole ebbed away as the government incurred the increasing unpopularity which derived from the deflationary measures which it had taken to deal with the economic situation. By 1932 the government majority over Social Democrats and Pan-Germans had declined to one. The opposition was encouraged by this situation to attempt obstructionist tactics in the Reichstag. Dollfuss was pushed further and further into the arms of the Heimwehr. Normal government soon became impossible in Austria.

Kraus watched the suicide of Austrian democracy with mounting disgust. From 1932 onwards he was concerned with the danger that threatened from Germany: it was the attitude which the Austrian parties adopted to the rise of Hitler in Germany which determined his political sympathies from now on. He became convinced that both the ideology and the phraseology of the Social Democrats in Germany and Austria prevented them from seeing the danger that was represented by the growing power of Nazism. The *Arbeiter Zeitung* claimed that Bismarck had persecuted the Social Democrats but had failed to crush them. Kraus did not feel the same optimism over Hitler and pointed out that, whatever the outcome of the intrigues between Schleicher, Von Papen and the Nazis, Hitler was bound to survive President Hindenburg.[63] The one person in Austrian politics, the satirist felt, who really understood the danger that now stemmed from Germany was the new Chancellor, Dollfuss. With that infuriating and irresponsible independence which only an intellectual and an aesthete utterly divorced from political responsibility can enjoy, Kraus moved almost overnight from a position on the Left of the Social Democratic party to one of support for Dollfuss. In December 1932, the last issue of the *Fackel* before Hitler's accession to power in Germany, the satirist did not deal with political problems at all, but with the problems of translating Shakespeare, in which he was concerned to criticise very severely the translations of Stefan George.[64] The stage was now set.

6   *The Reckoning*

1. *The Triumph of Nazism.*

Despite his preoccupation with Viennese affairs in the 1920s political events outside Austria were not entirely ignored by Kraus before 1932. In 1923 the satirist attacked the Viennese soprano Lucy Weidt who, after a visit to Italy, praised Mussolini's iron physique and the benefits of his dictatorship compared with the poverty and irritations of life in Austria: when she stressed the charm which the Italian dictator displayed on receiving from her a bunch of violets, Kraus wondered whether she would be able to evoke human feelings even in Hitler.[1] This was the first reference to Hitler in *Die Fackel*. In the same year the satirist ridiculed the racialism of Nazi placards and the speeches at the Nuremberg rally of right-wing extremists. Kraus was concerned to show that the figures of the Wilhelmine era—such as the Crown Prince, Ludendorff and Admiral Scheer—who attended this rally were not aware of the true nature of the company they were keeping. If Ludendorff was pressed to give a concrete explanation of what he meant when he exclaimed 'Forward with trust in God into the fight for our most holy possessions!' he could not do this: but when the inimitable Hitler urged that the commandment of love for the Fatherland should be enforced against others, he knew exactly what he meant—that rubber truncheons would be used to implement it.[2]

Already in the Innsbruck affair Kraus had experienced attacks from provincial anti-semites. He was to suffer, too, at the hands of the Nazis. When the Social Democrats in the Teplitz-Schönau area of Sudeten Czechoslovakia declared their intention in 1924 of performing the epilogue of *The Last Days of Mankind*, the local Nazis almost succeeded in preventing its performance at the town theatre. To the Sudeten Nazis Kraus was a perfect example of that type of left-wing Jewish journalist who, they believed, had maliciously turned against Germany during the First World War. As the Sudeten newspaper *Der Tag* said:

> Every person of völkisch sympathies who has been in politics in recent years knows what the *Fackel* stands for. It is a filthy magazine of almost unique shamelessness which during the war and even before the war, with an unparalleled Jewish gift for stirring up trouble, waged a veritable campaign of slander against everything that is and is felt to be German.[3]

In 1928, after a Munich performance of his play *Traumstück*, during which the Nazis threw stink bombs, Kraus was awarded 200 Marks and costs against the official Nazi party newspaper, the *Völkischer Beobachter*, which had described the play as 'the most impertinent ridicule of all those fighters of the front who died for the Fatherland, that has ever appeared on the open stage'.[4] It was a critic in the *Frankfurter Zeitung* of 13 April 1928 who after this attack on *Traumstück* pointed out the real significance of the hatred which was inspired among Nazis and others by the attack which Kraus had launched against the First World War.

> It is just like the workers who protested at the performance of Gerhart Hauptmann's *Weavers* (*Die Weber*), because they felt themselves to be ridiculed by the portrayal of their fate and suffering. From the point of view of logic that was indeed the case. Psychologically it is not difficult to understand the paradox why here it is not the victimisers but the victims who protest. Where ideology and reality lost contact with each other as in the last war, there can be no description of reality that is not a falsification. With blind rage those who took part in the war are protecting the very essence of their being.[5]

It was in a sense for this very reason that the Nazis to Kraus were beyond satire and even beyond the reach of polemic.

Partly, of course, it was a question of their vulgarity and cultural illiteracy. Several examples of this were to occur in the responses of the Nazis to the work of Kraus. Thus for example, when Streicher's *Der Stürmer* reviewed *Die Unüberwindlichen* it claimed that the play was a panegyric of the Jewish race against the Germans because its 'heroes' such as Bekessy and Castiglioni were Jewish.[6] Again, in 1931, Kraus was to be astonished at the spectacle of the *Völkischer Beobachter* printing one of his poems under the impression that it was by Grillparzer.[7] No wonder then that in 1933 the satirist did not publish anything in the *Fackel* until the October of that year, nine months after the accession of Hitler to power in Germany. Kraus's silence was not due to cowardice, as was alleged by many of his former admirers in the Social Democrat party. His real reason was explained in the poem which appeared in the *Fackel*:

Do not ask me what I have been doing all this time
I am silent;
And do not say, why.
And it is still, since the Earth collapsed.
No word, that could be found:
One speaks only in one's sleep.
And dreams of a sun which used to laugh.
It passes away:
Afterwards it was all the same.
The Word fell asleep, as that world awoke.[8]

As in the early months of the First World War, Kraus felt it impossible to grasp immediately the full significance of what had happened in Germany and, apart from the issue of October 1933, did not comment publicly upon these events until July 1934 when an extended issue of his magazine was published, entitled 'Why the *Fackel* does not appear'. Already in the summer of 1933, however, he had written a long examination of events in Germany, an examination that was originally intended to form a special issue of the *Fackel* but did not in fact appear until 1952 when it was published under the title of *Die Dritte Walpurgisnacht*. The principal reason why this document did not appear in 1933 was that, in Kraus's own words, 'This book includes among other things a description of the "mentality" of the Minister of Propaganda. It could happen that if his eyes saw my work he would, out of rage, order fifty Jews from Königsberg into the living death of a concentration camp. How could I be responsible for that?'[9] Yet another reason was the fact that, according to Heinrich Fischer, Kraus was afraid that in the nature of the events taking place in Germany, his book would be misunderstood by being interpreted in only a political sense.

And, indeed, any such attempt encounters serious difficulties: the style and language of the satirist, always difficult in its concentration and allusiveness, becomes at times almost incomprehensible to the average non-German reader. The student of *Die Dritte Walpurgisnacht* is reminded of what Kraus himself wrote of Lichtenberg: 'Lichtenberg goes deeper than any other, but he does not come up again. He speaks under the Earth. He is only heard by those who themselves dig deep.'[10] Kraus himself considered this work to be an artistic failure. Yet the full importance of the book only becomes meaningful in the context of the satirist's writings against the First World War; neither is complete without the other. The logic which the book follows is not the logic of politics or even the logic of culture, it is the logic of language—the German language which was being distorted out of recognition by the Nazis. This is the main theme of *Die Dritte Walpurgisnacht* and the reason for the style of Kraus himself becoming more abstruse and even gnomic as the full horror of Nazism is revealed. In the book, as he himself realised, he was attempting to do the impossible: to attack an opponent who spoke and wrote a language utterly different from that which he used himself. During the First World War men were still open to reason and the satirist could reasonably expect some result from his work. Now all that Kraus could do effectively to reveal the mentality of the Nazis was to oppose their style to his style, to let them condemn themselves in extensive quotations out of their own mouths. It is significant that the satirist could not bring himself to quote anything but a handful of phrases of

Hitler himself in *Die Dritte Walpurgisnacht*. Kraus could only attempt to deal with the minor characters of the Nazi drama: 'Nothing occurs to me worth saying about Hitler,' was the first sentence of this polemic.[11]

The very vocabulary of the Nazis surpassed in frightfulness such usage of the First World War as 'Menschenmaterial'. The Nazis invented new words such as 'Reichskulturkammer', 'Gaukulturwart' and 'Gestapo'. There was the constant use in the speeches of the Nazi leaders of words which they never defined: 'organisch', 'Konglomerat', 'Neuorientierung'. As for the use of the word 'Gleichschaltung', 'co-ordination', to describe the process by which Hitler suppressed the freedom of political and social groups and organisations (including the press) to achieve the totalitarian state, the word had only been used previously in the German language for technical descriptions of electrical circuits: by itself the word revealed the fusion of a perverted science and a perverted romanticism which lay at the heart of the Nazi experience. If the tragedy of 1914 had been caused by what Kraus had called 'the coexistence of thrones and telephones', that of 1933 was the result of 'the coexistence of electrical technique and myth'.[12]

The main responsibility for this development Kraus attributed to the decadence of modern journalism:

> National Socialism has not destroyed the press, but the press has created National Socialism. Seemingly only a reaction, in fact a fulfilment. . . . The alleged degradation of the German press might be the problem of a form of journalism that worked in freedom so long as it was not attacked by political power and ruthless masseuses did not employ terror. When, however, 'Commissars' burst into editorial offices and 'lay a revolver on the desk', this is only criminal in so far as two revolvers lie there.[13]

How unjustified and hypocritical the Nazi attack on Jewish influence in the press before 1933 had been is demonstrated by the fact that the power of the two great Jewish-owned press combines in Germany, the Ullstein and Mosse organisations, had been greatly reduced after the First World War as a result of the enormous growth of the Hugenberg newspaper and magazine empire, a group at the head of which was the leader of the German Nationalist party, Alfred Hugenberg, who gave support to Hitler in the elections of 1929.

The tendency for much of the press to be absorbed into one or other of the great newspaper empires was itself a reflection of the weak financial situation of Central European journalism, a weakness which could be seen before 1914. In Austria economic necessity was a contributory factor in the close dependence of the Liberal press on the major financial interests in Vienna. With the collapse of the Habsburg Empire, the circulation figures of the Austrian press received a severe blow, a fact which encouraged the kind of newspaper corruption pioneered by Bekessy. Finally, the lack in Germany and Austria of anything like the centralised mass-circulation press of England greatly reduced the ability of the former to stand up to the effects of the Great Depression. As a result of these factors in many ways the freedom of the press in Berlin and Vienna had already been eroded away before 1933. In Germany, after the collapse of the parliamentary system in 1930 and the spectacle of Brüning, without a majority within the Reichstag, maintaining himself as Chancellor by using the authority of Hindenburg's presidential decrees, and particularly after the huge Nazi gains in the elections of 1930, the Jewish-owned press, which up to that time had ardently supported the democratic republic, now adopted an increasingly nationalist line and attempted to 'Aryanise' itself by mass dismissals of Jewish staff.[14] When in 1933 Goebbels was faced with the task of subordinating the German press to the control of the new régime, he did not find the task very difficult.

In any case he was well equipped for his task. The methods and style of the Propaganda Minister were the apotheosis of that type of 'Asphalt literature' which it had been Kraus's life duty to attack and which it had been the claim of the Nazis to have ended. On the one hand Goebbels was the nearest thing to an intellectual within the Nazi leadership, having been a pupil at Heidelberg of the Jewish writer and literary critic Friedrich Gundolf, himself a disciple of Stefan George. It was a revealing comment on Goebbels's personality that it should have been rumoured that he had a complete set of *Die Fackel* in his private library.[15] On the other hand, a cynic and a nihilist in almost everything else, his scepticism did not extend to his hatred of the Jews (a hatred partly due no doubt to his failure to obtain a position as a journalist on the *Berliner Tageblatt* in 1924) or his reverence for the personality of Adolf Hitler. The press treatment of the personalities of Wilhelm II and Franz Josef during the First World War was pale in comparison with the banalities of the *Völkischer Beobachter* on the forty-fourth birthday of the Führer:

> On the barn floors of the cornlands in harsh East Prussia, from which the snow has hardly melted, and on the isolated valley farms of the Karawanken Alps, peasants meet together and their stern features relax as they send a heartfelt prayer to God above to sustain their Führer.[16]

Hitler was the friend of youth:

> His heart belongs to the young. The great man was particularly smitten by the schoolgirl from Oberstaufen with her swastika flag. The little girl called through the waiting crowds to the Führer: 'Today is my birthday', whereupon she was invited by Adolf Hitler to coffee and cakes and was given a photograph and autograph. To the left is Reich Youth Leader Baldur von Schirach.[17]

Readers of the *Völkischer Beobachter* were constantly reminded of Hitler's knowledge of art and his love of music. Thus Wilhelm Kube, the Gauleiter of Brandenburg and later, during the Second World War, regional commissar of Belorussia:

> If artists only knew how much Adolf Hitler is the embodiment of the musician, then he would have no enemies among them—this sentence, coined by Baldur von Schirach at the time of our most arduous struggle, brightened even the darkest hours like a star of hope.[18]

The music critic of the Austrian Nazi *Deutsch-Oesterreichische Tageszeitung* praised the composer of a Goethe symphony which was dedicated to the Führer: he joined with the composer in hailing 'the great men to whom his work does honour: Goethe and Adolf Hitler'.[19]

And yet there was ample evidence to refute this picture if the reader was careful in looking at the very same newspapers which praised the Führer. It was reported, for instance, that he did not read books and was only interested in the everyday problems of life; his reading consisted of illustrated papers.[20] Goebbels might announce his opposition to the kind of *Hurrakitsch* which had been performed on the Berlin stage in the 1920s but, claimed Kraus, the Nazi movement itself was only a mixture of blood and *kitsch*. How else could one describe the first visit of Hitler as Chancellor to the Berlin Rathaus when it was reported that 'on both sides of the vestibule heralds in historical costumes took up positions'? What else but *kitsch* was the poetry written under the auspices of the Ministry of Propaganda attacking the Jews?[21] The reality behind the Nazi talk of *Kultur* was revealed by a character in the Nazi dramatist Hans Johst's play *Schlageter* who exclaimed, 'When I hear the word culture, I take the catch off my Browning!'[22]

Two further examples of cultural policy from the very first months of the Third Reich may give an even more concrete idea of the kind of régime which Hitler and Goebbels had installed in Germany. The first affair was the situation created by the refusal of Toscanini to conduct at Bayreuth, despite a personal plea from Hitler that he should do so. The German public were not informed of this refusal, but the Nazi-inspired *Kampfbund für deutsche Kultur* issued a statement denying that any of their members had protested against Toscanini being invited to conduct at Bayreuth; by means of this trick the German public was led to believe that pressure had come from inside Germany to prevent Toscanini's appearance. This, however, was not the end of the story, for the affair was taken up by the *Deutsch-Oesterreichische Tageszeitung* which (unlike the German public) at least knew that the reason which Toscanini had given for his refusal was the proscription of Jewish conductors in Germany. This newspaper maintained that the German people would bring forth conductors of their own which would result in the Toscanini affair being forgotten. Kraus could only hope that, until this was achieved, Bayreuth would be closed: the only conductors available at the moment were Richard Strauss and Furtwängler, but when they raised their right arms it was not certain that they were about to conduct.[23]

The second example of Nazi *Kulturpolitik* at work was the case of the Oberammergau passion play; the local Nazis objected to the beards grown by the actors and the fact that they were going to act the part of Jews. It was suggested that, instead of the passion play, there should be substituted a dramatised version of the life of the Führer. But this idea was not carried through because it was considered, after reflection, that this would not attract foreign tourists. Instead a compromise was evolved: it was decreed that Christ should be played by a blond blue-eyed man with swastikas on his robes; the apostles should be Aryan Germans, while Judas should be played as 'a pronouncedly Jewish type'.[24]

Although in *Die Dritte Walpurgisnacht* Kraus was primarily concerned with the unspeakable atrocities committed by the Nazis against German language and culture, he also was at pains to show that in every sphere there was an impassable gulf between what the Nazis said and wrote on the one hand and what they did on the other. In economic affairs, for instance, it was clear to him that the Nazis had gained support from both the big industrialists and from the masses by pretending to be a party that was both capitalist and anti-capitalist. The only way out of this inconsistency was to deny that there was one or to claim that the other side was lying. As one Nazi speaker complained:

> They come along with the Party programme and with the Hitler book *Mein Kampf* and ask: Why has that not been implemented? Why are not the banks socialised yet? and

think that, in this way, they can impress us! . . . Those who
insinuate that the government wishes to rob people of their
interest and their rents, lie.[25]

The inconsistencies over foreign policy were even more glaring.
Kube, writing in the *Völkischer Beobachter*, outlined a plan for
German foreign policy under the new régime, a plan which
included not only the incorporation of Austria, German-speaking
Switzerland, Luxemburg, Danzig and Memel into Germany, but
also the right of German-speaking minorities in Eastern Europe
to recognition as members of a Greater Germany; Flanders was
to be separated from Belgium and should be given the right to
unite with Holland. Hitler had claimed that:

> Forty-eight hours after the taking of power by National
> Socialism the Treaty of Versailles lies in torn-up pieces at the
> feet of the French people.[26]

All this talk created anxiety abroad, and, in order to allay fears
outside Germany, Hitler's deputy, Rudolf Hess, was obliged to
clear away misunderstandings:

> In various quarters abroad propaganda directed against
> Germany has raised the false claim that the N.S.D.A.P. has
> as its aim the annexation of parts of Switzerland, Holland,
> Belgium, Denmark etc. However pointless the insinuation is,
> it is believed here and there. The Reich leadership therefore
> states categorically that no serious person in Germany has
> thought of even laying a finger on the independence of other
> states.

The word 'etc.', remarked Kraus, presumably included Austria
and Czechoslovakia.[27]

The same contradictions were to be found in statements by the
Nazis over the conditions that existed in the concentration camps.
These were explained to public opinion at home and abroad as
places not of torture, but merely of correction and training. Thus
the Nazi press pointed out that, even with the most hardened
Communists, patriotic feelings replaced Marxist ideology after
only a few weeks in a concentration camp; the camp routine of

early rising, bed-making, P.T. and hard manual work was likened to that of a sanatorium.[28] The Nazis denied that atrocities took place in the camps: had not Goering, Kraus pointed out, forbidden the vivisection of cattle because an animal could not just be treated as an object without feelings? Robert Ley, the Nazi Labour Minister, faced in Geneva with the charge that 'tens of thousands' of German workers were in prisons or concentration camps, refused, as he put it, to 'descend to the level' of his questioners, but added:

> You do not know Germany. I willingly invite the whole group to Germany at my own expense to inspect the concentration camps and build up a picture of Germany.[29]

But, on the other hand, the Prussian Minister of the Interior revealed that in the whole of Germany there were 18,000 people imprisoned by the régime, of whom 12,000 were in Prussia. Not to be outdone, the Minister of the Interior in Saxony claimed that his state contained twice as many prisoners as Prussia, although the latter was a much larger state.

As for the reports and denials of atrocities, Kraus preferred to trust the reports of the refugees who had seen the concentration camps for themselves:

> The camp was divided into different classes. The Communists and radical Socialists had things worst in the third class. The Jews were certainly fed by the Jewish authorities but had to perform the worst duties, clearing out the latrines, cleaning the boots of the S.A. men, kissing their feet and licking their boots if ordered. If they were reluctant the truncheon was used. . . . Many had nervous breakdowns, others were sick. Medical visits took place once a week. It was always: 'Next', 'Next', without listening to anyone. Someone near me said: 'Something is wrong with my lung, I am spitting blood': the answer was: 'Castor-oil'.[30]

Music and patriotic songs accompanied some of the most bestial atrocities. Alternatively the prisoners had to give recitations.

Kraus quoted the case of an Austrian seaman who, with a Jew, was forced to chant for half an hour:

The Jew: I—am—a—stink—ing—Jew!
The Austrian: And—I—wish—to—become—a—German![31]

There was the fate of a Munich lawyer who had inquired from the police about the arrest of one of his clients and was escorted through the streets of Munich, with trousers torn to shreds, and bearing the placard, 'I am a Jew, but I must not make complaints about the Nazis'. The man was then taken to a concentration camp where it was reported that he was shot while trying to escape. A photograph of this man's ignominy in the streets of Munich was published in French newspapers who entitled it 'Retour au moyen age'. Kraus likened it to the famous photograph of the corpse of Battisti that was circulated in Central Europe during the First World War.[32]

Occasionally, however, the truth was capable of revenging itself on the propagandists of the régime. In a radio programme from Stuttgart about conditions in the concentration camps, one of the journalists for the Press department of the Propaganda Ministry held what was publicised as a 'free conversation with prisoners'; and the programme was announced as being aimed 'as a refutation of lies that were being spread abroad'. Listeners were assured by the prisoners that they had nothing to complain of in the treatment which they received. Then followed the usual stereotyped questions and answers which could be expected from a programme held under such auspices. But, suddenly, one of the prisoners broke out with the words: 'No, my ears have not been cut off—but they have destroyed my being'. The programme was immediately broken off; an edited recording was broadcast on 8 April 1933.[33]

The lies and evasions of the Nazi régime were nowhere more apparent than in their dealing with the Jews. Hitler assured the Americans, 'We would give them a free ticket and 1,000 marks each for pocket money if we could get rid of them,' and Hitler hoped that in foreign countries 'the false talk about barbarism and terror would be silenced'.[34] As can be imagined, the Jewish population in Germany was subject to many conflicting pressures. Their situation was all the more senseless and tragic because of their attachment to the culture and civilisation that now rejected them. But if the majority of Jews who remained in Germany after 1933 still clung to the belief that the assimilationist position was still possible—if not in Germany, then in France, Britain or the United States—the appeal of Zionism became increasingly potent, especially to those who remained faithful to Judaism. After working with Franz Rosenzweig on a remarkable translation of the Old Testament into German in the 1920s, a translation that was a permanent addition to German literature, Martin Buber emerged in the years after 1933 as one of the major spiritual leaders of the Jews in Germany until his departure for Palestine in 1938.

On the other hand, a small minority of the German Jews, the 'Nationaldeutschen', attempted to ward off persecution by identifying themselves whole-heartedly with the régime. This group published a pamphlet entitled 'The propaganda about atrocities is lies!', a pamphlet which was described by the German Press Agency as 'the fulfilment of a natural feeling of honour, if with the Jews one can talk of honour'. The pamphlet illustrated the fundamental ambiguity of the position of the 'Nationaldeutschen'. They were concerned to refute some of the more lunatic of the claims of the antisemites by listing many of the scientific and medical (but not literary or philosophical) achievements of the Jews in Germany. On the other hand, there was the tragic plea for full Jewish assimilation into Germany:

> Although today we are treated by our fellow Germans of non-Jewish origin in a way that we must believe to be a grave injustice, this must not deter us from the one objective, and that objective is assimilation into Germany.[35]

Such atrocities against the Jews that had occured were:

> the exceptional actions of individuals who are found in any

people and in any organisation and who have used the opportunity to wreak personal feelings of vengeance against
Jewish people with whom they have had differences for a
whole variety of reasons. . . . At any rate we German Jews
. . . are convinced that on the part of the government and the
leadership of the N.S.D.A.P. there is an earnest determination to uphold law and order.[36]

There followed a plea to Jewish émigrés to cease attacking the
régime; otherwise the lot of the Jewish people would be far
worse. Einstein had not yet left for England but his opposition
to the Nazi régime was proving an embarrassment. As the
Jewish-owned *Neues Wiener Journal* pointed out, Einstein was
extremely unpopular:

The leaders of the German Jews would welcome it if he
moved his desk and his observatory to Jerusalem or some-
where in America, for science would not lose anything by this
change of location and Germany would only gain.[37]

The hopes for Jewish assimilation in Germany were illusory:
the only thing which the Nazis would allow Jews to share with
Germans was, Kraus said, a blood bath. Furthermore, maintained
the satirist, if the price of assimilation was the propaganda of the
'Nationaldeutschen', then it was too high: if their pamphlet was
a Jewish document, it was also a German communiqué which
so explained actions and atrocities that a mountain was made into
a mole-hill.[38] The foreign press might be assured by the Nazis
that less than twenty people had lost their lives as a result of the
revolution of 1933.[39] And the Nazis might pride themselves on
the compromise which they reached over the employment of
Jewish executives in the A.E.G. electrical combine (which had
been founded by the father of Walther Rathenau) by retaining
them to deal with foreign trade, which accounted for half of the
firm's output, while purging them from connection with the
domestic market.[40] But the Nazis, with their boycott of Jewish
shops and their placards against the Jews ('When Jewish blood
spurts from under the knife, things will be twice as good as

before.') were openly inciting their followers to violence. In the course of the same speech Goering both denied and accepted responsibility for this violence:

> I must defend myself against the charge now made by many people, that in my speech at Essen I gave the signal for the overthrow of discipline, the signal, indeed, for plunder and the like. But I am not such a coward that I repudiate what they did. I have, indeed, commended it. And if they made mistakes in the heat of the moment then we of the leadership bear the blame. For we have encouraged it. We will go further in our efforts to clean up, unmoved! . . . to extermi-
> nate. . . .[41]

As during the First World War Kraus was concerned in *Die Dritte Walpurgisnacht* to document the treason of the intellectuals in lending their prestige to the destruction of culture. Oswald Spengler had been the inspiration of many right-wing anti-democratic intellectuals during the Weimar Republic and had commented on the end of this régime 'nobody welcomes the national upheaval of these years more than I do'. He had been offered opportunities to lecture at Leipzig by the Nazis upon which Kraus commented that Spengler understood the *Untergangster* of the West and they understood him. [42]

But it was against another professed disciple of Nietzsche, Gottfried Benn, that Kraus was principally concerned. In 1933, Benn gave a series of broadcasts over Berlin radio defending the new régime against the attacks of foreign radicals like Romain Rolland. Benn refused to listen to the objections of the émigrés because they had not stayed in Germany to assess the realities of the German situation: the only people who could understand what had happened in Germany were those who had gone through the tensions of the previous months 'from hour to hour, from newspaper to newspaper, from one march to the next, from radio announcement to radio announcement'. Of course, remarked Kraus, Benn could not charge those people with cowardice who had remained in Germany and had been arrested in their beds by the Nazis. But Benn was more concerned to deal with the accusations of 'barbarism' which emanated from 'progressive' intellectuals outside Germany. They pictured events inside Germany as if culture and civilisation were being threatened by a wild horde; but, Benn asked, had the transition from the Romanesque to the Gothic style in the twelfth century been a subject for discussion, had there been debates on the relative merits of the rounded arch and the pointed arch? It seemed, said Kraus, that the Nazis had shed blood in order that architectual problems might be solved.

Indeed, far from dealing with the Nazi phenomenon in realistic terms, Benn concentrated exclusively on the prospect that, as a result of the events of 1933, there now might be evolved 'a new type of man'. This new biological type would combine the strength of primitive instincts with artistic achievement of a very high order; it was perhaps 'the last magnificent conception of the white race', a conception which had been heralded in Goethe's *An die Natur*. The most striking of Benn's imaginative flights was his analogy between this new type of man with the eternal spirit of the Quaternary age, as opposed to the last Ice Ages of mass democracy and the feuilleton. To Kraus, Benn's new epoch seemed more akin to the Ice Ages which he described so graphically than to the real Quaternary period itself. Under the pretext of prophesying the future, Benn was really advocating a return to Neandertal man; but, of course, with all the comforts of modern civilisation, including the radio. [43]

The disintegration of German culture was due not merely to the aberrations of individual writers such as Benn. There was the intellectual suicide of the German universities:

Johann Wolfgang von Goethe University, Frankfurt
Frankfurt, May 1933

The student Freikorps invites the whole professional body to the burning of Marxist and corrupt literature to take place on the Römerberg on Wednesday evening 10 May. In view of the great symbolic importance of this ceremony, the student body would welcome it if all the professors are seen there. I therefore invite colleagues to attend in large numbers.

March-off: from the university to the Römerberg on Wednesday evening at 8 o'clock, with music. The corporations will take part in uniform, as will the S.A. battalions.

Rector: Krieck.[44]

Ernst Krieck had enjoyed a meteoric rise under the auspices of the Nazis. From being a schoolteacher, he had been given a chair at Frankfurt after the accession of Hitler to power and was soon afterwards made Rector. A year later he took Rickert's chair at Heidelberg, from which position he wrote copiously on the aims of Nazi education in schools and universities. From the tone of his letter to his colleagues it could be inferred what amount of moral blackmail was going on within the German universities to secure uniformity. Jewish professors were dismissed and the students boycotted those teachers with marked anti-Nazi views. When prominent German academics such as the philosopher Martin Heidegger greeted the Nazi revolution Kraus was provoked to remark, 'I have always believed that a Bohemian cobbler came nearer to an understanding of the meaning of life than a new German thinker.'[45]

The crime of the new thinkers of Germany was compounded by their consistent invocation of the German cultural tradition in support of the revolution of 1933. Benn, for instance, after comparing Hitler to Napoleon had also put the Führer in the tradition of Goethe, Fichte and Hegel, Burckhardt and Nietzsche. But what, asked Kraus, had Goethe said about the Germans?

A comparison between the Germans and other peoples arouses painful feelings in us, which I seek to avoid in every way. Is the Volk really awakened?[46]

As for the so-called affinity between Hitler and Nietzsche, the Nazis did not represent the Superman, the advent of whom Nietzsche had prophesied, but the triumph of that very hard morality which he had despised. It was Nietzsche who had satirised the failings of the Germans and had admired the Jews.

He in his own day had felt the danger to European civilisation and to Germany's own cultural inheritance which was represented by the subordination of German idealism to the quest for military and political power. The culmination of this process was documented by Kraus in *Die Dritte Walpurgisnacht*. Well might Benn in his radio broadcasts address himself to the émigrés who had left Germany:

> It is the nation to which you belong by nationality, the nation whose language you speak, whose schools you attended . . . whose industry printed your books, whose theatre put on your plays . . . the nation that even now would have not have done much to you, if you had stayed here.[47]

But was it true, asked Kraus, that the émigrés spoke the same language as the Nazis? It was to be hoped that the émigrés had nothing in common with a people who could invent such slogans as:

> Germans, read Aryan newspapers only!
> Do not forget that you are a German!
> Germany awake!
> Perish Judah!

or the cry heard during one of the bonfires of banned books:

> Down with the disfigurement of the German language!
> Protect the most precious possession of our people.[48]

The picture which Kraus presents of the Third Reich in *Die Dritte Walpurgisnacht* is certainly open to some criticism. The events that he was documenting belonged to that particular period of confusion immediately after the accession of Hitler to power, a period in which rival groups within the Nazi movement fought for ultimate control and in which the process of *Gleichschaltung* was far from complete. As for the satirist's comments on the intellectuals it must be remembered that many of the artists and writers who greeted the advent of Hitler in 1933 were soon to be disillusioned. The conductor Wilhelm Furtwängler, for example, after becoming vice-president of the music section of Goebbels's Reichskulturkammer soon quarrelled with the Propaganda Minister over the proscription of Jewish conductors and the persecution of avant-garde composers such as Hindemith. Although Furtwängler made an uneasy reconcilliation with the régime, he resigned from his office in the Reichskulturkammer in 1934; in order to continue with his music, however, he was compelled to remain a member of that organisation. The composer Richard Strauss had become president of the music section for several reasons: one was his constant and obsessive concern that no hindrances should ever be put in the way of his creative work; another, less selfish, reason was his desire to protect his daughter-in-law who was of Jewish extraction. After Strauss's refusal to delete references in his work to two of his librettists, Hofmannsthal and Stefan Zweig (both of whom had Jewish blood in their veins) the enthusiasm of the Nazis for his co-operation diminished considerably.

As for the writers whom Kraus had attacked, it must be remembered that Spengler's attitude to the Nazis, outlined in his book *Hour of Decision* published in 1933, contained many reservations; and indeed he had completely broken with the Nazis by the time of his death in 1936.[49] Despite the glee which Gottfried Benn derived from the downfall of liberalism and democracy in Germany, he was never a member of the Nazi party and his type of intensely nihilistic aestheticism was soon condemned by the régime as degenerate: in 1937 Benn was forbidden to publish his work and fled from party persecution by re-entering the Army Medical Corps (in which he had served during the First World War), describing his action as 'the aristocratic form of emigration'.[50]

The mirror of satire is a distorting mirror. Kraus was not a historian and the full significance of his writings on Nazism does not lie in the realm of historical analysis. Since 1945 a variety of scholars have been able to investigate in a more systematic manner than Kraus the political implications of the Nazi prostitution of language.[51] The whole world has had time to digest the significance of the vocabulary of *The Final Solution*.

And yet if the Nazis were essentially beyond the reach of satire and even of polemic, at least the literalness of Kraus's approach was successful in laying bare the literalness of the movement that he was attacking. Constantly he had proclaimed that language would revenge itself on those who perverted it. The advent of the Nazis to power was both the fulfilment of a process which the satirist had foreseen during the First World War and a revenge on the invocations to violence which had been uttered by the politicians and intellectuals during that war. Stripped of all the lies and evasions of the Propaganda Ministry, the threats of Hitler and Goering, unlike those of the statesmen of 1914–18, must be taken literally. As a Nazi state president had proclaimed in 1933:

> We do not say: an eye for an eye, and a tooth for a tooth. No, whoever knocks out one of our eyes will have his head knocked off, and whoever knocks out a tooth, will have his jaw broken. [52]

Allied with this literalness was the apocalypticism of the Nazis. At last Kraus's own sense of the apocalyptic could reveal in full the diabolic implications of political phraseology. Had not Goebbels himself announced the world significance of the events of 1933?

> What we do today will be a measure for the whole world in ten years' time. What we do today will be decisive for the whole of Europe. [53]

In the twelve years that followed the accession of Hitler to power in Germany things were to happen that surpassed the most pessimistic insights of the satirist: the building of the concentration camp at Buchenwald around Goethe's beech tree, and the processions that took place into the extermination chambers of Auschwitz while elsewhere in the camp the orchestra played selections from Viennese light music—all this only becomes a little more explicable after reading the work of Kraus. Even in 1933, however, the extremism and utter lack of compromise of the satirist was able to reveal the extremism and limitless dynamism

Death mask of Karl Kraus

Swastikas cover the Burgtheater as Hitler drives towards the Rathaus, Vienna, 1938

of the movement which had seized power in Germany. Gottfried
Feder had written in the *Völkischer Beobachter*:

> Unlike other parties we refuse to modify our programme for
> reasons of expediency in the light of circumstances. We will
> modify circumstances to fit our programme by gaining control
> of the circumstances.[54]

Although Feder, the economic theorist of the party, was to be
cruelly disabused of his belief in the determination of Hitler to
implement many points of the original Nazi programme which
Feder had helped to draft, on matters of foreign policy and the
destruction of the Jewish threat the promises of *Mein Kampf*
were to be more than fulfilled. Although the Nazi movement
was far from monolithic, although even Himmler was driven to
disobey Hitler in the closing years of the war, many of the
quotations which Kraus reproduced in *Die Dritte Walpurgisnacht* already have the ring of Hitler's utterances from the
bunker in 1945.

Still, it was difficult, if not impossible for contemporaries to
appreciate the full significance of what had occurred in Germany
in 1933. Kraus himself experienced this acutely. The satirist
became aware, as he had never been aware before, that the
position which he had for so long occupied in Vienna was a
privileged one. As his enemies had pointed out over the years,
there was an enormous gulf between the revelation of brutality
in a newspaper and the reality of that brutality. Although during
the First World War Kraus had so bitterly criticised those journalists who had written despatches without ever having visited the
front, he himself had never visited the trenches. While Kraus,
like Sigmund Freud, might continually inveigh against the
crimes and follies of Viennese society, he was far more deeply
rooted in that city than he was ever prepared to admit. Although
he was able as no other writer to reveal the decadence and
disintegration of Austrian civilisation, the freedom that he
enjoyed to do so was also a feature of the society in which he
lived.

The clearer Kraus *did* see the tendencies of his epoch, the more he was alienated from it. The events in Germany in 1933 hastened the satirist's realignment with the forces of conservatism in Austria, a development which had already been apparent in the attacks which Kraus had made on the Austrian Social Democrats in the previous year. Nothing pained him more than the fact that the conservative forces inside Germany were the prisoners of Hitler. German newspapers reported that princes vied with each other to become the adjutants of the Nazi élite: Goebbels had a Schaumburg-Lippe and Goering a Prince of Hesse. As far as Hindenburg's relationship with Hitler was concerned, Kraus remarked that the marshal's baton had abdicated in favour of the kit-bag. The aged German President was reported by the *Nord-deutsche Allgemeine Zeitung* as saying of Hitler:

> Working with the new Reichschancellor gives me greater pleasure every day. The relationship between myself and Hitler is as delightful as that between grand-father and grandson. I am touched by the thoughtfulness which he displays to an old man like me. He is always anxious to help me, whether in sitting down or standing up. . . .[55]

The satirist could only compare Hindenburg to Duncan and Hitler to Macbeth:

> What need we to fear it who knows it, when none can call our power to account? Yet who would have thought the old man to have so much blood in him.[56]

2. *Austria 1933–36—The Beginning of the End.*

As has been pointed out earlier Dollfuss became Chancellor of Austria in May 1932 heading a government coalition with a majority of only one vote over an opposition of Social Democrats and Pan-Germans. Faced with the refusal of the Pan-Germans to support a government bloc which they held responsible for the mismanagement of the abortive customs union with Germany, a move which had produced a further ban on Anschluss from the

French, Dollfuss was forced into increasing dependence on the votes of the Heimwehr if his government was to survive. He was faced, too, with the monumental economic crisis following the failure of the Credit Anstalt and with the fact that in the local elections of April 1932, a month before he assumed office, there had been a marked upsurge of Nazi strength and a decline in the representation, not only of the Pan-Germans but also of his own Christian Socialists; the Social Democrats could now claim to be the most powerful political force in Austria.

The accession of the Nazis to power in Germany, therefore, only brought to a head the mounting political crisis in Austria. Terrified of the growth in Nazi strength now backed up by the power of Germany, Dollfuss was also faced by a desperate struggle to maintain his slender majority within the Austrian parliament where the deadlock finally resulted in the absurd suspension of parliament at its own hands on 4 March 1933.[57] Partly in response to this situation and partly from his own predilection for the idea of the corporative state, Dollfuss was led to attempt to do away with the party system inside Austria and launch instead the non-party Fatherland Front, or what his opponents of the Left called his experiment in Austro-Fascism. It has already been seen that attempts by Dollfuss to gain support among the moderate Social Democrats to meet the threat to Austrian independence from Germany were rendered futile both by the pressure of Mussolini and by the growing influence within his own ranks of the Heimwehr (led in particular by the minister of security, Major Fey, an embittered and intensely ambitious personality who was Starhemberg's chief rival within the movement). The Heimwehr attempted to gain control of the last centres of Social Democrat power in the provincial governments. Faced with this situation, a radical minority within the Social Democratic party and in the Schutzbund initiated a defensive action which pushed the party leadership into the desperate general strike of 12 February 1934. This was largely ineffective, but civil war broke out. The workers' flats of Vienna were shelled by elements of the Austrian army. The majority of Social Democrats and a significant number of the Schutzbund itself remained passive spectators of the destruction of their party.

As far as the Austrian Nazis were concerned, already in the summer of 1932 there had been disturbances instigated by them in which violence and threats of violence were employed. It was not however until after the advent of the Nazis to power in Germany and the self-extinction of the Austrian parliament in March 1933 that the Nazis committed themselves to a policy of systematic terrorism. A nation-wide offensive was accordingly launched, culminating between 12 and 19 June in a week of dynamite and hand-grenade outrages which led to a number of deaths. Dollfuss now banned the Austrian Nazi party and large numbers of their supporters fled across the border into Germany where Theo Habicht, a German citizen and Reichstag deputy whom Hitler had already officially appointed as Nazi 'Inspector General of Austria', formed the so-called 'Austrian Legion' with an estimated strength of nearly 15,000 men. Provocations from the Austrian Nazis in Germany and from the Nazi underground in Austria led to the abortive Nazi putsch of 25 July 1934 which resulted in the assassination of Dollfuss. The precise nature of Hitler's foreknowledge of the putsch is still not clear: it seems that he was misled by the Austrian Nazis into an exaggerated estimation of their strength and countenanced an action of which he did not know the full details.[58]

Although *Die Dritte Walpurgisnacht* was not published in the lifetime of Kraus, large sections which dealt with the Austrian situation did appear in the issue of the *Fackel* at the end of July 1934 (just before the assassination of Dollfuss) which was entitled 'Why the *Fackel* does not appear'. In this issue Kraus was concerned to point out the lies of the Nazis in their dealings with Austria. Thus the Bavarian government explained on behalf of itself and the leadership of the S.A. in Bavaria (which had been involved in numerous border incidents) that 'nobody in Bavaria thinks of involving themselves in Austrian internal affairs'.[59] Instead, the blame for the border incidents was put on the Austrian government, which was disturbing the international situation;

Habicht even threatened the Austrian government that Germany would have to bring the problem of Austrian provocation before the League of Nations.[60] Great play was made of the repressive policies of the Austrian government towards the Social Democrats and the Nazis. A film was made for release throughout Germany of 'shocking pictures of the distress of an enslaved people'.[61] The *Völkischer Beobachter* threatened that, when the revolution came, Austrian leaders would experience a frightful awakening to the fact that they could not repress a people and go unpunished.[62] Various excuses were put forward by the German press for the systematic policy of bomb-throwing in the summer of 1933. On the one hand everything was blamed on the Communists as 'irresponsible elements' and the Nazis disclaimed all responsibility:

> As long as the police does not publish the names of those it has arrested, it is impossible to prevent remarks and rumours.

On other occasions, however, the Nazis admitted responsibility for the bomb attacks, but it was explained that these had been directed at Jewish businessmen and had not been meant to harm Aryan customers and innocent Aryan passers-by.[63]

Just as in his analysis of the Nazi régime inside Germany, it was upon the self-revelatory and self-contradictory nature of its propaganda which Kraus concentrated. The German government protested at the arrest of harmless German 'tourists' in Austria but, as Kraus pointed out, they had been tourists who were plotting murder and violence; in any case genuine German tourists had been prevented from coming to Austria by the 1,000 mark tax on tourism which the Nazi régime had imposed in their offensive against the Austrian economy. And what about those Austrian tourists who had been interned in German concentration camps for alleged anti-Nazi activities? As for the pathos and the emotional blackmail which was continually employed by the Nazis concerning the special place which Austria and the Danube held in German hearts, Kraus could only applaud the words of Dr. Skubl, the Vice-President of police for

Vienna, who told the Nazi minister Hans Frank, on the latter's arrival at Aspern airfield in May 1933, that his visit was 'unwelcome'. In the satirist's view this deed was the best that had been done since the founding of the republic.[64] The visit of Frank to Austria, although ostensibly designated as 'private', had provoked everywhere he went noisy demonstrations from Nazi sympathisers. After Frank had taken the opportunity at a meeting of the Styrian Nazis publicly to appeal for increased resistance to the government in Vienna, he was politely escorted out of Austria. It was a fortnight after this deportation that Hitler launched his 1,000 mark blockade against the Austrian tourist trade; and, a fortnight after that, there commenced the series of bomb outrages which compelled Dollfuss to ban the Nazi party in Austria altogether.

The Austrian Chancellor was forced, however, to temper his firmness with prudence. The Viennese press was subjected to considerable pressure from the Austrian government to modify its coverage of the situation inside Germany in order that Hitler should be given no excuse for his campaign against Austrian 'provocation'. The *Neue Freie Presse* was particularly vulnerable to such pressure since in 1931 the Austrian government had bought a 50 per cent share in the newspaper from the Benedikt family.[65] Thus when in Germany in 1933 numerous atrocities were being committed by Roehm's S.A., the newspaper reported them, not as political crimes, but as ordinary civil murders, with no mention of who was responsible. The *Neue Freie Presse* also went in for the falsification of reports from the foreign press. When, for example, *The Times* wrote:

> In Great Britain public opinion has never been strongly in favour of the possible union of the Austrian and German peoples,

this was reproduced in Vienna in quite another sense:

> There has never been in England a strong feeling against the possible union of Germany and Austria.[66]

On 31 March 1933, the day before the boycott of Jewish shops in Germany, the newspaper ended an editorial: 'The propaganda about atrocities will be destroyed by the power of the truth'. On 2 April, the day after the boycott, the *Neue Freie Presse* admitted that it had received so many letters and telegrams that it could not publish them: it did, however, find room to reassure the public that business, including public business, had not been disturbed by the revolution that had taken place in Germany. A further touch of the grotesque was provided by a sentence which appeared in brackets below its columns:

(This information is entirely derived from the time before the imposition of the boycott.)[67]

There were further reasons, quite independent of the influence of the Austrian government, which were responsible for the circumspection of the *Neue Freie Presse* in commenting on the news from Germany. For a start the newspaper faced the same dilemma as that which confronted the Jews within the Third Reich. Should it broadcast the truth about the anti-semitic outrages, or should it suppress such news in the hope that somehow this pogrom would spend itself as earlier persecution had spent itself in the past? Felix Salten, author of (among many other things) the children's book *Bambi*, was one of the first to experience this particular difficulty. Salten, a leading feuilletoniste of the *Neue Freie Presse* and long the object of Kraus's attack, announced at the P.E.N. Club international meeting in Ragusa in 1933 that he had just returned from Germany, adding: 'I am a Jew and I was never questioned in Germany.' He ended his statement by appealing for caution before condemning the policies of the German government: 'Furthermore: without hatred. Above all, without hatred!'[68]

In any case the newspaper for which Salten worked was anxious that it should not be banned in Germany and lose still more of the circulation which it had lost since 1918: it was significant that in 1933 the *Neue Freie Presse* had to deny that it printed a separate Berlin edition which completely suppressed any news contrary to that permitted by the Nazis. The result of publishing one edition was that Austria suffered from the same sort of news censorship as Germany; it was all part of the kind of paralysis which Kraus felt to be afflicting Austria. As it was, the *Neue Freie Presse*, like other Viennese newspapers, was soon banned from Germany as the anti-Austrian campaign of the German government got under way. The ban was not lifted until the Hitler-Schuschnigg agreement of July 1936, in return for which the Viennese press had once again to moderate its tone on events in Germany. The catastrophic decline of the influence of the *Neue Freie Presse* since the proud days of Moritz Benedikt was symbolic of the situation of Austria after the collapse of the Empire.

It has been seen that, after the *Fackel* for October 1933, in which Kraus published his famous poem about his silence over events in Germany, no further issues of the magazine appeared until July 1934 when two issues appeared in the same month. During this time the satirist was under heavy attack from Czechoslovakia where exiles had gathered from Nazi Germany and from Austria after the crushing by Dollfuss of the riots of February 1934. It was in the first *Fackel* of July 1935 that Kraus printed, without comment, the attacks which had been made on him.

They varied in tone. From the unofficial Social Democrat *Aufruf* published in Prague on 1 November 1933 there was the pathetic appeal: 'Karl Kraus, do not leave us in the lurch'. The Communist *Gegenangriff* printed a more hostile article on 26 November, which ended: 'Karl Kraus is finished'. When several readers protested against this description and enumerated the services which the satirist had in the past rendered to the radical cause by his attack on bourgeois values, the newspaper sourly replied:

No, Kraus has not led many young men to our cause. He has taken away from the revolutionary movement those who were already dissatisfied with it. By his masterly satire and calls for repentance he has made the bourgeois intellectual world palatable again to rebels. And now he is silent again because 'his world has fallen to pieces'. As a consolation, he ought to make a belated study of Marx. And above all find the words to speak again.[69]

Not until the second issue of the *Fackel* of July 1914 did Kraus answer the charges of his enemies. 'Why the *Fackel* does not appear' was the last long and sustained polemic which the satirist completed before his death: it consists of a general résumé of his own attitude towards events in Germany and then of an attack on Austrian Social Democrats for not supporting Dollfuss.

It was the failure of the Left to distinguish between the Nazi régime in Germany and the Fatherland Front in Austria which aroused his sharpest comment. The Social Democrats claimed that Dollfuss was seeking the support of the Austrian Nazis when in fact he was trying to crush them and was sending many to concentration camps. These concentration camps were then equated by the Social Democrats with the concentration camps of Hitler; Wöllersdorf was put on the same level as Dachau. But they would not have things both ways, claimed Kraus. How absurd it was of Otto Bauer to proclaim that the policy of the Social Democrats should be that of fighting a war on two fronts, against brown as well as black fascism! The *Gegenangriff* from Prague suggested in 1934 that Dollfuss was worse than Hitler. Commenting on the decree of the Austrian government that workers who engaged in subversive activities should be dismissed, the newspaper pointed out that Dollfuss and his wife (whose charitable activities were frequently publicised) professed to be devout Catholics but were condemning workers to hunger; 'compared to him, Hitler almost looks like a man of culture'. Kraus pointed out that in Germany rebellious workers did not die of hunger; there were other methods of dealing with them. At a time of the most appalling danger for mankind, the Austrian Left could speak of fighting simultaneously the two fascisms of Austria and Germany—from Czechoslovakia of all places! This was frivolity and irresponsibility of classic Viennese proportions.[70]

Equally superficial to the satirist was the Marxist analysis of events in Germany and Austria which had given rise to Fascism. What had happened in 1933, the Social Democrats argued, was merely the result of international capitalism being shaken to its foundations.[71] The first battle might have been won by the Fascists but the dialectic of history revealed that the campaign would be won by the progressive forces. It was claimed that Bismarck had not been able to smash the workers by his proscription of the German Social Democratic party which had, indeed, emerged stronger after its ordeal: where Bismarck had failed, Adolf Hitler would not now succeed. Seitz, the Bürgermeister of Vienna, appealed in 1933 to the memory of 1848 when Vienna had held out against 'the forces of united reaction'.[72] After the failure of the 1934 riots Bauer from Brünn still maintained that the events of February had been only a temporary set-back; that fascism in Germany and Austria would inevitably lead to a war which, however ruinous, would result in victory for the workers' cause. It was in the period from 1934 onwards that, to Kraus's great dismay, Social Democrats throughout Europe began to look increasingly towards some form of co-operation with the Communists against the challenge of Fascism. Towards defectors from the ranks of the forces of socialism, the Social Democrats threatened in 1933 that punishment would follow 'in the not too distant future'.[73]

Throughout his life the satirist had been critical of the empty phraseology and the empty optimism of the Social Democrats. Both had now reached their apogee. In his view it was an insult to their German comrades suffering under the Third Reich glibly to compare the evils of Dollfuss with the evils of Hitler. How dare they attack the Austrian régime when a German Social Democrat émigré had congratulated them in 1933 on their good fortune in not being subjects of the Third Reich.[74] Faced with the consolidation of Dollfuss's authoritarian régime, the Social Democrats could only talk and write ceaselessly without actually doing anything. The contradictions which had plagued the party since the Linz Congress of 1926 now came to a head. On the one hand the party had since 1927 been pursuing a policy of greater flexibility which was directed at entering into the responsibilities of power even if the price for this was coalition with non-Socialist groups; on the other hand the Social Democrat programme still contained an element of revolutionary Marxism in the idea that the party might conceivably have to resort to violence if counter-revolution was threatened.

It appeared to the radicals in the party that the repressive policies of the Dollfuss régime exactly fulfilled this last condition. But both Renner and Bauer were extremely reluctant to draw the logical consequences from the Linz programme. The Social Democrats saw Dollfuss implement all those counter-revolutionary policies which had been laid down in the programme as a justification for retaliatory action; and yet the party as a whole did nothing to give effect to their threats of the use of force. Thus while in 1933 the *Arbeiter Zeitung* was equating brown with black fascism and Bauer was in public denouncing any compromise, secret negotiations had been initiated with the Dollfuss government. When violence did occur in February 1934 this was not the responsibility of the party itself but only of a small radical minority within it: and the party leadership, including Otto Bauer who rightly viewed with pessimism the outcome of an armed struggle between the Schutzbund and the Austrian army, did the best they could to limit the struggle. In his public apologia after these events, an apologia that was issued from Brünn in Czeschoslovakia, Bauer indeed regretted that the riots had not occurred earlier because they would then have had a greater chance of success. Why then, asked Kraus, had the party leadership not ordered action against the Austrian régime at an early date?

The truth was, and the satirist underlined this with heavy sarcasm, that the Austrian Social Democrats indulged in phraseology to conceal an inner fear of action and the exercise of will-power, a fatalistic acceptance that things would get worse before they got better. What had been their answer to the Nazi bomb outrages in 1933? Only slogans:

> There is a much more effective weapon against political acts of terror. Genuinely strong and creative democracy—that alone is an effective weapon against political terror.[75]

Did they really believe, Kraus had asked, that the Nazis threw bombs because there was no longer a parliament in Austria? It was the lack of dynamism in the German Social Democrat party which had rendered them impotent before Hitler: they were made, declared the satirist, not of blood but of paper resolutions. The same was true of the Austrian party which was weighed down with an antiquated ideology. Where the Social Democrats offered only phraseology, the Nazis offered romanticism; the latter offered madness, the former only emptiness.[76] The logic of the Social Democrat opposition to Dollfuss was pushing them into the arms of the Nazis who were asking for nothing else than the destruction of Austria and its union with Nazi Germany. The Social Democrats might try to disguise this fact by issuing in 1933 a 'declaration of neutrality' in the fight between Dollfuss and the Nazis: but especially after 1934 they could not disguise the fact that the impotence of the party was driving significant elements of its membership (particularly within the Schutzbund) over into the Communist camp; even the Nazis gained a number of disillusioned individuals after the disintegration of the Austrian Left in 1934.

Kraus realised, of course, that the Austrian Social Democrats had been put into an extremely difficult position by the simultaneous advent to power of Hitler in Germany and the emergence of the authoritarian régime of Dollfuss in Austria. He was also aware that a great deal of the hesitation which characterised party policy was due to the fact that neither the moderates nor the radicals could gain clear control and that in the desperate circumstances of 1933 and 1934 the unity of the party was now increasingly felt to be of more importance than the laying down of a coherent policy. As has been pointed out previously the

Austrian party had been well aware that one of the major weaknesses of the German party had been the split within the socialist movement in 1920 and the emergence in Germany of the largest Communist party outside the Soviet Union, a party which played an important rôle in bringing the Weimar republic to an end. The Austrian Social Democrats were determined to keep the Communist party in Austria as small as possible by including within their ranks many of the extreme radicals. Yet another lesson which the Austrian Left had derived from the German experience was a determination not to go under to Fascism without some form of resistance.

That the spectacle of Bauer's dilemma was material for tragedy as well as satire, Kraus was well aware. He wanted, he explained, so many of the things which the Social Democrats themselves wanted, but he believed that they would be better secured by supporting Dollfuss against the greater evil which threatened from Germany: all he could think of was, 'Anything, only not Hitler.'[77] During the fighting of February 1934 the satirist impressed his friends by his ability both to remain calm in this appalling situation and to display terrible grief at the suffering of harmless individuals, whether they were Social Democrats or supporters of Dollfuss. When a friend burst into his room in great agitation and cried: 'They are firing on women and children,' Kraus soothed him down and explained that nervous agitation would not solve anything: 'The first duty of a revolutionary is to keep calm.' He then left for the fighting area and helped in the evacuation of the wounded.[78]

And yet, understandably, the bitterness against Kraus for his attitude towards Dollfuss and the downfall of the party in 1934 has rankled ever since within Social Democratic circles: no enemy is more wholeheartedly hated than he who was formerly a friend. The followers of Otto Bauer have pointed out with considerable justification that the main burden of guilt for the civil war in 1934 must lie with Dollfuss who not only failed to conclude a compromise agreement with the Social Democrats but also made preparations for the elimination of the Social Democratic party as an independent political force. Other observers without any particular sympathy for Otto Bauer's leadership have also maintained that Dollfuss was guilty of several blunders in 1933 and 1934. Although admittedly under heavy pressure from Mussolini and the Heimwehr to destroy the Austrian Left, Dollfuss certainly had an exaggerated view of the strength of the Heimwehr whose effectiveness declined markedly after their failure in the elections of 1930 and after the emergence of the Nazis on the Austrian scene. This was shown very clearly in 1935 and 1936 when Schuschnigg was able to remove Fey and Starhemberg from his government without any great difficulty. Perhaps the greatest mistake which Dollfuss made, however, was his calculation that he could avoid a violent showdown with the Left by detaching the supporters of Renner from the Social Democrats and thus isolating the group around Bauer. Given the traditions of the Austrian Social Democrats, this assessment of the situation was somewhat naïve.

Kraus undoubtedly formed a sentimentalised picture of Dollfuss. The plain and unvarnished speech of the Austrian Chancellor seemed such a welcome relief after all the verbiage of the Social Democrats. The deeply religious, almost mystical, element in Dollfuss's character also recommended itself to the satirist who took pleasure in collecting photographs of the diminutive and unpretentious Chancellor in conversation with the resplendent princes of the Church. But there were other, less attractive, traits in this brief and ill-starred ruler of Austria. Dollfuss was possessed of a ruthless political instinct: if he was not concerned with the trappings of power, he was remorseless in pursuit of the reality. So weak was the position of Austria and so dependent was she on the goodwill of Mussolini that there was perhaps no policy which she could have adopted to avoid ultimate absorption by Nazi Germany. It was, however, the unintended but inevitable result of the policies pursued by Dollfuss that the Austrian people were to be deeply divided amongst themselves after 1934 and that the task of Hitler in gaining control of Austria was to be made much easier than it might otherwise have been.

The tragedy of the last years of the Austrian republic stemmed not from a dearth but an abundance of talent that could not accommodate itself to the crippling restrictions imposed upon the gifted individual by the collapse of the Empire in 1918. It has rightly been pointed out that both Dollfuss and Otto Bauer overestimated the possibilities which were offered to them: that Bauer still lived spiritually in the Habsburg Empire of before the First World War in which decisions taken in Vienna had repercussions all over the cosmopolitan world of international socialism; that Dollfuss, like Seipel, believed that Austria could give an example to Germany just as she had in the days of Metternich. Instead of a drab compromise between the Social Democrats and Christian Socialists for which Karl Renner and the Catholic labour leader Leopold Kunschak hoped, Bauer dreamt of a Socialist Austria that would be an inspiration to those dissatisfied with the brutality of the Bolsheviks and the reformism of the parties of Western Europe, while Dollfuss strove for a Catholic Austria that would regenerate Christendom. Kraus himself succumbed to this most Viennese of delusions. In 1933 and 1934 he praised Dollfuss for doing exactly what he had criticised Seipel for doing several years earlier—exaggerating the possibilities open to Austria.

To this dream there was a cruel awakening. On 25 July 1934 a group of Austrian Nazis penetrated into the Chancellery and Dollfuss was murdered in the building from which Metternich had decided the destiny of Europe. For some time it seemed that things were in the balance and that the attempted Nazi putsch might succeed. During this period of suspense the attitude of Major Fey was extremely ambiguous: even if, as now seems likely, he had no foreknowledge of the putsch, it is certainly clear that the Nazis had infiltrated into the police force to the extent that out of 8,000 policemen in Vienna it was estimated that 3,000 were Nazi sympathisers.[79] One of the most ambitious of Austrian politicians, Anton Rintelen, whom Kraus had attacked for his connections with Bekessy in the 1920's, was deeply implicated in the affair; and for a time the main radio transmitter in Vienna was under rebel control, broadcasting news of the 'resignation' of Dollfuss and the appointment of Rintelen as his successor. It was not until the Austrian army took the initiative that, after hours of delay, the putsch fizzled out.

At 6 o'clock in the evening on the day of the putsch, Kraus telephoned to one of his friends, Helene Kann, and asked her to come round to his flat. Already in 1934 he was feeling unwell and the heart ailment which was finally to kill him was showing its first symptoms. When she arrived at his flat, the satirist lay ill in bed and was listening on his phone to the news bulletins and music on the radio in the offices of the *Fackel*—Kraus had no radio of his own. At 7.30 Major Fey broadcast the news of Doll-fuss's death and immediately there followed a speech by the new Chancellor, Schuschnigg. Kraus remained quiet and seemed depressed; when his friends had told him earlier of the news of the assassination he had refused to pay attention to what he regarded as an unfounded rumour. A few hours later, Helene Kann met the satirist in the foyer of the Hotel Imperial and they sat there together through the warm summer night until the morning papers came out at 3 a.m. Kraus did not want to go home but remained silent, sunk in thought. The next day, on his instructions, Frau Kann sent a wreath to the Rathaus where the body of Dollfuss was lying.[80] On his next visit to Sidonie Nadherny in Czechoslovakia after the assassination, the satirist could not speak, but tears streamed down his face as he got out of the car.[81]

Kraus's public comment on the assassination came in a recital of readings from Shakespeare which was given in November 1934. The dark imagery of 'Macbeth', especially the scene in which the ghost of the murdered Banquo haunts the feast of his murderer, made a profound impression on the audience present on this occasion. In the speech of Ross on the situation of Scotland after Macbeth's seizure of power, there seemed to be a foreshadowing of the fate of Austria and of Europe:

Alas! poor country;
Almost afraid to know itself. It cannot
Be call'd our mother, but our grave; where nothing,
But who knows nothing, is once seen to smile;
Where sighs and groans and shrieks that rent the air
Are made, not mark'd; where violent sorrow seems
A modern ecstasy; the dead man's knell
Is there scarce ask'd for who; and good men's lives
Expire before the flowers in their caps,
Dying or ere they sicken.[82]

After the failure of the 1934 putsch, Hitler ordered a major
change of policy. Habicht, who was held responsible for the
failure of the rising, was removed and Hitler inaugurated his new
policy of taking Austria by sap rather than by storm by sending
Von Papen to Vienna as ambassador. It was a shrewd appointment which paved the way for the Austro-German agreement of
July 1936. Von Papen's arrival did not mean, however, that the
Nazi pressure on Austria had been relinquished. If the campaign
of bomb outrages was dropped, the 1,000 mark ban on German
tourists was maintained and a major propaganda offensive was
launched against Vienna. There the Nazi grip on the University
grew tighter. Goering promised prominent opera singers and
musicians twice the salary which they received in Austria if they
would come to Berlin; the departure for Berlin in 1934 of
Clemens Krauss, conductor of the Vienna State Opera, had
already been hailed as a major victory for Germany. Every
opportunity was taken by the illegal Nazi party within Austria
to show its strength. Thus, for instance, at a performance of
Rossini's *William Tell* in the Volksoper in 1935, Tell appeared
with white leggings (the unofficial emblem of the Vienna Nazis)
and at the words 'We wish to be a united people of brothers',
special emphasis was given to the word 'united' which received
loud applause.[83]

Schuschnigg, a more sensitive and less ruthless politician than
Dollfuss, was pushed into a quest for some sort of agreement with

Hitler not merely by the increasing strength of the Austrian Nazis but also by the growing evidence that Mussolini, who at the time of the assassination of Dollfuss had mobilised Italian divisions at the Brenner to show the Germans that he was prepared to defend Austria against external agression, was now preparing a complete reversal of policy. Hitler was indeed concerned to woo Mussolini away from his alignment with France and Britain against Germany, an alignment which had been made clear at the time of the Stresa Conference in 1935. The Italian dictator's invasion of Abyssinia in October of that year was Hitler's opportunity. The refusal of British public opinion to accept the agreement which had been reached between the British Foreign Secretary, Sir Samuel Hoare, and the French Prime Minister and Foreign Minister, Pierre Laval, to allow Mussolini a sphere of influence within Abyssinia had the effect of pushing Italy into an alliance with Germany, thus sealing the fate of the Austrian republic.

Sigismund von Radecki, a friend of Kraus, has recalled that during his last visit to see the satirist just before the latter's death, he was warned not to speak of England during his conversation because of Kraus's anger at English policy in repudiating the Hoare–Laval agreement.[84] The satirist was also concerned that Czechoslovakia stood in as great a danger from Germany as did Austria: his file of newspaper cuttings and comments for the year 1935 shows that he was worried that the Czech press seemed more preoccupied with Greta Garbo's visit to Prague than with the government campaign to step up the production of gasmasks and the construction of air-raid shelters.[85] Ever since the 'private visit' that Hans Frank had paid to Vienna in May 1933, Kraus had kept a wary eye on the career of the Nazi party lawyer and now Reich Minister Without Portfolio. After a visit which Frank had paid to Prague in 1935 to stimulate the nationalist ardour of the Bohemian Germans, the satirist protested at the laudatory treatment which the visit had received from sections of the German language press, pointing out in great detail that Frank was a disgrace to the legal profession.[86]

As it was, relations between Austria and Czechoslovakia did improve after 1933 as both governments became aware of their common interest in withstanding the expansionist pressure of Nazi Germany. Relations between the two countries could have been even better if there had not been increasing talk of a Habsburg restoration within Austria: that sense of identity which Austria had lost in 1918 and had not rediscovered in the republic of the 1920s or in the corporative state theories of Dollfuss was now to be found, it was hoped, in a return of the dynasty. Kraus himself felt the strength of this argument. Already in *Die Dritte Walpurgisnacht* the satirist had reminded the Austrian Social Democrats that their German comrades would have welcomed a return of the Hohenzollerns if they could have protected them against Hitler: he believed that in the last analysis they would support even the Habsburgs in Austria if that would save them from Nazi concentration camps. Shortly after the February riots of 1934, Kraus went further. On a visit to Prague he had long conversations with friends, among them Jan Münzer, editor of the newspaper *České Slovo*, an admirer of Otto Bauer and a fierce opponent of the Habsburgs. In vain the satirist tried to persuade Münzer that Bauer had been the greatest obstacle to Dollfuss's fight against the Nazis: not only because of Bauer's doctrinaire attitude, but also because he was unwilling to exchange his position as leader of the Social Democratic party for a more humble position in a coalition government with Dollfuss. Finally Kraus was driven to ask Münzer, 'Who would you rather have, the Habsburgs or the National Socialists?' It was, of course, a very unfair question.[87] There was little serious prospect of a return of the Habsburgs to Austria, let alone to Czechoslovakia. Although Schuschnigg was a convinced monarchist himself, he realised that such a solution was completely impracticable and, in the crisis which finally culminated in the *Anschluss* of 1938, rejected the offer of the Archduke Otto to return to Austria: he preferred, instead, to make desperate efforts to rally the remnants of Social Democracy with him in his stand against Hitler.

The real significance of Kraus's dispute with Münzer lay in the fact that it was indicative of the former's growing despair at the possibility of continued Austrian resistance to German demands and that, faced with the hideous nature of the reality outside, the satirist was moving more and more into a world of the imagination in which the artist and his message still counted. The almost complete isolation in which Kraus lived out the last two years of his life was in any case facilitated by the fact that he had lost many of his friends after his break with the Social Democrats. Some of his most devoted disciples on the extreme Left had now joined the illegal Revolutionary Socialist party in Austria, the underground successor to the old party which had been shattered in 1934. Others had gone over to the Communists.

Kraus did not gain new friends. Unlike Franz Werfel, long since disillusioned with revolutionary enthusiasm, and Werfel's remarkable wife Alma (the widow of Gustav Mahler and former mistress of Kokoschka), the satirist was never a member of the circle of intellectuals who were close to the Schuschnigg government; Social Democrat charges that the Austrian government had given its official blessing to the celebrations of Kraus's sixtieth birthday in 1934 have no basis in fact. This did not prevent the Viennese cabarets from talking of Kraus's 'pilgrimage to Canossa' and comparing his transfer of allegiance from the Left to the Fatherland Front with the departure of Clemens Krauss from Berlin.[88] Meanwhile the satirist was deeply distressed at rumours that elements in the Austrian Nazi party intended to use him as a propaganda weapon against the Jews. This may have been one of those sadistic jokes in which the Nazis delighted: if it was, it certainly caused the pain and anguish that was intended.

But still the satirist fought back. In the *Fackel* of 1935 Kraus reprinted the united attacks that were now directed against him from Social Democrats and Communists in Czechoslovakia. They continually referred to his ignorance of the economic factor in history and complained that *The Last Days of Mankind* was not realistic because it depicted the First World War, not as the death-throes of the capitalist order but as a permanent revelation

of the human condition. They charged that the work of Kraus
was pacifist, utopian, nihilistic, apocalyptic and fantastic. As the
cries against him from Prague and Brünn grew shriller and
shriller, the satirist could only reply that what the social
Democrats and the Communists called his 'fetish of language'
was better than being duped by Hitler and Stalin. One of the
last letters which he wrote was to Otto Bauer, protesting about
the terms in which he had been attacked by *Der Kampf* in April
1936, terms which certainly reveal the bitterness with which
Kraus was regarded in left-wing circles:

> At least in Germany the satirists have disappeared and no-
> where can it be read that they have levelled their wit at the
> martyrs of Fascism. In Austria there is a satirical practitioner
> who, out of his own prolonged puerility, has for some time
> denounced to the frontier-police men who were sacrificing
> themselves for an idea.

Kraus could only deny this charge and remind Bauer of the
praise which he himself had given to *The Last Days of Mankind*
when it had first appeared.[89] Perhaps it was no accident that two
of the plays which figured most prominently in the satirist's
public recitals during this last period of his life should have been
King Lear and *Timon of Athens* which he read in his own translations. Nor was it surprising that at his last recital, in November
1935, he should have turned in anger upon those Social Democrats who still attended his performances, despite his frequent
appeals that they should cease to do so.

It is true that Kraus continued to give entrancing performances
of the operettas of Offenbach. And yet some of those who attended
these last recitals became aware of a sense of mounting horror
when they contrasted the reality of Vienna in 1935 with the
synthetic, and at times desperate, gaiety that exists in parts of
Offenbach's work: they would have agreed with what François
Mauriac has written of *La Grande Duchesse de Gérolstein*, 'The
laughter I hear in Offenbach's music is that of the Empress
Charlotte gone mad.' The English reader, indeed, is uncomfor-

tably aware that, in the work of Kraus's last years, he is entering into a psychological dimension of which, for good and for ill, he has no experience. It was a world beyond polemic and satire in which the satirist retreated further and further into a private domain of the spirit. As Robert Scheu had feared, in his study of Kraus's work published as early as 1909, the more desperate the situation of Austria became, the more fanatically would Kraus cling to his idealism of language, so that Kraus, the enemy of abstraction, would himself become the victim of abstraction.[90]

Throughout 1934 and 1935 the satirist, despite the advice of his doctor, sat at his desk night after night trying to grapple with the Nazi horror. The decline in the readership of the *Fackel* following his break with the Social Democrats meant that it had to be subsidised out of the pocket of the editor. Kraus would soon have been forced to cease publication for financial reasons, had death not intervened. In the summer of 1935 he asked his friend Heinrich Fischer to accompany him on a trip to the scenes of his childhood. They walked through the Wienerwald, Kraus breathing heavily, to the house where he had spent his early years. They sat down on a bank and on the satirist's face there was an expression so full of dejection and grief that Fischer could never forget it. Kraus lamented that ever since Hitler had come to power, the trees and shrubs had lost their greenness; everything was now grey. They then went swimming, an activity which Kraus normally enjoyed. But he was breathless and his face was strained when they left the water: 'Last year', he gasped, 'I could swim a hundred strokes but now only fifty. What will it be like next year?'[91]

This was the last summer of his life. In 1936 his condition worsened and, after a short illness, he died on 12 June. Nestroy had possessed a pathological fear of death, a fear which Kraus had shared and had expressed in his poetry.[92] The end, however, when it came, was peaceful.

Epilogue

ON 11 July 1936, one month after Kraus's death, Von Papen secured his greatest triumph by the signing of the Austro-German agreement according to which Schuschnigg, in return for promises that the Austrian Nazis should be kept in control by Berlin, was forced to admit into his government two members of the quasi-Nazi 'National Opposition'. Eighteen months followed in which the Nazis continued to provoke unrest inside Austria and in which frantic attempts were made by the Austrian government to build up the strength of the ramshackle Fatherland Front. In February 1938, at the height of the Carnival season in Vienna, Schuschnigg was summoned by Hitler to Berchtesgaden and was there brow-beaten into making concessions which would have had the effect of reducing Austria to the status of a satellite of Germany. On his return to Vienna, Schuschnigg attempted to preserve the independence of his country by calling for a nation-wide plebiscite on the question of Austria's future. This provoked Hitler into setting into motion those military and diplomatic manoeuvres which resulted, in the second week of March 1938, in the absorption of Austria by the Third Reich.

As the German troops entered Vienna, they were greeted with a hysteria that was unparalleled even in Germany itself since 1933. The effusive nature of this welcome was due in part to the volatile nature of the Viennese: in part to the release of the tension in which Austria had been living for so long. For one section of the population, however, the *Anschluss* brought catastrophe. The Austrian Nazis erupted into the streets and instigated a

THE LAST DAYS OF MANKIND

hideous attack on the Jews: the palace of Baron Rothschild was looted of its art treasures; Jewish shops and department stores in the Kärntnerstrasse and the Mariahilferstrasse were systematically plundered. Jews were forced to dance and adopt all kinds of humiliating postures in the Prater, the amusement park of Vienna: while in the city itself numbers of the officers of the German army were disgusted by the spectacle of jeering mobs compelling aged Jews to scrub Dollfuss crosses and stencilled portraits of Schuschnigg from public buildings and pavements, using for this purpose acid preparations which made the victims scream with pain.

Hundreds, if not thousands, of Jews committed suicide during these days to avoid arrest and maltreatment. Meanwhile the main railway stations of Vienna were thronged with Jews trying to escape; anywhere—Switzerland, Prague or Budapest—it did not matter. Terrible scenes took place when the trains were stopped and boarded by the Gestapo before reaching the frontier. Even at the frontier the misery of the refugees was not alleviated, since many of them were turned back or left to starve in the no man's land between the frontier posts.[1]

In the years after the *Anschluss* the world which Kraus had known was almost completely obliterated. Various members of his family, including the satirist's favourite niece, were eventually deported by the Nazis to concentration camps from which they never returned.[2] The same fate was in store for Richard Lanyi, the bookseller who had been responsible for the business side of Kraus's recitals. Helene Kann left Vienna for Switzerland, taking with her many of the papers and documents from the office of *Die Fackel*. But not everything was saved. In 1938 a squad of S.S. men broke into Kraus's flat in the Lothringer Strasse, not far from the Opera. In the satirist's study there was, under a glass cover, the death mask of one of his friends; one of the intruders smashed this with the butt of his rifle. Kraus's books and papers, including the manuscripts of his translations of Shakespeare, were thrown on a truck and driven away.[3]

Among the Jewish intellectuals and artists to whom Viennese

culture owed so much, the aged Freud, was forced in 1938 to leave Vienna for London where he died of cancer in the next year. Franz Werfel managed to reach the South of France, but was forced to continue his wanderings after the German conquest in 1940. With his wife Alma (who carried with her the manuscript of Bruckner's Third Symphony) he crossed the Pyrenees on foot and entered Spain; they eventually reached the United States where Werfel died in Beverly Hills, California, in 1945. Three years earlier Stefan Zweig and his wife Charlotte had committed suicide in Brazil.

Among the suicides in the first few days after the German entry into Vienna was Dr. Müller, editor of the *Neue Freie Presse*. The Austrian Nazis had at first suggested that this newspaper should be purged of its Jewish staff but allowed to continue as a showpiece of the new régime, much in the same way as the *Frankfurter Zeitung* or the *Vossische Zeitung* had been allowed to remain in Germany: this project was killed by the personal opposition of Hitler who hated this newspaper as a symbol of all that he felt had made his youthful stay in Vienna so bitter and frustrating. The *Neue Freie Presse* was eliminated.[4] A different fate was accorded to the *Neues Wiener Journal* which, although Jewish-owned, had possessed links with the moderate elements among the Austrian Nazis, in addition to its main commitment to the cause of the Heimwehr. This newspaper continued to appear but its Jewish proprietor and staff were removed.

Various were the fates of the politicians who have appeared in this study. Schuschnigg was imprisoned in a variety of German prisons and concentration camps—an experience which he survived; in 1945 he was liberated after leaving Dachau where he had been moved together with such personalities as Léon Blum, Admiral Horthy and Dr. Schacht, one time president of the Reichsbank. Schuschnigg subsequently left Europe for the United States where he became a university professor in political science. His former rival, Prince Starhemberg, escaped to Paris after the *Anschluss* and during the war fought for a time on the side of the Free French. He then moved to South America, returning after the war to Austria where he died in 1956. The other leader of the Heimwehr, Major Fey, committed suicide with his wife in Vienna in 1938 as soon as he heard the news of the German invasion. For Anton Rintelen 1938 was a year of disillusionment: emerging hopefully from imprisonment he expected that some reward might be his for the rôle which he had played in the putsch of 1934. But the Nazis were now masters of Austria and there was no place in the New Order for the old-fashioned style of intrigue in which he was such an expert. Rintelen had to be content with writing his memoirs: he died in 1946.

On the Left the impact of Hitler's victories was shattering. Otto Bauer died in Paris four months after the German occupation of Austria. His position had, of course, been seriously weakened after the collapse of the Social Democratic party in 1934: after that date power inevitably shifted to the underground leadership inside Austria, although his name and prestige still commanded respect. Already before Bauer's death the onset of Stalin's purges was a cruel disillusionment to the former's hope that in the influence and power of the Soviet Union there might emerge a counterpoise to the menace of Fascism.

After the Anschluss and the death of Otto Bauer, continual quarrels rent the exiled Social Democrats now congregated in Paris. In addition to the disputes between the former underground movement in Austria and those who had left for Czechoslovakia in 1934, the party was also split over the policy to be adopted towards the Communists: there were those who hated the Communists for their subservience to Moscow and their unprincipled opportunism in wanting to ally even with the monarchists to form an anti-fascist front: Julius Deutsch, on the other hand, wanted the Social Democrats to collaborate with both the Communists and the monarchists (whose support was deemed valuable since they had the ear of the French Foreign Office). With the fall of France in 1940 and the dispersal of the emigration between Britain and North America the task in achieving a co-ordinated policy became even more impossible.

Finally, in 1941 Friedrich Adler felt compelled formally to dissolve the party organisation.[5]

Meanwhile, ever since February 1934, Karl Renner had remained in Austria, refusing to participate in any of the party's underground activities which he condemned as futile and irrelevant. In 1938 he prudently issued a public statement welcoming the *Anschluss* while admitting that he regretted the circumstances in which it had occurred. Understandably this statement was greeted with cries of outrage from the emigrés. During the next seven years Renner lived quietly in retirement, largely undisturbed by the Nazis. In 1945 he became first Chancellor and then first President of the Second Austrian Republic, partly due, at least, to the mistaken belief of the Russians that he would be an acquiescent instrument of their policies. In fact until his death in 1950 Renner rendered considerable services to the new Austrian Republic in resisting politely but firmly every attempt by the Russians to tamper with the unity and integrity of his country. One of his principal aims was to overcome the deep divisions that had been left in Austrian society by the quarrel between the Social Democrats and the Christian Socialists in the 1930s. The radical wing of the Social Democrats was muzzled and it was intimated to a number of the émigrés that their return to Austria was not particularly desirable. Renner was one of the architects of that coalition government of the two dominant parties of the Republic which lasted so successfully until 1966.

The stability and economic prosperity which Austria has enjoyed after the war and particularly after the peace treaty of 1955 cannot, however, conceal the terrible impoverishment from which Viennese intellectual life has suffered since the Jewish element was almost entirely dispersed or annihilated. Friedrich Adler, that pure and idealistic spirit, who at the end of the war resumed his work for the Socialist International, was appalled by the atmosphere of the new Austria:

The intention of creating an 'Austrian nation' is, in my opinion, entirely utopian. But if this reactionary, as well as nauseous, Utopia should ever be realised—should the Austrians, in fact, be faced with the choice between the 'Austrian nation' and the 'German nation' (which situation I shall fortunately not live to see), I would be one of those who would, without hesitation, elect to remain with the nation, for which, for example, Goethe's Faust, Wagner's Ring of the Nibelungen, Freiligrath's poems of the revolution and Lassalle's speeches do not belong to a *foreign* culture.[6]

Adler was never so obviously the spokesman of his generation than in this repudiation of the political and cultural provincialism of post-war Vienna. He died in 1960.

At evening meetings in Hampstead and New York during the war, admirers of Kraus held readings from his work, readings which sometimes produced heated discussions amongst Social Democrats who were present. After the war, the debate was resumed within Austria itself. In a newspaper article published in 1946 one party member who had been imprisoned in Dachau described some of the ways in which prisoners had been able to maintain their morale. One day in 1943, for example, an S.S. officer brought a lorry-load of books from private Jewish libraries in Vienna and ordered prisoners to sort them out so that he could sell them at a profit for himself: the prisoners were thus able to smuggle into the camp works such as *The Last Days of Mankind* which were surreptitiously passed from hand to hand. For Viktor Metejka, the writer of this article, the message of Karl Kraus was highly relevant to the Austria of 1945.[7]

But there were many who disagreed. Oskar Pollak, one of the few members of the party's radical old guard to return to Vienna in 1945, maintained a resolute hostility to the memory of the satirist in the pages of the *Arbeiter Zeitung*. Further fuel for Pollak's campaign was provided by the brief appearance in Vienna after the war of a small red-covered magazine *Der Plan*, which posed as a successor to *Die Fackel*. The combination of Communism and Aestheticism propagated by this magazine soon proved unstable, however, and this venture came to a speedy end.

Nevertheless it seemed to point to the truth of Julius Braunthal's contention, that one of the reasons for the decline in the effectiveness of the Austrian Social Democratic party after 1918 was the wilful and erratic behaviour of many of those intellectuals who had been attracted to Socialism through the influence of Karl Kraus.[8]

It was easy to think of further examples. There was Emil Franzel, editor of the Prague newspaper *Sozialdemokrat* who had in the 1920s supported Kraus in many of his quarrels with the Austrian Social Democrats. Franzel flirted with Communism in the 1930s but during the war became director of the Urania publishing house in Prague which was under the ultimate control of Heydrich, the Nazi 'Protector of Bohemia and Moravia'. Since the war Dr. Franzel has been active as a Catholic publicist.[9] Then there was the case of yet another admirer of Kraus, the journalist Willi Schlamm, an active Trotskyist in the 1930s who, for a short while after the German editor Carl von Ossietzky had been put into a concentration camp by the Nazis in 1933, continued to publish a Viennese edition of Ossietzky's left-wing magazine *Die Weltbühne*. After the Second World War, by contrast, Schlamm was to become one of the most vociferous anti-Communist voices in America during his period working for the *Time-Life* Corporation.

The satirist's posthumous influence is still at work, it is true, within a small group of Catholic intellectuals in Vienna who publish a magazine significantly entitled *Wort und Wahrheit* (Word and Truth). But it is also clear that there are aspects of Kraus's work which Christians find hard to accept. The writer Karl Thieme, a Social Democrat and a Catholic who had long been a supporter of the satirist but was distressed by his apostasy from the Church in 1922, summed up the feelings of many of Kraus's erstwhile admirers in both the Socialist and the Catholic camps when, in September 1936, several months after the satirist's death, he accused him of portraying God as the God of Hell and Damnation, the very view against which Christ had protested; because Kraus could not reconcile reality with his ideal, he turned in revenge to vent his hatred and disillusionment on mankind.[10] The same point was made from a more sympathetic point of view by Kraus's friend and literary biographer, Leopold Liegler, in his funeral speech on the satirist in 1936: mourning the loss of a friend who had stood like an unshakeable rock amidst all the troubles that were closing in on Austria, Liegler pointed to the tragedy of Kraus's unfulfilled idealism which, like that of Plato, was rooted not in the reality of this world, but in another that was not yet born.[11]

It is not easy to pass a judgement on Karl Kraus. Perhaps the most balanced comment has come from Theodor Haecker, the Catholic philosopher and translator of Kierkegaard, who had, in his study of Kierkegaard published in 1913, praised Kraus as a worthy successor to the Danish writer, as the one great ethical polemicist and satirist of his time. In November 1940, however, after listening to a radio speech from Goebbels, who had boasted about the dropping of 300,000 kilograms of bombs on Birmingham, Haecker was prompted to reflect in his diary on the life and work of Kraus:

> I think that Karl Kraus was a great writer, but I would not wish to have written *Die Fackel*. It is more than a matter of writing. . . . A matter of what? I can clarify this in some way by the following observation: I do not hold Hilty to be a great writer or a great philosopher—but I would like to have written many things of his, for he was a friend of God.[12]

And yet, this can hardly be the note on which to end a study such as this. One thing is certain: if the society which produced the satirist has now disappeared, it still lives in the claustrophobic intensity of his work. As Brecht said of him, 'As the epoch raised its hand to end its life, he was this hand.'[13]

Notes and References

ABBREVIATIONS

F.   *Die Fackel*. Page references to *Die Fackel* indicate the first page of the article or section from which the quotation is taken.

L.T.M.   *Die Letzten Tage der Menschheit*, Vienna, 1922. New edition, Munich, 1957.

D.W.   *Die Dritte Walpurgisnacht*, Munich, 1952.

K.A.   Kraus—Archiv, Stadtbibliothek, Vienna.

INTRODUCTORY NOTE

1. A. Wandruszka, *Geschichte einer Zeitung. Das Schicksal der 'Presse' und der 'Neuen Freie Presse' von 1848 zur zweiten Republik*, Vienna 1958, p. 122.
2. L.T.M., Act III, Scene 41.
3. 'Nachts', F. 360–2, November 1912, p. 6.

CHAPTER 1. KARL KRAUS, PORTRAIT OF THE ARTIST

1. S. von Radecki, *Wie ich glaube*, Cologne, 1953, p. 28.
2. E. Jones, *Sigmund Freud*, London, 1953–7, Vol. II, p. 133.
3. W. Haas, *Die literarische Welt, Erinnerungen*, Munich, 1960, p. 23.
4. W. Kraft, *Karl Kraus, Beiträge zum Verständnis seines Werkes*, Salzburg, 1956, p. 46.
5. H. Fischer, 'The Other Austria and Karl Kraus', in H. J. Rehfisch (ed.), *In Tyrannos. Four Centuries of Struggle Against Tyranny in Germany*, London, 1944, p. 324.
6. Ibid., p. 326.
7. Caroline Kohn, *Karl Kraus*, Paris, 1962, pp. 63–4.
8. 'Vom grossen Welttheaterschwindel', F. 601–7, November 1922, p. 1.
9. A. Mahler-Werfel, *Gustav Mahler, Memories and Letters*, London, 1946, pp. 89–90.
10. Quoted in J. H. Nicholls, *Force and Freedom*, New York, 1943, pp. 277–8.
11. H. von Hofmannsthal, *Selected Prose*, New York, 1952, p. 133.

12. P. Rieff, *Freud, The Mind of the Moralist*, London, 1960, pp. 78–9.

13. F. Kafka, *Erzählungen*, Frankfurt am Main, 1948, p. 169.

14. This quotation is taken from the poem 'Der Irrgarten', K. Kraus, *Worte in Versen*, Munich, 1959, p. 83.

15. 'Aus der Branche', F. 339–40, December 1911, p. 30.

16. 'Nachts', F. 445–53, January 1917, p. 110.

17. Information from Dr. Marie Jahoda.

18. Radecki, op. cit., p. 24.

19. 'Nachts', F. 389–90, December 1913, p. 28.

20. Fischer, loc. cit., p. 314.

21. 'Der Ankläger', F. 324–5, June 1911, p. 7.

22. 'Grosser Sieg der Technik', F. 347–8, April–May 1912, p. 1.

23. 'Antworten des Herausgebers', F. 158, November 1904, p. 22.

24. A. Koestler, *Arrow in the Blue, An Autobiography*, London, 1952, p. 171.

25. A summary of Kraus's views on Heine may be found in *Heine und die Folgen*, Munich, 1910.

26. E. Heller, *The Disinherited Mind*, 2nd. edn., London, 1957, p. 238.

27. F. 69, February 1901, p. 1.

28. F. 138, May 1903, p. 14.

29. F. 1, April 1899, p. 1.

30. Kraus's principal essay on Nestroy was 'Nestroy und die Nachwelt', F. 349–50, May 1912 (published on the fiftieth anniversary of Nestroy's death).

31. Alban Berg's admiration for Kraus, 'one of the greatest Austrian artists, one of the greatest German masters', was expressed in the Festschrift, *Stimmen über Karl Kraus zum 60. Geburtstag*, Vienna, 1934, p. 43.

32. Karin Michaelis, 'Ein Karl Kraus Abend', F. 336–7, November 1911, p. 45.

33. F. 51, August 1900, p. 19.

34. *Der Brenner*, Vol. XVIII, Innsbruck, 1954, pp. 234–48. For the importance of *Der Brenner* in Austrian intellectual life between its foundation in 1910 and the outbreak of the First World War: A. Fuchs, *Geistige Strömungen in Österreich*, 1867–1918, Vienna, 1949, p. 81.

35. E. Heller, 'Ludwig Wittgenstein', in *Encounter*, No. 72,

September 1959, p. 40. See also Heller's contribution to 'Ludwig Wittgenstein: a Symposium', in *The Listener*, 28 January 1960, p. 163.

36. F. Heer, 'Perspektiven österreichischer Gegenwarts-Dichtung' in W. Kaiser (ed.), *Deutsche Literatur in unserer Zeit*, Göttingen, 1959, p. 125.

37. *Rundfrage über Karl Kraus* (published by *Der Grenner*), Innsbruck, 1917, p. 21.

38. For an examination of the relationship between the work of Kraus and that of Schoenberg, see E. Křenek, 'Karl Kraus und Arnold Schönberg', in *23*, No. 15–16, Vienna, 25 October 1934. See also E. Křenek, *Ansprache bei der Trauerfeier für Karl Kraus*, Vienna, 1936.

39. 'Warum "Die Fackel" nicht erscheint', F. 890–905, July 1934, p. 1.

40. This line is taken from the poem 'Bekenntnis', *Worte in Versen*, p. 79.

41. E. Heller, *The Disinherited Mind*, p. 256.

42. H. Broch, *Gesammelte Werke*, Zürich, 1955, Vol. I, pp. 76 passim.

43. The neo-positivist philosophy of Ernst Mach exercised considerable influence on the intellectual life of Vienna in the early years of this century. The philosophy of the young Wittgenstein and the later work of the Vienna circle in the 1920s was directly inspired by his teaching. Mach further influenced the positivist school of law which developed around Professor Hans Kelsen who was largely responsible for the constitution of the first Austrian Republic. Mach's theories were also important for their impact on the theoreticians of the Austrian Social Democratic party, especially Friedrich Adler who made use of Mach to criticise the metaphysical basis of Marx's materialism.

44. Quoted in W. A. Jenks, *Vienna and the Young Hitler*, New York, 1960, pp. 95–6.

45. R. Musil, *Tagebücher, Aphorismen, Essays und Reden*, Hamburg, 1955, p. 565.

46. Quoted in L. Liegler, *Karl Kraus und Sein Werk*, Vienna, 1920, p. 53.

47. Kraft, op. cit., p. 177.

48. A. Hitler, *Mein Kampf*, unexpurgated edition, London, 1949, p. 116.

49. 'Tagebuch', F. 251–2, April 1905, p. 34.

CHAPTER 2. 'RESEARCH LABORATORY FOR WORLD DESTRUCTION': AUSTRIA, 1899–1914

1. Heller, op. cit., p. 245.

2. On Harden's relations with Kraus, see H. F. Young, *Maximilian Harden, Censor Germaniae*, The Hague, 1959, pp. 143–5. Harden was in many ways the pioneer of a species of highly individual radical magazine which was to have many imitators in Central Europe after the First World War. This type reached its apotheosis in the Berlin *Weltbühne* of Carl von Ossietzky who in the 1920s fearlessly attacked the secret rearmament of Germany.

3. E. V. Zenker, *Ein Mann im sterbenden Österreich*, Reichenberg, 1935, p. 106.

4. H. W. Steed, *The Habsburg Monarchy*, 2nd edn., London, 1914, p. 182.

5. An example of government appeasement of the Press by these methods was the lifting in 1900 of revenue taxes upon the Viennese newspapers. The government compensated itself by levying a tax on postcards. With the exception of the *Arbeiter Zeitung* and the *Deutsches Volksblatt*, the Viennese press did not accordingly reduce the price of newspapers. It was Kraus who exposed this fact—F. 35, March 1900, p. 1.

6. Steed, op. cit., p. 187. Count Thun had said in 1900 that no Austrian government could rule against the will of the *Neue Freie Presse*.

7. 'Bismark und die Presse', F. 142, July 1903, p. 1.

8. Jenks, op. cit., pp. 95–6.

9. For Liebknecht's articles, see: 'Nachträgliches zur "Affaire"', F. 18, September 1899, p. 1; 'Nachträgliches zur "Affaire"', F. 19, October 1899, p. 1; 'Schlusswort', F. 21, October 1899, p. 1.

10. 'Nachträgliches zur "Affaire"', F. 26 December 1899, p. 8. One of the reasons why Liebknecht had in fact written in

Die Fackel was that at this time it was widely read in France, particularly among sympathisers of the *Action Française* who admired its wit and its attacks on the Jewish bourgeoisie, if not its general position of sympathy for the Austrian Social Democrats.

11. 'Schimpfen', F. 143, October 1903, p. 1.

12. F. 81, June 1901, p. 1. See also obituary of Schöffel: F. 296–7, February 1910, p. 1.

13. For Kraus's attack on the corruption in railway administration and the links between the companies and the Press, see especially 'Die Sequestration der Südbahn', F. 36, March 1901, p. 1. For Kraus's attack on the links between the Viennese press and the Austrian sugar cartel: F. 95, February 1902, p. 6.

14. See, for example, F. 47, July 1900, p. 12.

15. For a typical early attack on the Social Democrats: F. 64, January 1901, p. 1.

16. Kraus's attack on clerical demagogy against the Jews, which had a long tradition in Vienna from the days of the great preacher Abraham a Sancta Clara in the late seventeenth century, can be seen in the article 'Peter Abel, S. J.', F. 22, November 1899, p. 10.

17. F. 12, July 1899, p. 1.

18. For a typical attack on Milan of Serbia: F. 41, May 1900, p. 12.

19. In *Die Fackel* of January 1910 there is a complete list of other contributors to the magazine. Kraus also explained there that he did not wish *Die Fackel* up to issue 154 (February 1904) to be considered as part of his collected work.

20. J. Braunthal, *In Search of the Millennium*, London, 1945, p. 114.

21. 'Die Wahlreform, ein offener Brief an Karl Kraus', F. 194, January 1906, p. 1. Scheu had been a frequent contributor to *Die Fackel* and was to contribute later an extremely perceptive article on Lueger after the latter's death: 'Karl Lueger', F. 301–2, May 1910, p. 37.

22. 'Apokalypse', F. 261–2, October 1908, p. 1.

23. 'Antworten des Herausgebers', F. 157, March 1904, p. 20.

24. With his eye for the right quotation, Kraus was later able to condemn Aerenthal out of his own mouth: 'We live in a

time when people thirst for sensations', 'Zitate', F. 319–20, April 1911, p. 20.

25. Masaryk's gratitude was expressed to Kraus in a letter of 8 January 1910: K. A.

26. 'Prozess Friedjung', F. 293, December 1909, p. 1.

27. 'Conrad von Hötzendorf', F. 366–7, January 1913, p. 1.

28. 'Herbstzeitlosen, oder Heimkehr der Sieger', F. 366–7, January 1913, p. 37.

29. 'Offiziöses', F. 374–5, May 1913, p. 12.

30. 'Das ist der Krieg—c'est la guerre—das ist der Moloch!', F. 360–2, November 1912, p. 39.

31. 'Alles wohlauf', F. 398, April 1914, p. 1.

32. 'Übersetzung aus Harden', F. 251–2, April 1908, p. 15.

33. 'Die deutsche Schmach', F. 253, May 1908, p. 1.

34. 'Maximilian Harden, eine Erledigung', F. 234–5 October 1907, p. 1.

35. 'Schoenebeckmesser', F. 305–6, July 1910, p. 1.

36. 'Die Kinderfreunde', F. 187, November 1905, p. 1.

37. 'Prozess Riehl', F. 211, November 1906, p. 1.

38. Ibid.

39. S. Zweig, *Die Welt von Gestern, Erinnerungen eines Europäers*, Berlin, 1955, p. 84. English translation: *The World of Yesterday*, 2nd edn., London, 1944, p. 74.

40. For a discussion of the disintegration of bourgeois morality through contact with aristocratic culture in Vienna see C. E. Schorske, 'Politics and the Psyche in fin de siècle Vienna, Schnitzler and Hofmannsthal', *American Historical Review*, LXVI, No. 4, July 1961, p. 930.

41. 'Unbefugte Psychologie', F. 387–8, November 1913, p. 17. Further correspondence from Freud to Kraus may be found in: E. L. Freud, *The Letters of Sigmund Freud, 1873–1939*, London, 1961, Letter No. 122.

42. 'Die Kinderfreunde', F. 187, November 1905, p. 1.

43. 'Unbefugte Psychologie', F. 387–9, November 1913, p. 17.

44. 'Nachts', F. 376–7, June 1913, p. 8.

45. Jenks, op. cit., p. 115.

46. P. G. J. Pulzer, *The Rise of Political Antisemitism in Germany and Austria*, New York, 1964, p. 10.

47. Ibid., p. 347.

48. Steed, op. cit., p. 184. The proportion in Budapest Steed put as high as 90 per cent.

49. Discussion of the rise of the ideology of antisemitism may be found in: Pulzer, op. cit., chapters 3–8; F. Stern, *The Politics of Cultural Despair, A Study in the Rise of the Germanic Ideology*, Berkeley and Los Angeles, 1961; E. G. Reichmann, *Flucht in den Hass, Die Ursachen der deutschen Judenkatastrophe*, Frankfurt am Main, 1956.

50. Pulzer, op. cit., p. 204.

51. W. B. Simon, 'The Jewish Vote in Vienna', *Jewish Social Studies*, XXIII, 1961, pp. 38–48. It was also true that, precisely because of the large numbers of Jewish intellectuals inside the party, there were antisemitic elements—particularly in the provinces—hostile to the influence of 'Jewish' Vienna within the Social Democratic leadership. These elements were to be revealed after the defeat of the party at the hands of the Dollfuss dictatorship in 1934.

52. A useful study of Weininger is to be found in: H. Kohn, *Karl Kraus, Arthur Schnitzler, Otto Weininger. Aus dem jüdischen Wien der Jahrhundertwende*, Tübingen, 1962.

53. 'Dietrich Eckhart told me that in all his life he had known just one good Jew: Otto Weininger who killed himself on the day when he realised that the Jew lives upon the decay of peoples.' *Hitler's Secret Conversations 1941–44*, New York, 1961, p. 156 (conversation of night of 1st-2nd December 1941).

54. T. Lessing, *Der Jüdische Selbsthass*, Berlin, 1930, p. 125. Lessing, who fled to Czechoslovakia in 1933 on the accession of Hitler to power, was tracked down by Nazi agents and murdered in Marienbad on 31 August 1933.

55. F. Kafka, *Briefe 1902–1924*, Frankfurt am Main, 1958, p. 334. Kafka's opinion of Kraus was undoubtedly affected by the bad relations which existed between the satirist and Max Brod: 'Selbstanzeige', F. 326–8, July 1911, p. 34.

56. Lessing, op. cit., p. 43.

57. Articles by Chamberlain included: 'Der vorraussetzunglose Mommsen', F. 87, December 1901: 'Katholische Universitäten', F. 92, January 1902.

58. *Rundfrage uber Karl Kraus*, Innsbruck, 1917, p. 26. The

article was first published in *Studien über Karl Kraus*, published by *Der Brenner* in 1913.

59. Radecki, op. cit., p. 334.
60. C. Kohn, op. cit., p. 98.
61. Kraft, op. cit., pp. 104–5.
62. D. W., p. 139.
63. L.T.M., Act III, Scene 14.
64. *Worte in Versen*, p. 109.
65. K. S. Pinson, *Modern Germany, Its History and Civilization*, New York, 1954, p. 197.
66. 'Heine und die Folgen', F. 329–30, September 1911, p. 1. Even Kraus had to exempt from his strictures some of the poetry in which Heine, during the long and terrible illness before his death, moved to a deeper understanding of religious truth, an understanding which embraced the virtues of Judaism as well as those of Christianity.
67. H. W. Puner, *Freud: His Life and Mind*, London, 1949, p. 161.
68. F. Weltsch, 'The Rise and Fall of the Jewish-German Symbiosis. The Case of Franz Kafka', *Year Book of the Leo Baeck Institute*, London, 1956, p. 255.
69. H. H. Stuckenschmidt, *Arnold Schoenberg*, London, 1959, p. 110. After reading 'Jacob's Ladder' aloud Franz Werfel said of Schoenberg, 'Now I know the entire conflict of this man. He is a Jew—the Jew who suffers from himself': A. Mahler-Werfel, *And the Bridge is Love*, London, 1959, p. 90.
70. F. 649–56, June 1924, p. 137.
71. The line is taken from the poem 'Grabschrift', *Worte in Versen*, p. 516.
72. Quoted by H. Kohn, op. cit., p. 64.
73. 'Franz Ferdinand und die Talente', F. 400–3, July 1914, p. 1.
74. Ibid.
75. 'Innsbruck', F. 531–43, April 1930, p. 1. 'Ich habe es nicht gewollt' was a phrase attributed to the Emperor Wilhelm II with reference to the First World War. It was frequently used by Kraus to symbolise the impotence of politicians in the grip of phraseology.
76. 'In dieser grossen Zeit', F. 404, December 1914, p. 1.
77. 'Die Lage der Deutschen in Europa', F. 400–3, July 1914, p. 6.

CHAPTER 3. THE FIRST WORLD WAR—FIRST PHASE

1. L.T.M., Act I, Scene 1.
2. Jones, op. cit., Vol. I, p. 192.
3. 'In dieser grossen Zeit', F. 404, December 1914, p. 1. Although this was published in December 1914, it was first read by Kraus at a public recital on 19 November 1914.
4. 'Der Ernst der Zeit und die Satire der Vorzeit', F. 405, February 1915, p. 14.
5. Zweig, op. cit., p. 222: English translation, p. 185.
6. 'Eine Bombe', F. 431–6, August 1916, p. 78. Kraus quoted from a report of the 'atrocity' in the *Deutsche Medizinische Wochenschrift* of 16 March 1916 and a corrected report in the issue of 18 May after a reply from the municipal authorities of Nuremberg.
7. 'Die Denkgesetze', F. 431–5, August 1916, p. 57.
8. 'Eine Feststellung', F. 431–6, August 1916, p. 52.
9. Wandruszka, op. cit., p. 120.
10. 'Solche Kontraste gibt's nur an der Front', F. 431–6, August 1916, p. 68.
11. 'Wie die Schalek in Serbien gehaust hat', F. 413–17, August 1915, p. 36. See also L.T.M., Act II, Scene 19.
12. 'Die Schalek irgendwo an der Adria', F. 418–22, April 1916.
13. 'Solche Kontraste gibt's nur an der Front', F. 431–6, August 1910, p. 68.
14. 'Die einzelne Frauengestalt', F. 462–71, October 1917, p. 134.
15. For the relevant documents to this case: 'Prozesse', F. 521–30, January 1920, p. 9.
16. C. E. Montague, *Disenchantment*, London, 1922, Chapters VII and VIII.
17. *The War Dispatches of Sir Philip Gibbs*, Douglas, Isle of Man, 1964, p. ix.
18. 'Die Wahrheit ist immer in der Mitte', F. 431–6, August 1916, p. 94.
19. L.T.M., Act II, Scene 10.
20. 'Aus dem Herrenhaus', F. 462–71, October 1917, p. 58.

21. 'Der englische Benedikt und der österreichische Northcliffe', F. 445–53, January 1917, p. 33.

22. 'Kriegsnamen', F. 418–22, April 1916, p. 30.

23. 'Der tragische Karneval', F. 426–30, June 1916, p. 35.

24. 'Eine der schlimmsten Folgeerscheinungen die der Krieg auf dem Gewissen hat', F. 445–53, January 1917, p. 27.

25. ''s gibt nur an Durchhalter!', F. 418–22, April 1916, p. 89.

26. '1916', F. 418–22, April 1916, p. 25.

27. 'Spiele', F. 406–12, October 1915, p. 34.

28. 'Lehár spricht', F. 431–6, August 1916, p. 92.

29. 'Das übervolle Haus jubelte den Helden, die stramm salutierend dankten', F. 462–71, October 1917, p. 1. This piece originally appeared in *Die Fackel* in May 1916 but was immediately censored. It was subsequently published in the following year.

30. O. Jászi, *The Dissolution of the Habsburg Monarchy*, Chicago, 1961 edn., p. 116.

31. L.T.M., Act IV, Scene 29.

32. L.T.M., Act III, Scene 24.

33. Ibid.

34. L.T.M., Act III, Scene 41.

35. With particular reference to the treatment of Czech deserters and the dissolving of Czech regiments for cowardice in 1915: 'Für ewige Zeiten', F. 632–9, October 1923, p. 34.

36. For the Battisti Affair: 'Nachts', F. 406–12, October 1915, p. 166: L.T.M., Act IV, Scene 29. When Count Lützow, president of the Jockey Club of Vienna, claimed that the treatment meted out to Battisti was no worse than that accorded by the English to Sir Roger Casement, Kraus replied that, however horrible the hanging of Casement had been, no official photograph had been taken of it: 'Nachruf', F. 501–7, January 1919, p. 1.

37. 'Gruss an Bahr und Hofmannsthal', F. 423–4, May 1916, p. 41; L.T.M., Act I, Scene 19. Less than one year before Bahr's open letter, Hofmannsthal had written to Richard Strauss on 19 December 1913: 'Bahr wrote about me at least twenty times in the old days, always as a partisan, but it never gave me any pleasure; it was always shallow, biased and fundamentally without impact, without consistency, without

the truth of conviction. Nothing more unpleasant could happen to me than for someone to try and induce him now to devote his prattle to anything that involves me.' *The Correspondence between Richard Strauss and Hugo von Hofmannsthal*, Introduction by E. Sackville-West, London, 1961, p. 181. Even when Bahr announced his support in 1917 for the efforts of Lammasch and others to make a compromise peace with the Allies, Kraus did not forgive him: 'He has more principles than pretty bath-robes . . . I warn the new Austria'. 'Ich warne das neue Österreich', F. 462–71, October 1917, p. 25.

38. L.T.M., Act II, Scene 30.
39. 'Blinder Eifer', F. 462–71, October 1917, p. 49.
40. 'Das Schwert der Professoren', F. 437–42, October 1916, p. 4.
41. 'Na und ihr zwei Beede?', F. 462–71, October 1917, p. 18.
42. 'Eine wahre Meldung. Die Bedeutung Belgiens für Deutschland's Verteidigung', F. 484–98, October 1918, p. 199.
43.   'Mit uns sind die himmlischen Scharen all
    Sankt Michael ist unser Feldmarschall'.
L.T.M., Act III, Scene 32.
44. 'Fanatismus', F. 462–71, October 1917, p. 119.
45. 'Philosophie', F. 406–12, October 1915, p. 6.
46. L.T.M., Act I, Scene 29.
47. 'Ein Kantianer und Kant', F. 474–83, May 1918, p. 155; L.T.M., Act IV, Scene 37.
48. The full German text of this poem is as follows:
    Unter allen Wassern ist—'U'
    Von Englands Flotte spürest du
    Kaum einen Hauch. . . .
    Mein Schiff ward versenkt, dass as knallte
    Warte nur, balde
    R-U-hst du auch.
'Fanatismus', F. 462–71, October 1917, p. 119; L.T.M., Act III, Scene 4.
49. L.T.M., Act II, Scene 10.
50.   Aus Schleswig und Elsass, Tirol, Mähren, Krain—
    Nur Deutscher wollt endlich jeder sein—
    Und was kommt hinterdrein noch getönt,
    Was stampft so eisern die Erde,

Dass uns die Wand des Herzens dröhnt?

Das waren die deutschen Pferde.

'Warum die Pferde wiehern', F. 462–71, October 1917, p. 22.

51. L.T.M., Act I, Scene 1.

52. L.T.M., Act I, Scene 29.

53. Ibid. Kraus maintained that from the first day of the war he had hoped for the defeat of the Central Powers: 'Nachruf', F. 501–7, January 1919, p. 1.

54. L.T.M., Act I, Scene 29.

55. 'Nachts', F. 445–53, January 1917, p. 6.

56. L.T.M., Act I, Scene 29.

57. L.T.M., Act IV, Scene 37.

58. L.T.M., Act V, Scene 54.

59. 'Der Wille zur Macht', F. 431–6, August 1916, p. 36.

60. For an attack on Sieghart and others: 'Zu den mächtigsten Männern Österreichs', F. 445–53, January 1917, p. 131.

61. 'Die Historischen und die Vordringenden. Ein Wort an den Adel', F. 418–22, March 1916, p. 50.

62. 'Diana-Kriegs-Schokolade', F. 413–17, December 1915, p. 85.

63. 'Schonet die Kinder!', F. 462–71, October 1917, p. 30.

64. The text of this letter, intercepted and copied by an officer in his capacity as censor of his men's mail, was contained in a letter from Moritz von Lempruch to Kraus, dated 26 January 1917: K.A. The satirist used this letter in L.T.M., Act V, Scene 34.

65. 'Kinder und Vögel sagen die Wahrheit', F. 413–17, December 1915, p. 80.

66. 'Feierfage', F. 431–6, August 1916, p. 1; L.T.M., Act III, Scene 16.

67. 'Ungefähr sagt das der Papst auch, nur mit ein bisschen anderen Worten', F. 445–53, January 1917, p. 20; L.T.M., Act I, Scenes 27 and 28. See also 'Zwei Stimmen', F. 406–12, October 1915, p. 1.

68. L.T.M., Act III, Scene 8.

69. 'Zitate', F. 443–4, November 1916, p. 13.

70. Cissy von Ficker to Kraus, 12 October 1916: K.A. It was Ficker who had tried on several occasions to help the writer Georg Trakl, of whose poetry Kraus had been an early admirer. Before the outbreak of the war, Ficker had attempted to give

to Trakl and Rilke some of the money which Wittgenstein had donated to him. Rilke accepted the financial assistance, but Trakl refused the help which he so desperately needed, insisting that he could not believe in such a disinterested action as Ficker's offer. After being conscripted into the medical corps in 1914 Trakl either threatened or, indeed, attempted suicide in protest against the impossible conditions—the lack of proper clothing and medical supplies—which prevailed on the Eastern Front. As a result he was removed to an army sanatorium in Cracow. Ficker asked Wittgenstein, who was also serving in Poland, to visit Cracow and keep an eye on Trakl, a hypersensitive neurotic who already before the First World War had become addicted to drugs. When Wittgenstein arrived, however, Trakl had already died of an overdose of cocaine: M. Hamburger, *Reason and Energy, Studies in German Literature*, London, 1957, p. 245.

71. 'In Memoriam Franz Janowitz', F. 474–83, May 1918, p. 69.

72. Janowitz to Kraus, 15 October 1917. K.A.

73. L. Sternbach-Gärtner (Caroline Kohn), '*Die letzten Tage der Menschheit* und das Theater von Bertolt Brecht', *Deutsche Rundschau*, Vol. 9, September 1958, p. 836.

74. It is doubtful whether the author ever intended that it should be acted—Kraus himself estimated that the play would take ten evenings to be performed. Friedrich Torberg, the Austrian critic and editor of the Viennese magazine *Forum*, judged the Vienna performance of 1964 to be a failure. Despite the episodic structure of the play, it is essentially static in its concentration on the theme of language: F. Torberg 'Das Wort gegen die Bühne', *Forum*, Vol. XI, No. 128, August 1964, p. 383.

75. The comments of Fried, Bauer, and Masaryk on Kraus's play were quoted in 'In dieser Kleinen Zeit', F. 657–66, August 1924, p. 1. Fried's review was originally published in the magazine *Friedenswarte*, Vol. XXII, May 1920.

76. There was indeed in 1918 an attempt by a German financial group to buy the *Neue Freie Presse* for the German government in order to curb Austrian defeatism: Wandruszka, op. cit., p. 121.

77. L.T.M., Act IV, Scene 37. Kraus's source for this incident was

the book by Kontreadmiral Persius, *Der Seekrieg*, Charlottenburg, 1919: 'Innsbruck', F. 521–43, April 1920, p. 1.

78. 'Verwandlungen', F. 462–71, October 1917, p. 171.

79. Reimann to Kraus, 14 November 1916. K.A.

CHAPTER 4. THE FIRST WORLD WAR—FINAL PHASE

1. 'Edda', F. 484–98, October 1918, p. 72.

2. 'Wahhalla mit Exportabteilung', F. 437–42, October 1916, p. 116.

3. L.T.M., Act II, Scene 20.

4. 'Der Geist', F. 474–82, May 1918, p. 130.

5. 'Das moralische Moment', F. 484–98, October 1918, p. 195.

6. 'Wie ein König, mit Bomben beladen, wie ein Gott!', F. 418–22, April 1916, p. 38.

7. 'Ein deutsches Buch', F. 462–71, October 1917, p. 148. This was an extract from Richthofen's book, *Der rote Kampfflieger*, Berlin, 1915.

8. 'Mit der Uhr in der Hand', F. 437–42, October 1916, p. 121; L.T.M., Act II, Scene 10.

9. L.T.M., Act II, Scene 10.

10. 'Eine Lügennachricht', F. 437–42, October 1916, p. 34.

11. 'Ein Zwischenspiel', F. 437–42, October 1916, p. 35. This was an extract from the *Neue Freie Presse* for 14 October 1916.

12. 'Nachts', F. 445–53, January 1917, p. 17.

13. 'Gerüchte', F. 484–98, October 1918, p. 188. This was originally written in 1917 but was not passed by the censor until the following year.

14. 'Lange vor dem Erwachen', F. 474–98, October 1918, p. 153. This was an extract from the *Neue Freie Presse* for 15 June 1918.

15. 'Aus der Riesenzeit', F. 484–98, October 1918, p. 154.

16. 'Das Verbluten Frankreichs für England', F. 484–98, October 1918, p. 155.

17. 'Vor dem Einschlafen der Welt', F. 474–83, May 1918, p. 147.

18. 'Wie Hindenburg und Ludendorff unter Paul Goldmanns

Einwirkung zu Pazifisten wurden', F. 474–83, May 1918, p. 95. Goldmann, a German, combined his position on the *Neue Freie Presse* with work for the German Foreign Office: Z.A.B. Zeman, *The Break-up of the Habsburg Empire*, London, 1961, pp. 150–1.

19. 'Stellen wir uns vor', F. 474–83, May 1918, p. 67.

20. Zeman, op. cit., p. 142.

21. 'Das sind Brave', F. 474–83, May 1918, p. 144.

22. A typical example of Kraus's analysis of the vocabulary of war may be found in L.T.M., Act IV, Scene 29.

23. 'Kein Mensch wird glauben', F. 445–53, January 1917, p. 20.

24. L.T.M., Act V, Scene 42; M. Bullock, *Austria 1918–1938, A Study in Failure*, London, 1939, p. 6.

25. 'Der begabte Czernin', F. 474–83, May 1918, p. 1.

26. Ibid.

27. 'Der zweite Teil', F. 474–83, May 1918, p. 136.

28. 'Peripetie', F. 474–83, May 1918, p. 104.

29. 'Die Kombination', F. 484–98, October 1918, p. 32.

30. 'Eine prinzipielle Erklärung', F. 484–98, October 1918, p. 232.

31. Ibid.

32. 'Der begabte Czernin', F. 474–83, May 1918, p. 1.

33. 'Klärung', F. 474–83, May 1918, p. 135.

34. 'Getreide aus der Ukraine', F. 474–83, May 1918, p. 103.

35. 'Ein Kronzeuge für die österreichische Regierung', F. 474–83, May 1918, p. 26.

36. 'In unserer äusseren Politik steuern wir, Gott sei Dank, den deutschen Kurs', F. 484–98, October 1918, p. 13.

37. 'Ausgebaut und vertieft', F. 484–98, October 1918, p. 1; L.T.M., Act V, Scenes 8 and 9.

38. 'Aber-Aber', F. 484–98, October 1918, p. 38.

39. 'Der begabte Czernin', F. 474–83, May 1918, p. 1.

40. O. Czernin, *Im Weltkriege*, Vienna, 1919, p. 100.

41. 'Nachruf', F. 501–7, January 1919, p. 1.

42. 'Niemand geringer als', F. 474–83, May 1918, p. 23.

43. This view is taken by so bitter a critic of Czernin as Bauer: O. Bauer, *Die oesterreichische Revolution*, Vienna, 1923, p. 59.

44. 'Am Sarge Alexander Girardi's', F. 474–83, May 1918, p. 120.

45. 'Die Zeit ist also doch gross', F. 431–6, August 1916, p. 25.

46. 'Sonderling', F. 418–22, April 1916, p. 38.

47. 'Der soziale Standpunkt von Tieren', F. 437–42, October 1916, p. 30.

48. In 1920, one year after the murder of Rosa Luxemburg during the Spartacist uprising, Kraus read at one of his public recitals the letters which she had written from prison during the First World War, letters which breathed a joy in life that enabled her spirit to transcend the miseries of captivity: 'Vorlesungen', F. 546–50, July 1920, p. 3; 'Antwort an Rosa Luxemburg von einer Unsentimentalen', F. 554–6, November 1920, p. 6.

49. 'Verwandlungen', F. 462–71, October 1917, p. 171.

50. 'Das Geistige im Krieg', F. 462–71, October 1917, p. 62.

51. 'Die Sozialdemokratie geht in die Opposition', F. 462–71, October 1917, p. 164.

52. 'Revolution in Deutschland', F. 462–71, October 1917, p. 165; L.T.M., Act IV, Scene 11.

53. Kraus had been a vigorous supporter of the Hague Conferences: F. 13, August 1899, p. 4.

54. 'Ein besserer Oesterreicher', F. 445–53, January 1917, p. 66.

55. 'Für Lammasch', F. 474–83, May 1918, p. 46.

56. 'Der darbende Bürger', F. 474–83, May 1918, p. 52.

57. 'In dieser kleinen Zeit', F. 657–67, August 1924, p. 1.

58. 'Lammasch und die Christen', F. 521–30, January 1920, p. 153.

59. 'In dieser kleinen Zeit', F. 657–67, August 1924, p. 1.

60. 'Nachruf', F. 501–7, January 1919, p. 1.

61. Ibid.

62. 'Vorlesungen: An alle die die Wahl haben', F. 508–13, April 1919, p. 30.

63. 'Notizen', F. 552–3, October 1920, p. 23.

64.   'Man fühlt es schmerzlich und betroffen:
      Herr Kitchener ist nun zwar ersoffen—
      Doch Grey? Da bleibt noch viel zu hoffen!
'Der ruhmlose Abschluss', F. 431–6, August 1916, p. 50. In Kraus's opinion Grey was the only honourable statesman of the war; L.T.M., Act III, Scene 41.

65. The following are typical verses from Kerr's *Rumänenlied*;
Verse I   In den klainsten Winkelescu
           Fiel ein Russen—Trinkgeldescu.

> Fraidig ibten wir verratul—
> Politescu schnappen Drahtul.

Verse III
> Gebrüllescu voll Triumphul
> Mitten im Korruptul—Sumpful,
> In der Hauptstadt Bukurescht
> Wo sich kainer Fisse wäscht.

'Ein deutsches Kriegsgedicht', F. 437–42, October 1916, p. 7; L.T.M., Act III, Scene 20.

Kerr denied that he was the author of the poem 'Aus Russland' in which reference was made to the drowning of Russian soldiers in the Masurian Lakes:

> Nun hat man im Reiche des weissen Despoten
> Den ersten sittlichen Anlauf genommen,
> Und hat den Branntweinverkauf verboten,
> Den wackeren Truppen zu Nutz und Frommen.

> Sie sollten sich fern von der Wodkiflasche
> Allmählich gewöhnen ans Wassertrinken
> Damit der Geschmack sie nicht überrasche
> Wenn sie in die seen Masurens versinken.

'Kerr in Paris', F. 717–23, March 1926, p. 47. The series of legal suits over this poem between Kraus and Kerr were inconclusive. For details: 'Der grösste Schuft im ganzen Land. (Die Akten zum Fall Kerr)', F. 787–94, September 1928, p. 1.

66. 'Wenn jemand eine Reise tut', F. 583–7, December 1921, p. 9.

67. Zweig, op. cit., p. 214: English translation, p. 179.

68. See, for example, 'Der Kleine Pan ist tot', F. 319–20, March 1911, p. 1.

69. Werfel's attack on Kraus may be found in the article 'Die Metaphysik des Drehs', Die Aktion, April 1917, p. 127. Werfel also attacked Kraus in his play Spiegelmensch, Munich 1920.

70. For Kraus's attack on Zweig and Rilke for being associated with the official Austrian propaganda magazine Donauland: 'Literaten unterm Doppelaar', F. 457–61, May 1917, p. 22. Sidonie Nadherny had pleaded with Kraus to use whatever influence he possessed to obtain Rilke's release from military service after the latter had been conscripted. Kraus replied that he was deeply moved by the plight of Rilke but perhaps

his fate was better than having to work for the War Office: Kraft, op. cit., p. 350. In fact, after collapsing on the parade-ground in Vienna, Rilke was transferred to the Kriegsarchiv for a few months before Princess Marie Taxis and other influential friends secured his release from the Austrian army in June 1916: E. C. Mason, *Rilke*, London, 1963, p. 97.

71. 'Notizen', F. 484–98, October 1918, p. 127. Zweig, for his part, considered that Kraus was too concerned with notoriety to be a real artist: *Rundfrage über Karl Kraus*, Innsbruck, 1917, p. 36.

72. For the most important attack on Bolshevism by Kraus: 'Gespenster', F. 514–18, July 1919, p. 21.

73. 'Proteste', F. 514–18, July 1919, p. 1.

74. 'Gespenster', F. 514–18, July 1919, p. 21.

75. Ibid.

76. Ibid.

77. 'Die Sintflut', F. 499–500, November 1918, p. 28.

78. 'Die Kriegsschreiber nach dem Krieg', F. 474–83, May 1918, p. 156.

79. 'Die Sintflut', F. 499–500, November 1918, p. 28.

80. Kraft, op. cit., p. 142.

81. 'Gespenster', F. 514–18, July 1919, p. 21.

82. 'Österreich's Fürsprech bei Wilson', F. 499–500, November 1918, p. 15.

83. L.T.M., Act I, Scene 29.

84. Heller, op. cit., p. 249.

85. In 1919 Kraus published in full those pieces which had never been allowed to pass by the censor. On the whole, apart from Kraus's attacks on military jurisdiction, there was nothing sensational in them. The main preoccupation of the censor seems to have been with references to royal personages: 'Konfiskationen der Fackel', F. 508–13, April 1919, p. 56. Wandruszka (op. cit., p. 120) also comments on the inefficiency of the Austrian censor during the First World War.

86. At a performance of Beethoven's Ninth Symphony in Vienna in 1918, at which the Emperor and members of the imperial family were present, students demonstrated in favour of peace at the beginning of the last movement. (Private infor-mation.)

87. 'Ad Acta', F. 508–13, April 1919, p. 81: this contains, in full, the correspondence between Kraus and the police.
88. 'Tages Anzeiger', Zurich, 16 June 1945.
89. 'In dieser grossen Zeit', F. 404, December 1914, p. 1.
90. The charge seems to have originated with the Western Allies and was then copied by the Central Powers: A. Ponsonby, *Falsehood in War-Time*, London, 1928, pp. 102–14; 'Eine prinzipielle Erklärung', F. 484–98, October 1918, p. 232.

CHAPTER 5. REPUBLICAN INTERLUDE

1. 'Er hat so Heimweh gehabt!' F. 568–71, May 1921, p. 1.
2. 'Der Fürst von Ragusa', F. 588–94, March 1922, p. 37.
3. 'Vorlesungen', F. 546–50, July 1920, p. 3.
4. 'Notizen', F. 717–23, March 1926, p. 32. *Die Fackel* was banned in Rumania, too, as Kraus reminded the Rumanian embassy in Vienna when it wrote to him asking him for a year's subscription for the Rumanian Ministry of Foreign Affairs.
5. 'Die Letzte Nacht', F. 613–21, April 1923, p. 62.
6. 'Vorlesungen', F. 546–50, July 1920, p. 3.
7. For the whole affair: 'Innsbruck', F. 531–43, April 1920, p. 1.
8. 'Gespenster', F. 514–18, July 1919, p. 21.
9. 'Die vornehmen Gäste aus der Kulturstadt Wien', F. 601–7, November 1922, p. 31.
10. 'Die Gesellschaft der Freunde', F. 557–60, January 1921, p. 1.
11. 'Brot and Lüge', F. 519–20, November 1919, p. 1. The tapestries were eventually pledged in return for credit from the Entente: 'Genua', F. 595–600, July 1922, p. 1.
12. 'Klarstellung', F. 554–6, November 1920, p. 1.
13. 'In dieser kleinen Zeit, F. 657–67, August 1924, p. 1.
14. 'Kreuzbrav', F. 622–31, June 1923, p. 30.
15. 'Selbsthilfe', F. 622–31, June 1923, p. 142.
16. Braunthal, op. cit., pp. 250–1.
17. O. Pollak, 'Ein Künstler und Kämpfer', *Der Kampf*, Vol. XVI, March 1923, p. 1.

18. D. J. Bach, 'Der unpopuläre Karl Kraus', *Der Kampf*, Vol. XVI, April 1923, p. 77.

19. '*Hétfoi Napló* 19 April 1927.

20. 'Metaphysik der Haifische', F. 632–9, October 1923, p. 150.

21. 'Ehre wem Ehre gebührt', F. 640–8, January 1924, p. 137.

22. On Stolper's legal suit with Bekessy: T. Stolper, *Ein Leben in Brennpunkten userer Zeit; Wien, Berlin, New York, Gustav Stolper, 1888–1947*, Tübingen, 1950, pp. 151–8.

23. 'Hinaus aus Wien mit dem Schuft!' F. 697–705, October 1925, p. 145.

24. 'Entlarvt durch Bekessy', F. 691–6, July 1925, p. 68.

25. 'Die Stunde des Todes', F. 732–4, August 1926, p. 1.

26. 'Bekessy's Sendung', F. 640–8, January 1924, p. 84.

27. A. Kuh, *Karl Kraus, der Affe Zarathustras*, Vienna, 1925, p. 9.

28. 'Entlarvt durch Bekessy', F. 691–6, July 1925, p. 68.

29. For details of this scandal: H. Benedikt (ed.), *Geschichte der Republik Österreich*, Munich 1954, pp. 142–3.

30. 'Die Stundes des Todes', F. 732–4, August 1926, p. 1.

31. 'Das reine Banditenblatt', F. 706–11, December 1925, p. 71.

32. 'Das geht nicht', F. 717–23, March 1926, p. 89.

33. 'Der nicht Genannte', F. 717–23, March 1926, p. 78.

34. 'Die Stunde des Gerichts', F. 730–1, July 1926, p. 1.

35. 'Der verlorene Sohn', F. 759–65, May 1927, p. 7. Stolper, who was conducting a campaign against Ahrer, seems subsequently to have accepted Ahrer's explanation that he went to Cuba for family reasons only: C. A. Gulick, *Austria from Habsburg to Hitler*, Berkeley and Los Angeles, 1948, Vol. I, p. 706.

36. 'Der nicht Genannte', F. 717–23, March 1926, p. 78.

37. For the Hammerbrotwerke affair: Gulick, op. cit., Vol. I, pp. 326–9.

38. Ibid., pp. 245–6.

39. 'Ein Plakat das seine Wirkung vor dem Erscheinen getan hat', F. 759–65, May 1927, p. 117.

40. O. Pollak, 'Noch einmal Karl Kraus', *Der Kampf*, Vol. XIX, June 1926, p. 261.

41. F. Austerlitz, 'Der wahre Karl Kraus', *Der Kampf*, Vol. XIX, July 1926, p. 309.

42. O. Pollak, 'Noch einmal die Karl Kraus Anhänger', *Der Kampf*, Vol. XIX, August 1926, p. 353.

43. 'Briefe Wilhelm Liebknechts', F. 717–23, March 1926, p. 6; 'Hungerlohn aus Idealismus', ibid., p. 76.

44. 'Ich und wir', F. 743–50, December 1926, p. 133.

45. *Commentary*, Vol. III, No. 5, May 1947.

46. These details are taken from the book by Bekessy's son, Hans Habe: *Ich stelle mich. Meine Lebensgeschichte*, Vienna-Munich, 1954, p. 529.

47. Braunthal, op. cit., p. 75.

48. 'Der Hort der Republik', F. 766–70, October 1927, p. 1.

49. 'Blut und Schmutz, oder Schober entlarvt durch Bekessy', F. 778–80, May 1928, p. 1.

50. G. E. R. Gedye, *Fallen Bastions. The Central European Tragedy*, London, 1938, p. 34.

51. Peter Lorre played the rôle of 'Barkassy' with suitably sinister charm.

52. 'Der Hort der Republik', F. 766–70, October 1927, p. 1.

53. Gulick, op. cit., Vol. I, p. 694.

54. 'Rechenschaftsbericht', F. 795–9, December 1928, p. 1.

55. 'Demokratisierung und Isolierung', F. 811–19, August 1929, p. 158.

56. Gulick, op. cit., Vol. II, p. 879.

57. Nachrichtenblatt, Sozialdemokratische Vereinigung 'Karl Kraus', April 1931: K.A.

58. Social Democrat party secretariat to Vereinigung 'Karl Kraus', 11 March 1931: K.A.

59. Nachrichtenblatt, Sozialdemokratische Vereinigung 'Karl Kraus', February 1931.

60. 'Der treue Eckhardt', F. 857–63, August 1931, p. 20.

61. Pulzer, op. cit., pp. 320–1.

62. 'Hüben und Drüben', F. 876–84, October 1932, p. 1.

63. Ibid.

64. 'Sakrileg an George oder Sühne an Shakespeare', F. 885–7, December 1932, p. 45.

CHAPTER 6. THE RECKONING

1. 'Mussolini's Bezähmung', F. 622–3, June 1923, p. 5.
2. 'Sehnsucht eines Schweidnitzers mit seinen Gedanken allein zu sein', F. 632–9, October 1923, p. 40.
3. 'Die Sudeten', F. 657–67, August 1924, p. 74.
4. 'Vorlesungen', F. 800–5, February 1929, p. 50; *Völkischer Beobachter*, 3 March 1928.
5. 'Notizen', F. 800–5, February 1929, p. 60.
6. 'Notizen', F. 806–9, May 1929, p. 51.
7. 'Grubenhund und Hakenkreuz', F. 852–6, May 1931, p. 29.
8. Man frage nicht, was all die Zeit ich machte.
   Ich bleibe stumm;
   und sage nicht, warum.
   Und Stille gibt es, da die Erde krachte.
   Kein Wort, das traf:
   man spricht nur aus dem Schlaf.
   Und träumt von einer Sonne welche lachte.
   Es geht vorbei:
   nachher war's einerlei.
   Das Wort entschlief, als jene Welt erwachte.

   F. 888, October 1933, p. 4.
9. D.W., p. 308.
10. K. Kraus, *Beim Wort genommen*, Munich, 1955, p. 127.
11. 'Mir fällt zu Hitler nichts ein': D.W., p. 9.
12. Ibid., p. 20.
13. Ibid., pp. 280–1. The reference to 'ruthless masseuses' applies of course to the *Neue Freie Presse* and other newspapers which had carried thinly disguised advertisements for prostitutes. In this quotation Kraus is also playing on the fact that the word 'Revolverblatt' was a word used to refer to the gutter press.
14. Koestler, op. cit., pp. 223–4.
15. Radecki, op. cit., p. 334.
16. D.W., p. 12.
17. Ibid., p. 181.
18. Ibid., p. 52.
19. Ibid., p. 53.

20. Ibid., p. 181.

21. Ibid., p. 45.

22. The complete quotation from Johst was:
'Nein, zehn Schritt vom Leib mit dem ganzen
Weltanschauungssalat—hier wird scharf geschossen!
Wenn ich Kultur höre—entsichere ich meinen
Browning.' Ibid., p. 85.

23. Ibid., pp. 142–4.

24. Ibid., pp. 253–4.

25. Ibid., p. 141.

26. Ibid., p. 146.

27. Ibid., p. 147.

28. Ibid., p. 189.

29. Ibid., p. 161.

30. Ibid., p. 61.

31. Ibid., p. 193.

32. Ibid., p. 50.

33. Ibid., p. 206.

34. Ibid., p. 46.

35. Ibid., p. 87.

36. Ibid., p. 89.

37. Ibid., p. 90.

38. Ibid., p. 90.

39. Ibid., p. 160.

40. Ibid., p. 177.

41. Ibid., p. 157. The last sentence reads, in Kraus's quotation:
'Wir werden weiter säubern, unerbittlich! . . . ausrotten . . .'

42. Ibid., p. 64. A reference, of course, to Spengler's major work,
Die Untergang des Abendlandes.

43. Ibid., pp. 66–75. Benn's radio broadcasts were printed in
book-form: *Der neue Staat und die Intellektuellen*, Berlin, 1933.

44. Ibid., p. 32. Krieck is one of the leading Nazi theorists whose
work is discussed in A. Kolnai, *The War against the West*,
London, 1938.

45. D.W., p. 58.

46. Ibid., p. 56.

47. Ibid., p. 109.

48. Ibid., pp. 111–12.

49. H. S. Hughes, *Oswald Spengler*, London, 1952, pp. 127–31.

50. Hamburger, op. cit., p. 276.

51. W. Betz, 'The National Socialist Vocabulary', in M. Baumont (ed.), *The Third Reich*, London, 1955, p. 784; D. Sternberger, *Aus dem Wörterbuch des Unmenschen*, Hamburg, 1957; C. Berning, *Vokabular des Nationalsozialismus*, Berlin, 1964.

52. D.W., p. 122.

53. Ibid., p. 254.

54. Ibid., p. 145.

55. Ibid., p. 155.

56. Ibid., p. 156.

57. For a description of the events of 4 March 1933: G. Brook Shepherd, *Dollfuss*, London, 1961, pp. 97–8.

58. Ibid., pp. 231–2; J. Gehl, *Austria, Germany, and the Anschluss 1931–38*, London, 1963, pp. 87–100.

59. D.W., p. 167. So much material from *Die Dritte Walpurgisnacht* was subsequently incorporated into *Die Fackel* that, for the sake of convenience, references have been taken from the former. For Kraus's views on events during and immediately after the riots of February 1934: 'Warum die Fackel nicht erscheint', F. 890–905, July 1934, passim.

60. D.W., p. 171.

61. Ibid., p. 166.

62. Ibid., p. 172.

63. Ibid., p. 168.

64. Ibid., p. 208.

65. At one time in the 1920s there was an attempt by the Czech government to buy the newspaper. Wandruszka, op. cit., p. 145.

66. D.W., p. 94.

67. Ibid., p. 92.

68. Ibid., pp. 105–7.

69. F. 889, July 1934, p. 6.

70. 'Warum die Fackel nicht erscheint', F. 890–905, July 1934, p. 1.

71. D.W., p. 219.

72. Ibid., p. 231.

73. Ibid., p. 222.

74. Ibid., p. 225.

75. Ibid., p. 229.

76. Ibid., p. 219.

77. 'Ich denke an nichts als an Alles nur nicht Hitler', ibid., p. 239.

78. H. Kann, 'Erinnerungen an Karl Kraus', *National Zeitung*, Basel, 22 April 1944.

79. For the Nazi evaluation of the situation in Vienna in 1934: *Die Erhebung der österreichischen Nationalsozialisten im Juli 1934.* (Akten der Historischen Kommission des Reichsführers S.S.), Vienna, 1965.

80. Kann, loc. cit.

81. Kraft, op. cit., p. 354.

82. D.W., p. 256. For Kraus's comparison between Dollfuss and the murdered Banquo: 'Vorspruch und Nachruf', F. 912–15, August 1935, p. 69.

83. These and other incidents are recorded in Kraus's newspaper cuttings for 1935: K.A.

84. Radecki, op. cit., p. 27.

85. Newspaper cuttings and comments, in particular *Prager Montagsblatt* and *Prager Tagblatt* for 6 March 1935: K.A.

86. Kraus to *Prager Tagblatt*, 29 January 1935: K.A.

87. Kann, loc. cit. Still, there was some validity in the satirist's position: Otto Bauer was foolishly to urge in exile that, since a return of the Habsburgs to Austria was a more immediate danger than a Nazi take-over, Social Democrats would be forced into a situation in which they would have to struggle along with the Nazis against a monarchical restoration. Bauer held this view even though he recognised that the 'next day' after overthrowing the Clerical-Fascist régime the workers would probably have to fight the Nazis. Gulick, op. cit., Vol. II, pp. 1678–9.

88. Kraus to Samek, 24 June 1935: K.A.

89. Kraus to Bauer, 13 May 1936: K.A. It is quite clear from a mass of Kraus's newspaper cuttings and comments for the year 1935–6 (dealing in particular with Léon Blum's negotiations with the French Communists) that the satirist was utterly opposed to the idea of a Popular Front: in any coalition between Bauer and the Communists, Kraus was convinced that the former would be eaten up by the latter. Regarding the situation in France Kraus complained that fellow-travellers like Romain Rolland now saw the road to

humanity lying through Russian equipment for gas-warfare: as for Dollfuss, he had done more for the wretched proletariat of Germany and Austria than Litvinov (the Russian Foreign Minister) and the group of French intellectuals who were entertained by him to breakfast at the Soviet embassy in Paris. Kraus to Alice Asriel, 22 November 1934: K.A.

90. R. Scheu, *Karl Kraus*, Vienna, 1909, pp. 34–6.
91. H. Fischer, 'Erinnerungen an Karl Kraus', *Forum*, Vienna, June 1961, p. 225.
92. See particularly the poem 'Todesfurcht', *Worte in Versen*, p. 375. For a comparison between Kraus and Nestroy in their attitude towards death: P. Schick, 'Der Satiriker und der Tod: Versuch einer typologischen Deutung', *Festschrift um hundertjährigen Bestand der Wiener Stadtbibliothek*, Vienna, 1956.

EPILOGUE

1. For a painfully vivid description of events in Vienna immediately after the entry of German troops into Austria: Gedye, op. cit., pp. 300–14.
2. C. Kohn, op. cit.
3. Radecki, op. cit., p. 34.
4. Wandruszka, op. cit., p. 146.
5. For the history of the Social Democratic party between 1934 and 1941: J. Buttinger, *Am Beispiel Österreichs, Ein geschichtlicher Beitrag zur Krise der sozialistischen Bewegung*, Cologne 1953. English translation: *In the Twilight of Socialism. A History of the Revolutionary Socialists in Austria*, New York, 1953.
6. J. Braunthal, *The Tragedy of Austria*, London, 1948, p. 154.
7. V. Metejka, 'Karl Kraus und das Österreich von heute,' *Vorwärts*, Basel, 1 June 1946.
8. 'A Viennese writer with an abundance of bitter sarcasm and an utter dearth of human wisdom and political character.' J. Braunthal, *In Search of the Millennium*, London, 1945, p. 284.

9. Evidence for Dr. Franzel's war-time activities may be found in *Der Spiegel*, 18 November 1964.

10. K. Thieme, 'Der Apokalyptiker Karl Kraus', *Die Erfüllung*, Vienna, September 1936, p. 109.

11. L. Liegler *In Memoriam Karl Kraus*, Vienna, 1936, p. 12.

12. T. Haecker, *Tag- und Nachtbücher*, Munich, 1949, p. 169. Carl Hilty (1833–1909) was professor of law at the University of Berne and a persistent critic of German militarism.

13. 'Als das Zeitalter Hand an sich legte, war er diese Hand.' Quoted in Kraft, op. cit., p. 13.

Select Bibliography

THE following list of works by and on Karl Kraus is by no means complete. Reference is made only to those works which have particular relevance to the theme of this study. For a complete bibliography reference must be made to: O. Kerry, *Karl Kraus-Bibliographie*, Vienna, 1954, and C. Kohn, *Karl Kraus*, Paris, 1962.

I. WORKS BY KARL KRAUS

Die Demolierte Literatur, 2nd edn., Vienna, 1897.

Eine Krone für Zion, Vienna, 1898.

Die Fackel, 1–922, Vienna, 1899–1936.

Sittlichkeit und Kriminalität, Vienna, 1908; new edn., Munich, 1963.

Sprüche und Widersprüche, Vienna, 1909.

Die Chinesische Mauer, Vienna, 1910.

Heine und die Folgen, Munich, 1910.

Pro Domo et Mundo, Munich, 1912.

Nestroy und die Nachwelt, Vienna, 1912.

Nachts, Munich-Leipzig, 1918.

Weltgericht, Munich-Leipzig, 1919.

Gedicht und Rede am Grabe Peter Altenbergs, Vienna, 1919.

Die letzten Tage der Menschheit, Vienna, 1922; new edn., Munich, 1957.

Untergang der Welt durch schwarze Magie, Vienna, 1922; new edn., Munich, 1960.

Wolkenkuckucksheim, Vienna, 1923.

Traumstück, Vienna, 1923.

Traumtheater, Vienna, 1924.

Epigramme, Vienna, 1927.

Die Unüberwindlichen, Vienna, 1928.

Literatur und Lüge, Vienna, 1929; new edn., Munich, 1958.

Zeitstrophen, Vienna, 1931.

Rede am Grabe von Adolf Loos, Vienna, 1933.

Shakespeare-Sonette, Nachdichtung, Vienna, 1933.

Die Sprache, Vienna, 1937; new edn., Munich, 1954.

Dokumente und Selbstzeugnisse, Zurich, 1945.

Die Dritte Walpurgisnacht, Munich, 1952.

Beim Wort genommen (which includes the aphorisms from *Sprüche und Widersprüche, Pro Domo et Mundo* and *Nachts*), Munich, 1955.

Widerschein der Fackel (An anthology from *Die Fackel*), Munich, 1957.

Worte in Versen, Munich, 1959.

Mit vorzüglicher Hochachtung (Letters), Munich, 1962.

TRANSLATIONS

Poems, translated by A. Bloch, Boston, 1930.

Ventures in Verse, after the German of Karl Kraus, translated by A. Bloch, New York, 1947.

II. BOOKS AND ARTICLES RELATING DIRECTLY TO KARL KRAUS

Altenberg, P., *Vita ipsa*, Berlin, 1919.

Austerlitz, F., 'Der wahre Karl Kraus', *Der Kampf*, Vol. XIX, Vienna, 1926.

Bach, D. J., 'Der unpopuläre Kraus', *Der Kampf*, Vol. XVI, Vienna, 1923.

Benjamin, W., *Schriften*, Vol. II, Frankfurt, 1955.

Brock-Sulzer, E., 'Karl Kraus und das Theater', *Akzente*, Vol. II, No. 6, Frankfurt, 1955.

Brügel, F., 'Die letzte Fackel', *Der Kampf*, New Series, Vol. I, No. 5, Brünn, 1934.

Dallago, C. (ed.), *Studien über Karl Kraus*, Innsbruck, 1913.

Ehrenstein, A., *Karl Kraus*, Vienna, 1920.

Engelmann, P., *Dem Andenken an Karl Kraus*, Tel Aviv, 1949.

Ficker, L. von (ed.), *Rundfrage über Karl Kraus*, Innsbruck, 1947.

Fischer, H., *Karl Kraus und die Jugend*, Vienna, 1934.

— *Karl Kraus, Abschiedsworte am Grabe*, Vienna, 1936.

— 'The Other Austria and Karl Kraus', in H. J. Rehfisch (ed.), *In Tyrannos. Four Centuries of Struggle Against Tyranny in Germany*, London, 1944.

— 'Erinnerungen an Karl Kraus', *Forum*, Vol. VIII, No. 90, Vienna, 1961.

Goblot, G., 'Karl Kraus et la lutte contre la barbarie moderne', *Revue d'Allemagne*, Vol. III, No. 8, Paris, 1929.

— 'Les parents de Karl Kraus', *Études Germaniques*, Vol. V, No. 1, Paris, 1950.

Heller, E., *The Disinherited Mind*, London, 1957.

Kann, H., 'Erinnerungen an Karl Kraus', *National Zeitung*, Basel, 22 April 1944.

Kohn, C., 'État des recherches sur Karl Kraus', *Allemagne d'Aujourd'hui*, Nos. 4 and 5, Paris, 1957.

Kohn, H., *Karl Kraus, Arthur Schnitzler, Otto Weininger. Aus dem jüdischen Wien der Jahrhundertwende*, Tübingen, 1962.

Kraft, W., *Karl Kraus: Eine Einführung in Sein Werk und eine Auswahl*, Wiesbaden, 1952.

— *Karl Kraus, Beiträge zum Verständnis seines Werkes*, Salzburg, 1956.

Křenek, E., 'Karl Kraus und Arnold Schönberg', *Dreiundzwanzig*, Nos. 15 and 16, Vienna, 1934.

— *Ansprache bei der Trauerfeier für Karl Kraus*, Vienna, 1936.

— 'Erinnerungen an Karl Kraus', *Dreiundzwanzig*, Nos. 28–30, Vienna, 1937.

Kuh, A., *Karl Kraus, der Affe Zarathustras*, Vienna, 1925.

Kurzweil, B., *Die Fragwürdigkeit der jüdischen Existenz und das Problem der Sprachgestaltung*, Tel-Aviv, 1965.

Lasker-Schüler, E., *Briefe an Karl Kraus*, Cologne/Berlin, 1956.

Lichnowsky, M., 'Karl Kraus zum Gedächtnis', *Merkur*, Vol. X, No. 2, Stuttgart, 1956.

Liegler, L., *Karl Kraus und die Sprache*, Vienna, 1918.

— *Karl Kraus und sein Werk*, Vienna, 1920.

— *In Memoriam Karl Kraus*, Vienna, 1936.

Loos, C., *Adolf Loos Privat*, Vienna, 1936.

Metejka, V., 'Karl Kraus und das Österreich von heute', *Vorwärts*, Basel, 1 June 1946.

Nadler, J., *Literaturgeschichte Österreichs*, Salzburg, 1951.

Pollak, O., 'Karl Kraus, ein Künstler und Kämpfer', *Der Kampf*, Vol. XVI, Vienna, 1923.

— 'Nochmals Karl Kraus', *Der Kampf*, Vol. XIX, Vienna, 1926.

— 'Nochmals die Karl Kraus-Anhänger', *Der Kampf*, Vol. XIX, Vienna, 1926.

— 'Karl Kraus', *Berner Tagwacht*, 15 February 1946.

Radecki, S. von, *Wie ich glaube*, Cologne, 1953.

Rollett, E., *Karl Kraus zum 60. Geburtstag*, Vienna, 1934.

Rychner, M., *Karl Kraus*, Vienna, 1924.

Schartner, G., *Karl Kraus und die politischen Ereignisse bis 1914* (Unpublished dissertation, University of Vienna, 1952).

Schaukal, R., *Karl Kraus, Versuch eines geistigen Bildnisses*, Vienna, 1933.

Scheu, R., *Karl Kraus*, Vienna, 1909.

Schick, P., 'Zu den Briefen Karl Kraus an Alfred Berger', *Das Silberboot*, Vol. V, No. 2, Salzburg, 1949.

— 'Karl Kraus, der Satiriker und die Zeit', *Études Germaniques*, Vol. XII, No. 3, Paris, 1957.

— 'Der Satiriker und der Tod: Versuch einer typologischen Deutung', *Festschrift zum hundertjährigen Bestand der Wiener Stadtbibliothek*, Vienna, 1956.

Schick, P., *Karl Kraus*, Hamburg, 1965.

Stephan, J., *Satire und Sprache. Zu dem Werk von Karl Kraus*, Munich, 1964.

Stern, J. P., 'Karl Kraus's Vision of Language', *Modern Language Review*, Vol. LXI, No. 1, London, 1966.

Sternbach-Gärtner, L. (C. Kohn), 'Neue Kraus Dokumente', *Neue Deutsche Literatur*, Vol. IV, No. 9, 1956.

— '*Die letzten Tage der Menschheit* und das Theater von Bertolt Brecht', *Deutsche Rundschau*, Vol. 9, 1958.

Thieme, K., 'Der Apokalyptiker Karl Kraus', *Die Erfüllung*, Vienna, 1936.

Viertel, B., *Karl Kraus, ein Charakter und die Zeit*, Dresden, 1921.

— *Karl Kraus, Festrede zum fünfzigsten Geburtstag*, Vienna, 1924.

Wagenknecht, C. J., *Das Wortspiel bei Karl Kraus*, Göttingen/ Zürich, 1966.

Index